American Railroads
in the Nineteenth Century

American Railroads
in the Nineteenth Century

Augustus J. Veenendaal

Greenwood Guides to Historic Events, 1500–1900
Linda S. Frey and Marsha L. Frey, Series Editors

GREENWOOD PRESS
Westport, Connecticut • London

385
VEE

Library of Congress Cataloging-in-Publication Data

Veenendaal, A. J.
    American railroads in the nineteenth century / Augustus J. Veenendaal.
        p.   cm.—(Greenwood guides to historic events, 1500–1900, ISSN 1538–442X)
    Includes bibliographical references and index.
    ISBN 0–313–31688–0 (alk. paper)
        1. Railroads—United States—History.   I. Title.   II. Series.
TF23.V44   2003
385′0973′09034—dc21   2002032068

British Library Cataloguing in Publication Data is available.

Library of Congress Catalog Card Number: 2002032068
ISBN: 0–313–31688–0
ISSN: 1538–442X

First published in 2003

Greenwood Press, 88 Post Road West, Westport, CT 06881
An imprint of Greenwood Publishing Group, Inc.
www.greenwood.com

Printed in the United States of America

The paper used in this book complies with the
Permanent Paper Standard issued by the National
Information Standards Organization (Z39.48–1984).

10 9 8 7 6 5 4 3 2 1

CONTENTS

Photo essay follows page 59.

SERIES FOREWORD

American statesman Adlai Stevenson stated that "We can chart our future clearly and wisely only when we know the path which has led to the present." This series, Greenwood Guides to Historic Events, 1500–1900, is designed to illuminate that path by focusing on events from 1500 to 1900 that have shaped the world. The years 1500 to 1900 include what historians call the Early Modern Period (1500 to 1789, the onset of the French Revolution) and part of the modern period (1789 to 1900).

In 1500, an acceleration of key trends marked the beginnings of an interdependent world and the posing of seminal questions that changed the nature and terms of intellectual debate. The series closes with 1900, the inauguration of the twentieth century. This period witnessed profound economic, social, political, cultural, religious, and military changes. An industrial and technological revolution transformed the modes of production, marked the transition from a rural to an urban economy, and ultimately raised the standard of living. Social classes and distinctions shifted. The emergence of the territorial and later the national state altered man's relations with and view of political authority. The shattering of the religious unity of the Roman Catholic world in Europe marked the rise of a new pluralism. Military revolutions changed the nature of warfare. The books in this series emphasize the complexity and diversity of the human tapestry and include political, economic, social, intellectual, military, and cultural topics. Some of the authors focus on events in U.S. history such as the Salem Witchcraft Trials, the American Revolution, the abolitionist movement, and the Civil War. Others analyze European topics, such as the Reformation and Counter Reformation and the French Revolution. Still others bridge cultures and continents by examining the voyages of discovery, the Atlantic slave trade, and the Age of Imperialism. Some focus on intellectual questions that have shaped the modern world, such as Darwin's *Origin of Species* or on turning points such as the Age of Romanticism. Others examine defining economic, religious, or legal events or issues such as the building of the railroads, the Second Great Awakening, and abolitionism. Heroes (e.g., Lewis and Clark), scientists (e.g., Darwin), military leaders (e.g., Napoleon), poets (e.g., Byron), stride across its pages. Many of these events were seminal in that they marked profound changes or turning points. The Scientific Revolution, for example, changed the way individuals viewed themselves and their world.

The authors, acknowledged experts in their fields, synthesize key events, set developments within the larger historical context, and, most important, present a well-balanced, well-written account that integrates the most recent scholarship in the field.

The topics were chosen by an advisory board composed of historians, high school history teachers, and school librarians to support the curriculum and meet student research needs. The volumes are designed to serve as resources for student research and to provide clearly written interpretations of topics central to the secondary school and lower-level undergraduate history curriculum. Each author outlines a basic chronology to guide the reader through often confusing events and a historical overview to set those events within a narrative framework. Three to five topical chapters underscore critical aspects of the event. In the final chapter the author examines the impact and consequences of the event. Biographical sketches furnish background on the lives and contributions of the players who strut across this stage. Ten to fifteen primary documents ranging from letters to diary entries, song lyrics, proclamations, and posters, cast light on the event, provide material for student essays, and stimulate a critical engagement with the sources. Introductions identify the authors of the documents and the main issues. In some cases a glossary of selected terms is provided as a guide to the reader. Each work contains an annotated bibliography of recommended books, articles, CD-ROMs, Internet sites, videos, and films that set the materials within the historical debate.

These works will lead to a more sophisticated understanding of the events and debates that have shaped the modern world and will stimulate a more active engagement with the issues that still affect us. It has been a particularly enriching experience to work closely with such dedicated professionals. We have come to know and value even more highly the authors in this series and our editors at Greenwood, particularly Kevin Ohe. In many cases they have become more than colleagues; they have become friends. To them and to future historians we dedicate this series.

Linda S. Frey
University of Montana

Marsha L. Frey
Kansas State University

PREFACE

Few forces have been more instrumental in forging the American nation into one entity than the railroad. From a largely agricultural country, with its small population mostly concentrated in towns and villages along the Atlantic seaboard and the navigable rivers, the United States was transformed in the nineteenth century into an integrated and highly industrialized country. Railroads, after having conquered mountains and deserts, linked the different parts together and made possible the rapid exchange of people, goods, and ideas. Travel from one end of the country to the other became possible without much hardship or danger and at a fairly low price that was affordable for a large majority of Americans.

Of course, a library-full of books has been written about American railroads. From serious studies about the technology, the business methods, and impact of railroads on society to glossy picture books and the like, everything seems to be available. Therefore, this book does not pretend to fill a gap in the historiography, but it will be useful for students as a concise entry into the complicated world of railroad technology, economics, finance, and personalities. An extensive annotated bibliography will enable readers to delve deeper into chosen subjects.

In common with other modern historians, I consider the long nineteenth century to end with America's entry into World War I in 1917. The succinct chronology of events with which the book opens reflects that basic assumption. Chapter 1 then presents a historical overview of the expansion of railroads in America as related to developments elsewhere in the world, chiefly in Great Britain, the cradle of railways. Chapter 2 explains the technology of the steam railroad, its infrastructure, rolling stock, and other equipment necessary for the safe running of trains. Chapter 3 covers the thorny field of railroad finance and describes the different sources of the multimillion-dollar investment needed to construct and operate the railroad network. Chapter 4 is devoted to one special subject, the role of the railroads during the Civil War, in which railroads were first employed as tools of war. Chapter 5 covers the epic—and sometimes sordid—story of the building of the transcontinental railroads, starting with the Union Pacific–Central Pacific combination and ending with the last one, the ill-fated Chicago, Milwaukee & St. Paul Pacific extension. Chapter 6 describes the movement from regional lines toward larger entities, covering large parts of the country. The quest for monopoly and all the abuses connected with that object and its ensuing regulation is also covered in that chapter. The last, Chapter 7, gives an overview of the impact of railroads on the American economy, their role in the economic growth, and recent discussions of that role.

Brief biographies of fifteen personalities who made marks in the railroad world are also included. These figures range from technicians and engineers to managers, directors, and robber barons. Twenty-three documents, which cover many aspects of railroad construction and operation, make up the last part of the book. The book concludes with an annotated bibliography and a general subject index.

ACKNOWLEDGMENTS

I owe a great debt to the series editors, Linda and Marsha Frey. They came up with the idea of asking me to write this book. Of course, as a non-American historian, I at first hesitated to agree, but they managed to persuade me to undertake the work. They read through all my first trial pieces and commented extensively on the final manuscript. As I had cooperated with them in an earlier project not related to American railroads, I knew their way of working and that they would react quickly to all my questions and ideas. I owe them a great deal. Being a resident of the Netherlands, I did not always find it easy to locate documents and material pertaining to the book in hand. My good friends H. Roger Grant of Clemson University, South Carolina, and W. Thomas White of the James Jerome Hill Library at St. Paul, Minnesota, provided me with advice and ideas for documents and the like. The actual search for some documents was partly done by my friend Margriet B. Lacy of Butler University at Indianapolis, who went about this with a great deal of enthusiasm, although the subject was far removed from her usual fields of interest. I also want to thank Paul Hanson, then chairman of the history department of Butler University, for introducing me to the librarians when I was in Indianapolis myself, and for helping me in every way. Last, I want to thank my patient wife Jannie, who had to listen to ever more stories about railroads and railroaders. For years she has had to bear up with my seemingly endless research into American and Dutch railroads, but she never tires of urging me on and encouraging me when my spirits are low.

Augustus J. Veenendaal
Pijnacker, The Netherlands

CHRONOLOGY OF EVENTS

1806	Cumberland Road Act passed by Congress as first part of National Road.
1807	Robert Fulton tries out his first steamboat *Clermont* on the Hudson River.
1818	Cumberland Road opened for traffic to Wheeling, Virginia.
1825	Erie Canal, Albany-Buffalo, opened.
	First steam locomotive in America built by John Stevens.
1826	Baltimore & Ohio Railroad chartered, first public carrier.
1829	British built *Stourbridge Lion* locomotive in service on Delaware & Hudson Railroad.
1830	South Carolina Railroad opened, with steam locomotive *Best Friend of Charleston*.
1831	First railroad in New York, Albany-Schenectady, with steam locomotive *DeWitt Clinton*.
1834	Pennsylvania's Main Line canal, rail, and inclined-plane route opened.
1835	Baltimore-Washington, D.C., railroad opened.
1837	First crude sleeping car built.

1841	Boston-to-Albany railroad completed.
1842	Railroad route between Albany and Buffalo opened.
1848	Railroad route between Boston and New York City opened.
1850	First Land-Grant Act, in favor of Illinois Central and Mobile & Ohio Railroads.
1851	New York & Lake Erie Railroad opened.
1852	Telegraph first used for train dispatching.
1853	Chicago and New York City connected by all-rail route.
1855	Railroad across Isthmus of Panama opened.
1856	First railroad bridge across the Mississippi opened at Davenport, Iowa.
	Illinois Central Railroad opened, longest railroad in the world.
1859	George M. Pullman constructs his first sleeping car.
1862	Pacific Railroad Act signed by President Abraham Lincoln.
	First experimental car for sorting mail en route introduced on Hannibal & St. Joseph Railroad.
1863	Ground broken for Union Pacific and Central Pacific Railroads.
	First railroad union founded, Brotherhood of Locomotive Engineers.
1865	First oil tank car in service.
	First steel rails rolled in America.
1867	First railroad refrigerator car patented.
	First shipment of Texas longhorns by rail, from Abilene, Kansas.
1868	Automatic coupler patented by Eli H. Janney.

1869	First transcontinental railroad, the Union Pacific and Central Pacific, completed.
	George Westinghouse patents his first airbrake.
1871	First narrow-gauge (3 foot) railroad opened, in Colorado.
	First Granger railroad legislation in Illinois and Minnesota.
1872	George Westinghouse patents his automatic air brake.
1874	James B. Eads opens his Mississippi railroad bridge at St. Louis.
1877	Widespread railroad strike, starting on the Baltimore & Ohio.
	First use of telephone communication by railroad companies.
1879	First successful electric locomotive tried out by Werner von Siemens at Berlin.
1881	Steam heating introduced for passenger trains.
1883	Northern Pacific Railroad, third transcontinental railroad, opened.
	Standard time adopted by all American railroads.
1886	Last of the southern railroads narrowed to standard gauge.
1887	Interstate Commerce Commission set up by Congress.
	First trains with electric lighting introduced on Pennsylvania Railroad.
1893	Railroad Safety Appliance Act passed, requiring installation of airbrakes and automatic couplers on all trains.
1894	Great Pullman Strike, led by Eugene V. Debs and the American Railroad Union.
1895	First electric mainline railroad opened, in Baltimore.

1903   Penalties for discriminatory railroad rates established by Elkins Act.

1904   Northern Securities Company dissolved by the Supreme Court.

1905   First steel railroad cars in regular service.

            Hepburn Act passed by Congress, giving the Interstate Commerce Commission (ICC) greatly enhanced powers.

1910   Mann-Elkins Act passed by Congress, further strengthening the authority of the ICC.

1914   Panama Canal opened.

1916   Eight-hour day for railroad operating staff introduced by the Adamson Act.

1917   Operations of all railroads taken over by U.S. Railroad Administration (USRA) on December 28.

CHAPTER 1

HISTORICAL OVERVIEW

Early Transportation in America

In early America, freight and passengers were conveyed by water where possible. Rivers, lakes, and the ocean provided smooth surfaces for slow but heavy haulage. Soon surfaced roads were laid out to supplement the waterways, and many states helped to finance the construction of these turnpikes and toll roads. The National Road, running from Washington westward, was easily the most ambitious road project. It had been finished to Wheeling, Virginia, on the Ohio River, in 1818, but it took another fifteen years before Columbus, Ohio, was reached. Although fairly well built, it soon deteriorated through heavy usage and lack of maintenance. Traffic on most other turnpikes was heavy, both with passengers and freight, but rates and tolls were high, and the lumbering freight wagons were slow.

Canals were built about the same time, first to get around natural obstacles in rivers but soon also to extend navigation where rivers were too shallow or otherwise inadequate. The greatest canal project was undoubtedly the Erie Canal, 364 miles in length, connecting Albany, on the Hudson River, with Buffalo and the Great Lakes. It was built by the state of New York at a cost of eight million dollars, a staggering sum at the time, and opened in 1825. It was an immediate success and channeled a great deal of trade to the port of New York. Other ports, such as Philadelphia and Baltimore, immediately felt the impact and saw the necessity of improving their own connections with the hinterland. Eventually Pennsylvania constructed a system of canals, called the "Main Line," all the way to the Ohio River, 395 miles long, with 174 locks and a number of inclined planes on both sides of the mountains where the gradients were too severe for a canal.

Most of the canal traffic was moved by horses on towpaths along the banks, but steam propulsion promised faster and cheaper haulage. Robert Fulton had demonstrated the advantages of steamboats back in 1807, and soon steamboats were to be seen on most rivers. They were relatively fast, cheap, and luxuriously appointed, especially those on western rivers. In 1839 a trip from Pittsburgh to New Orleans, 2,064 miles, including meals on board, cost only forty-five dollars.[1] But steamboats were dangerous craft, flimsily built and with high-pressure boilers. Accidents were all too common, sometimes with great loss of life.

The First Railroads

The idea that wheels on a smooth surface encountered relatively little friction had occurred to miners in Europe in the Middle Ages. In Bohemian silver mines, carts with wooden wheels running on wooden "rails" were used, and elsewhere similar contraptions were developed. By the end of the eighteenth century a fairly large number of railways—or "plateways," as they were called then—were in use in England. Coal from inland mines was transported to the ports in four-wheel carts, which descended chiefly by gravity; empties were hauled back by horses. The first railroad on which traction with steam locomotives was used was the English Stockton & Darlington Railway, opened in 1825 and engineered by George Stephenson—"the Father of Railways," as he was later called. Stephenson also used inclined planes, where stationary steam engines hauled up carts by means of hemp ropes or cables.

The great breakthrough of the railway as a means of transportation came with the Liverpool & Manchester Railway, opened in 1830 and, again, engineered by George Stephenson, with help from his son Robert. Steam locomotives, constructed in the factory of Robert Stephenson & Company at Newcastle, were used exclusively after Stephenson's *Rocket* proved itself vastly superior to all competitors at the Rainhill Trials of 1829. All the interested world was present at the opening of the L & M, and its technological and economic success made a great impression everywhere. The railway was here to stay.

These developments in England did not go unnoticed in America. American engineers such as Horatio Allen, John B. Jervis, and others went to England to study railroads in their country of origin. Several short railroad lines were built in America in the late 1820s, most of them intended to haul stone or coal over relatively short distances. The great breakthrough in this country came with the founding of the Baltimore & Ohio Railroad in 1827. Where Philadelphia had opted for a system of canals to tap the western trade, Baltimore, then the third-largest city in the country, boldly chose the newfangled railroad for its own western connection. The first stone was laid on July 4, 1828, by the aged Charles Carroll, sole surviving signer of the Declaration of Independence. Carroll considered this to be "among the most important acts of my life, second only to my signing of the Declaration of Independence, if even it be second to that."[2] By 1830 the line had been extended to Ellicott's Mills, thirteen miles from Baltimore, and traffic had begun, with horse-drawn cars. Steam traction came soon after, when the distances became too great for horses. Harpers Ferry was reached in 1836, and a branch to Washington was opened in the same year, but it was 1852 before Wheeling was at last connected by rail to Baltimore. Steam had already been tried out in 1828, on the Delaware & Hudson Canal Company, when a locomotive imported from England, the *Stourbridge Lion*, had been put on the rails. It proved to be too heavy and was not used in regular service, but the seed had been sown.

Meanwhile, another coastal city, Charleston, South Carolina, had encountered the same decline in trade, and to stem the tide a railroad was projected from the city all the way to Hamburg, opposite Augusta, Georgia, on the Savannah River. This line was the first to use steam traction right from the start: on Christmas Day of 1830, the *Best Friend of Charleston*, a steam locomotive constructed by the West Point Foundry in New York City, hauled the first scheduled passenger train in the country. In 1833 the line was opened all the way to Hamburg, 136 miles from Charleston, making it the longest continuous railroad in the world. The success of the Baltimore & Ohio and the South Carolina railroads soon prompted others to try the same.

One of the first to do so was the Camden & Amboy of New Jersey, first begun in 1830 under the vigorous leadership of Robert L. Stevens, the inventor of the T-rail (that is, railroad rail with the now-familiar T-shaped cross section) and builder of steamboats and locomotives. The line from Camden, opposite Philadelphia on the Delaware River, to South Amboy on the Raritan River was opened throughout in 1834; with later extensions it constituted a second mainline between New York and Washington, with connections to Baltimore. Boston constructed its Western Railroad, chartered in 1833 and finished in 1841, across the Berkshires to Albany. New York State opened its first railroad, the Mohawk & Hudson between Albany and Schenectady, engineered by John B. Jervis, in 1831, and many other lines were chartered in that state after the success of this first one. All of these lines were "common carriers," expected to carry all passengers and freight within reason for certain set rates and on fixed schedules.

By 1840, only four states—Arkansas, Missouri, Tennessee, and Vermont—had no railways running within their borders; of the total of almost 3,000 miles of railroad lines in place, Pennsylvania, New York, and Massachusetts accounted for about half. The financial panic of 1837 brought some states—notably Michigan, Indiana, and Ohio, which had indulged in too much canal building and other internal improvements— to the verge of bankruptcy, and railroad construction languished for a time. Steam traction had become commonplace, speeds had risen to an un- believable thirty or forty miles per hour on some lines, and passenger cars providing more comfort than had the first crude boxes on wheels were gradually being introduced.

Still, there was no national network, and large gaps still existed be- tween the several lines or systems. Generally, however, American railroads were built more cheaply than comparable British or European roads. Land was cheap in America, in some places even free, while in heavily built-up Europe acquiring the land for rights of way could absorb millions. Also, American railroads were laid out with as little earthmoving as possible, following the lay of the land, though in some places that resulted in ex- cessive curvature and stiff gradients. But labor was scarce and expensive, and so the lesser quality of most of the railroads had to be accepted, at least in the early years. Later, extensive realignment and straightening of many lines would become necessary.

Growth was fast in the 1840s, and by 1850 the railroad network had grown to some 9,000 miles, still largely concentrated in New England and the Middle Atlantic states. But Georgia and South Carolina also had size- able networks, and in the old Northwest, Ohio was easily the leading state. Among the important lines constructed in this decade was the first stretch of the Pennsylvania Railroad, westward from Philadelphia by way of Harris- burg to Pittsburgh. When finished, the Pennsylvania RR quickly made the cumbersome Main Line canal across the mountains completely superflu- ous. Another significant addition was a string of seven railroads parallel- ing the Erie Canal; in 1853 they were united under the name of New York

Central Railroad, forming the nucleus of one of the great American railroad systems. In the southern part of the state of New York, the broad-gauge New York & Erie was being pushed forward. Dunkirk on Lake Erie, 483 miles from line's terminus on the Hudson River across from New York City, was reached in 1851.

The decade between 1850 and 1860 saw an enormous growth of the national network, from 9,000 to no less than 30,000 miles. The American economy expanded as never before and with it the railroads. Chicago and St. Louis had been reached from New York City, Chicago being served in 1860 by no less than eleven different railroads from all directions.

Indeed, Chicago had become the nation's great railroad center, having passed St. Louis as the commercial and industrial metropolis of the Midwest. By 1850 the city, with 30,000 residents, had been served by an extensive network of plank roads, stretching into the prairies in all directions. The first railroad in town was the Galena & Chicago Union Railroad (later part of the Chicago North Western), built to tap the lead-mining region to the west. Others soon followed after this first line had proved that railroads were better than the quickly rotting plank roads. From the east and southeast came such lines as the Michigan Central and the Michigan Southern; from the south, the Illinois Central; and to the west and southwest ran the first lines of the future systems of the Chicago, Burlington & Quincy and the Chicago, Rock Island & Pacific.[3]

The Rock Island became involved in a legal case that attracted widespread attention. The first line to bridge the Mississippi River en route to Davenport, Iowa, it aroused the enmity of the established steamboat interests, who naturally felt threatened in their very existences. In 1856, two weeks after the Rock Island's bridge was opened for rail traffic, a steamboat, the *Effie Afton*, hit the span and burst mysteriously into flames, burning a large part of the wooden bridge as well. The steamboat owners then sued the Rock Island for damages and complete removal of the bridge as a hindrance to shipping, but the Rock Island's attorney, Abraham Lincoln, the future president, managed to turn back the suit. This case clearly established that, in the future, navigable rivers could be bridged and that river steamboats would soon lose their monopoly. General traffic patterns in America were changing in any case; much of the north-south river traffic was gradually being superseded by a west-east pattern over the new railroads.[4]

Railroads were the nation's big business during this period.[5] Investment in the railroad network had been gigantic—around $1,150,000,000, largely from domestic sources, although foreign capitalists were becoming aware of the possibilities of American railroads as a profitable investment. The 700-mile Illinois Central, running from Chicago to Cairo at the confluence of the Ohio and Mississippi Rivers and completed in 1856, was one of the first railroads to be financed largely from abroad, in this case from England and the Netherlands. South of Cairo, the Mobile & Ohio continued the line, and another road—the New Orleans, Jackson & Great Northern—provided a connection with the Crescent City on the Gulf. Steam ferries connected the railheads on the Illinois and Kentucky shores of the Ohio River. A bridge at Cairo would have to wait until 1889.

At the outbreak of the Civil War, a fairly dense railroad network covered most of the states east of the Mississippi River. Ohio was now first in railroad mileage, with Illinois a close second. Pennsylvania and New York had fallen to third and fourth places, with Indiana only just behind New York. The South trailed far behind, with some 9,000 miles of the total of 30,000. West of the Mississippi only a few lines penetrated into the vast unknown, with the Hannibal & St. Joseph one of the most important. Around Galveston and Houston some primitive lines were opened and became the beginnings of the later extensive network in Texas. California counted one short line out of Sacramento.

On paper, then, the American railroad network by this time looked substantial and fully interconnected, but this was not the case in reality. Many different track gauges were in use, even in New England and the old Northwest. Some were made compatible by means of extra-wide wheel treads, but generally they were not compatible at all, necessitating transfer of through freight and passengers to other cars. This transfer was for passengers a nuisance at best, but for freight it was an expensive and labor-intensive process that delayed shipments and drove up rates. In wartime, as Americans were soon to find out, it could mean disaster when supplies and reinforcements could not be brought forward in time. But whatever their shortcomings, railroads had managed to bring down transportation costs substantially, and rates per ton-mile continued to fall in late 1850s. By 1860 one could travel from Boston to St. Louis in forty-eight hours. One could even buy a coupon ticket for the entire journey from Bangor, Maine, to New Orleans, a journey that, although it included several changes of cars, was much more safe and comfortable than the same trip had been ten or fifteen years before.[6]

Railroads after the Civil War

The important role played by the railroads during the Civil War is discussed in a separate chapter in this book. The Northern railroads came out of the war virtually undamaged—apart from the Baltimore & Ohio— and generally in good shape. Financially they had done well too, with money in hand for improvements and extensions. Traffic had boomed on most lines, and after the end of the war the many transatlantic steamship lines brought an ever larger influx of immigrants from Europe. In the South things were much different: extensive damage had been done to almost every railroad line, and rolling stock and locomotives were lacking. Some roads had built up large cash reserves and had paid out large dividends during the war, they had done so in greatly depreciated Confederate currency; after 1865 this money was worthless, and the companies had to start anew. Federal help came forward in the shape of cheap rolling stock and engines from the former U.S. Military Railroads and iron rails from government stockpiles, but even so, the 104-mile direct line between Charleston and Savannah, for instance, was put back in service only in 1870. The activities of carpetbaggers who laid hands on many southern rail systems, not for the public cause but chiefly for their own good, did not help either. Venal state government representatives and officials joined forces with these northerners and managed to steal millions from the already depleted state treasuries. Fraud was everywhere, corruption the normal way of life, and the railroad system suffered accordingly. It was many years before some measure of normalcy had returned to southern railroads.

In the 1860s the first two of the great transcontinental railroads were chartered, the Union Pacific–Central Pacific combination and the Northern Pacific. The transcontinentals form the subject of a separate chapter in this book and so need not detain us here. But apart from these trunklines, a large number of branch lines and other independent roads were being constructed west of the Missisippi River as well. From a paltry 3,500 miles in this area in 1865, mileage grew to a respectable 32,000 miles by 1880 and to 87,000 miles at the end of the nineteenth century. Some of the railroads serving the large agricultural area of the prairie states were called

"Granger" roads, as their chief commerce was in agricultural products. Most important of these were the Chicago, Burlington & Quincy, the Chicago, Milwaukee & St. Paul, the Chicago & North Western, and the Chicago, Rock Island & Pacific. Between them these companies covered the prairies with a closely woven network of branches, centered on Chicago and, to some extent, St. Louis and the twin cities of Minneapolis and St. Paul. Almost all of them put out feelers deep into the mountain area of Colorado or Montana. Most of them had acquired large land grants from the federal government in the then still unorganized territories; these tracts furnished them with a basis for obtaining credit in the East and in Europe. The extent of these land grants has been greatly exaggerated over the years by opponents of the railroads. Maps put out by detractors, chiefly Democrats out to blacken their Republican opponents before the elections of 1884, showed almost 90 percent of Iowa as railroad land, while in reality only 13 percent could be marked as such; for Kansas it was 62 percent against 16, and for Michigan 75 percent instead of 9. Apparently no one questioned the accuracy of these faulty figures; they were repeated uncritically again and again until finally exploded in the 1940s.[7] In reality the grants were fairly modest, and in return the railroads in question carried government mail, personnel, and supplies at 50 percent of the going rate.

The railroads played a conspicuous part in the development of the range cattle industry. In 1867 Abilene, Kansas, on the Kansas Pacific, was the first of the stations where Texas longhorns were loaded for slaughter in the Chicago market; other stations, such as Newton and Dodge City, soon followed. By 1880, however, corn (as well as wheat and other grains) had supplanted cattle as the major industry, and cattle shipments fell off. Without the railroads, agriculture in the whole area would not have experienced its phenomenal growth; only the availability of cheap transportation made it profitable for the farmers to sell their products in the markets of Chicago and other cities. A vast agricultural-industrial complex grew up in the area, comprising the Chicago wheat pit, the flour mills of Minneapolis, the slaughterhouses of Kansas City, and the farm-implement industries of Rock Island and Davenport. Railroads served them all.

Similarly, the mining industries of Colorado, Utah, and Montana could not have been developed without railways. Ores were heavy and difficult to transport by wagon, and all supplies, from food to shovels and black powder, had to be brought in from afar. A dense network of narrow-gauge lines, adapted to the mountainous terrain, sprang up in Colorado. Every new gold or silver strike was soon followed by a railway line, and some of the more spectacular mining towns, such as Leadville, were served by more than one railroad. Competition between the several companies was keen, and much superfluous construction was undertaken, just to make sure that one's competitor was not the only one to haul away the riches of the earth.

Labor relations deteriorated in the 1870s. Some railroad workers had already started to organize—the locomotive engineers first of all in 1863, followed by the conductors five years later, the firemen in 1873, and the trainmen in 1883. A general downturn of the economy after 1873 caused many layoffs and wage cuts; when the Baltimore & Ohio announced a further cut of 10 percent in 1877, B & O crews went on strike. Soon other railroads were affected too, and the strike spread as far as Chicago, St. Louis, and Omaha. Federal troops finally suppressed the strike after much bloodshed and destruction of property, especially in the Pittsburgh area, where the strike had been most violent. Labor relations improved somewhat after this, but the attitude of railroad management toward the unions remained hostile well into the twentieth century.

A particularly nasty conflict was the Pullman Strike of 1894. The general downturn of the economy after the Panic of 1893 had caused a severe setback for the Pullman Palace Car Company. George Pullman started to lay off workers and cut the wages of those remaining by 25 percent, but without lowering the rents in his model town of Pullman (south of Chicago). After many protests his workers walked out in May 1894; the strikers were supported by the American Railway Union of Eugene V. Debs, the members of which refused to handle Pullman cars. After much bloodshed and damage to property, federal troops were called out to suppress the strike, which embittered labor relations for many years to come. It also broke George M. Pullman.[8]

The High Noon of Railroads

In the 1890s railroad construction slowed down somewhat, the more so after the Panic of 1893, when many railroad companies, including even such giants as the Union Pacific and the Santa Fe, went under and had to be reorganized. But late in the 1890s new construction picked up again, and the trend continued well into the twentieth century, especially in new states such as Oklahoma and New Mexico. Oil strikes in Oklahoma and Texas caused a new boom, as every railroad wanted to get into the business of hauling oil and oil products (as usual, much overbuilding resulted). The nation's shift from a largely agricultural to a heavily industrialized society took place in this era, and the railroads were a major factor.

Most mainlines were in place by 1900, but a few latecomers should be mentioned. The Kansas City, Pittsburg & Gulf—today the Kansas City Southern—was the last great north-south mainline, opened in 1899 and profiting from the big Beaumont oil field in East Texas. It was the brain-child of an outsider, Arthur E. Stilwell, and financed exclusively from the Netherlands—hence the large number of Dutch place-names along the route. The last mainline ever was the Western Pacific, meant to provide the railroad empire of George Gould with an outlet of its own to the Pacific coast, but in the end, it was a financial disaster.

It was an era of major railroad mergers, whereby smaller roads were grouped together in giant corporations. Bankers played a major role here; railroad managers had to take a back seat as Wall Street took over. Bankers like J. Pierpont Morgan, James Stillman, Jacob Schiff, and Kuhn Loeb & Company, afraid of endangering the return on their investments, abhorred what they considered wasteful competition between the mutually hostile companies and tried to collect railroads in friendly combinations. They were soon to find themselves in a morass of litigation and government antimonopoly measures.

The years before 1914 also saw the high tide of railroad passenger traffic. Never before had it been possible to travel in such luxury as most carriers now provided. Sumptuous accommodations became commonplace for the happy few who could afford to pay the price, and in a time when there was no alternative to railroad travel, the well-heeled classes were willing to pay. On all major transcontinentals, which competed strongly for the traffic, luxury trains were introduced, with parlor cars, lounge cars, dining cars, sleeping cars, and observation cars, as well as excellent meals and superb service to woo the traveler from the competition next door. Electric lighting, comfortable heating, and ventilation became the norm, and high speeds became possible after the introduction of the automatic coupler and continuous airbrake. The names of such trains as the "Over-land Limited" on the Union Pacific, the "Oriental Limited" of the Great Northern, and the "North Coast Limited" of the Northern Pacific became household words. Even more prestigious was Santa Fe's "California Limited," launched in 1892 and in 1911 supplemented by the "de-Luxe," the last word in luxury and the pinnacle of rail travel in the world. It made the trip between Chicago and Los Angeles once a week in sixty-three hours and carried, apart from the usual luxurious sleepers and restaurant cars, baths, showers, and a library—all for an extra twenty-five dollars over the first-class rate.[9] In the East, the New York Central and the Pennsylvania competed strongly for the New York–Chicago traffic, with the luxury "20th Century Limited" of the New York Central, introduced in 1902, and the "Pennsylvania Special" (later the "Broadway Limited") begun in the same year. They were of about the same quality in speed and luxury, and each commanded a dedicated ridership.

On the other side of the spectrum was the daily (except Sundays) mixed train, ambling leisurely along the track, setting out and picking up cars at every depot and spur, easily taking a whole day for a trip. Even so, it provided transportation in a time when country roads were impassable in most weather, or simply nonexistent. The railroad depot in every rural town and hamlet was the center of civilization, connected to the outside world by the telegraph, and the station staff was the best source of news. The growth of mail-order houses such as Sears, Roebuck and Co. could not have taken place had not the railroads entered almost every remote mountain valley or sleepy prairie town. The free rural delivery of the Post Office, introduced in 1896, went, after all, chiefly by train.

Monopoly and Government Measures

Nonetheless, not all was well in the railroad industry. Business ethics were lenient generally, but in the railroad world it seemed that nearly anything was allowed. Stock speculation on Wall Street was perhaps the most widely accepted way of acquiring private wealth or control over competing lines. "Stock watering," whereby the share capital of a company was raised artificially to obtain a majority on the board, was common too; dividends, when paid at all, were accordingly spread very thin. The ordinary shareholders suffered. (The "Erie Wars" and all other mergers and struggles for monopoly are the subject of a separate chapter and need not be discussed here.)

Another sore point caused by the railroad monopoly was the question of rates and the rebates given to favored shippers. Railroad rates west of the Mississippi were considerably higher than east of the river, 2.2–2.5

cents per ton/mile against 1.25–1.6 cents; despite continuing protests, this margin was still 1.03 to 0.83 cents in 1900. Railroad rates fell all over the country after the Civil War, but farmers still complained.[10] A counter movement, led by the National Grange of the Patrons of Husbandry, founded by Oliver H. Kelley in 1867, gained strength. Around 1875 the Grange, as it was generally called, had grown to 800,000 members and was becoming a force to be reckoned with. Regulation of railroads started on the state level in Illinois in the 1870s; other agricultural states soon followed and passed similar laws. Of course, the railroads fought these state laws in the courts, denying states' right to establish maximum rates. In the end the U.S. Supreme Court, in the notorious case of the *Wabash, St. Louis & Pacific v. Illinois,* decided that individual states in fact could not establish rates on freight passing over their borders—only the federal government could regulate interstate traffic.

The idea of a federal railroad commission had been aired in 1871, but nothing had come of it. By the 1880s, however, the clamor for regulation had swelled to such an extent that President Chester Arthur in 1883 urged Congress to act to protect the public from railroad abuses. The ultimate result was the Interstate Commerce Act, signed by President Grover Cleveland on February 4, 1887. At first the commissioners appointed under the new law had little power to establish the "reasonable and just" rates mentioned in the act, and abuses continued. However, the Progressive movement, embodied by President Theodore Roosevelt, gained strength in the early twentieth century, and in 1906 a new act greatly enlarged the powers of the ICC. Monopolies and Big Business came under fire and were severely restricted in power. Under Roosevelt's successor, William H. Taft, this process continued, and in 1910 the ICC obtained further powers to regulate rates and service.

In 1917, with the entry of the United States into World War I, the railroads could hardly meet the vastly increased demand for transportation. A complicating factor was the Adamson Act of 1916, stipulating eight-hour days for railroad workers and thereby necessitating large numbers of new personnel to keep railroads running day and night. Lack of cooperation between many carriers, shortages of cars, the inadequacy of many railroad yards and ports, and lack of suitable freight power caused an almost complete breakdown. Yards became clogged with freight trucks that could not be unloaded on time, ships that were to carry much-needed

Railroad Mileage in the United States

1830	23
1840	2,808
1850	9,201
1860	30,626
1870	52,922
1880	93,267
1890	163,597
1900	193,346
1910	240,439
1916	254,037
1920	252,845
1930	249,052
1940	233,670
1950	223,779

Source: Stover, *American Railroads*, 205.

supplies for the allies had to wait in port for cargoes because trains could not get through, and trains out on the line were delayed beyond belief. Around Christmas 1917 the crisis had become a disaster, and the federal government felt obliged to take over the management of all railroads in the country; it did so through the U.S. Railroad Administration, under the able leadership of William G. McAdoo, already secretary of the treasury. The crisis soon passed, but it was not until 1920 that the railroads were handed back to their owners.

Notes

1. John F. Stover, *American Railroads*, 2nd ed. (Chicago: University of Chicago Press, 1997), 8.

2. James D. Dilts, *The Great Road: The Building of the Baltimore and Ohio, the Nation's First Railroad, 1828–1853* (Stanford, Calif.: Stanford University Press, 1993), 10–11.

3. William Cronon, *Nature's Metropolis: Chicago and the Great West* (New York: Norton, 1991).

4. Louis C. Hunter, *Steamboats on the Western Rivers: An Economic and Technological History* (Mineola, N.Y.: Dover, 1993).

5. Alfred D. Chandler, *The Railroads: The Nation's First Big Business* (New York: Harcourt, Brace & World, 1965).

6. Stover, *American Railroads*, 48.

7. Stover, *The Routledge Historical Atlas of American Railroads* (New York and London, 1999), 32–33.

8. W. Thomas White, "Eugene Victor Debs," in *Railroads in the Nineteenth Century: Encyclopedia of American Business History and Biography*, ed. Robert L. Frey (New York: Facts On File, 1988), 79–83.

9. Mike Schafer, *The American Passenger Train* (St. Paul, Minn.: MBI, 2001), 41–42.

10. Stover, *American Railroads*, 92.

CHAPTER 2

THE TECHNOLOGY OF RAILROADS

Railroad technology did not come ready-made but evolved slowly over the early years of the nineteenth century. Most of the technology came from Great Britain, where the new mode of transportation spread in the 1820s and 1830s. Other countries followed. American engineers were few, but some army engineers, educated at the U.S. Military Academy at West Point, New York, became civilian railroad engineers or were lent out by the government to make surveys for railroad lines. Land surveyors branched out in railroad engineering, and not a few were self-made men with only their own wits to guide them, as handbooks of railroad engineering hardly existed. A few of these former surveyors were sent to England to study railway practice and place orders for ironwork and engines, but soon a new breed of men arose, reared in the railroad world and fully able to develop the American railroad into a modern, widely used, and dependable system of transportation. During most of the nineteenth century the railroad industry was on the cutting edge of modern technology, a position it was to relinquish in the twentieth century to the automotive and aircraft industries and still later to electronics.

Rails

George Stephenson had used short cast-iron rails on his Stockton & Darlington line and again on the Liverpool & Manchester. Iron was plentiful and fairly cheap in England, and although brittle, it was adequate for the comparatively light loads of the time. The rails were fastened in "chairs" resting on stone blocks, but when it proved difficult to keep the rails in gauge, transverse wooden sleepers, or ties, were used instead. Other systems were tried, such as Isambard Kingdom Brunel's wrought-iron rails of a "hat," or inverted U, profile on longitudinal wooden stringers. It was used on the English Great Western Railway in the early 1830s and also elsewhere in the world.

If iron was cheap in England, it was not in America. Most of its iron had to be imported from England, as foundries and rolling mills were a rarity in early America. The first American railway engineers, such as John B. Jervis, were forced to use wooden stringers with flat strips of wrought iron nailed across their tops as rails. With light loads they worked, but the nails had a tendency to work loose, with the result that an iron strap could suddenly buckle and force itself up through the flimsy floor of a car and derail the train. These "snake heads," as they were called, could kill or maim the occupants of the car and were much feared. When heavier loads and higher speeds became possible with better and stronger locomotives, the strap rail was no longer adequate.

In 1830 Robert L. Stevens, engineer of the Camden & Amboy Railroad in New Jersey, came up with the idea of using wrought-iron rails of an inverted T profile. The wide portion of the T formed the base, and the wheels of the train ran on the slightly enlarged top edge. The Pennsylvania Railroad Company, always in the forefront of technology, adopted the Stevens T-rail in 1845, and others soon followed.[1] In England, almost simultaneously, Charles Blacker Vignoles, who probably did not know of Stevens's work, invented a flat-bottomed rail profile that resembled Stevens's and is still in general use worldwide. The first American T-rails were rolled in England, but in the late 1840s domestic rolling mills started the production of iron rails on a large scale, although imports from England, Germany, and Belgium continued to be used from time to time when American mills were swamped with orders. In 1861 the protective Morrill Tariff effectively put an end to foreign imports; from that year on American mills and foundries developed quickly.

Steel rails were first rolled in England in 1860, using the Bessemer process, and although much more expensive they soon came into general use, as they proved much harder and longer lasting than the soft iron rails used until then. In America the first steel rails were rolled in 1865 by the North Chicago Rolling Mills, soon followed by the Cambria Iron Works of Johnstown, Pennsylvania, and others.[2] Where traffic was light, the use of the cheap iron rail continued, even for new construction; even in 1889 only twenty-nine percent of all American railroad lines were being laid with steel rails.[3] But by the turn of the century iron rails were to be found only in sidings and spurs; all mainlines were laid with steel.

T-rails came originally in short lengths, fifteen feet being about the maximum. They were at first simply spiked down end to end, but these joints lacked stability, and rail joints with bolted-on fishplates became common. Rail weights of thirty pounds per yard were common, but gradually longer and heavier rails, thirty feet long (thirty-nine feet after 1893) and fifty to sixty pounds per yard, came into use. Only toward the end of the nineteenth century did rail weights increase to ninety pounds per yard, again in longer rails by then being produced by the rolling mills.

Most early primitive railroads buried in the ground the stone blocks or wooden ties that carried the rails and spread the weight of the trains, but gravel or stone chips were soon used as ballast to give better drainage and slow the rotting of the wood. Hardwood was preferred, but when it was not available other, softer, woods had to be used as well. Several methods were tried to postpone the inevitable rotting process. Surface burning of ties was practiced in some places, but more successful was the "Kyanizing" process (invented by J.H. Kyan in 1832), saturating the wood with a solution of mercury chloride or zinc chloride. It was too expensive, however, and a cheaper means was found in creosote. At first ties were simply immersed in creosote for days or weeks, but later it was found out that impregnating the ties under pressure was much more effective. Ties treated in this way could last for twenty or even thirty years. Steel ties were used by some companies, but on a limited scale only.

The Battle of the Gauges

George Stephenson had used for his Stockton & Darlington line a track gauge (rail separation) of four feet, eight and one-half inches, because that was the width at which most of the plateways or wagonways in his native Northumberland were laid. Purportedly this rather arbitrary gauge went back to the dimensions of ancient Roman horse carts. However that may be, the Stephensonian gauge was to become the standard gauge of today, but it did not do so without competition in both directions. Many engineers found the standard gauge too narrow and opted for wider gauges to accomodate larger engines and cars and to give more stability at higher speeds. Brunel built his Great Western Railway with a gauge of seven feet, and it lasted in England until 1892, despite the nuisance of transshipment at points where the GWR touched other lines laid to the Stephensonian "standard" gauge. In Europe other gauges—of five feet or five feet, six inches—were, and still are being, used (in Ireland, Russia, and Spain, for instance). Other countries, such as the grand duchy of Baden (Germany) and the Netherlands, converted to the standard gauge only after laying their first lines to wider gauges.

Small wonder, then, that in America a number of different gauges were used. Most of the first railroad lines in the northeastern part of the country used the standard gauge, because their first engines were ordered from England. But soon lines were being laid to a width of five feet, especially in the southern states; as most early lines were purely local or regional, the question of connections between them hardly arose. Other lines, such as the New York & Erie (and its subsidiary the Atlantic & Great Western) and the Ohio & Mississippi, adopted a wide gauge of six feet on the false assumption that the competition could be kept out in this way. By 1864 a broad-gauge line from New York all the way to St. Louis was available. Ohio prescribed an official gauge of four feet, ten inches; Pennsylvania specified four feet, nine inches; and most southern states had five feet, with important exceptions in Virginia and North Carolina.[4]

Of course, questions of connections arose when the railroad network grew, and when they did, technical solutions were sought. Gauges between four feet, eight and one-half inches and four feet, ten inches were more or less interoperable using cars with wide wheel treads, but they were not considered completely safe. Between the standard gauge and five- or six-foot gauges no through traffic was possible; passengers had to change trains. At some transfer points freight cars were lifted off their trucks so the trucks could be rolled away and replaced by others on the new gauge. This operation took time; the only real solution was complete conversion, and this happened fairly early. Ohio abolished its wide gauge in the late 1860s and early 1870s, the Ohio & Mississippi converted in 1871, and the Erie laid a third rail to the standard gauge in that same year and abolished its six-foot gauge completely by 1880. The Illinois Central, itself a standard-gauge road, converted its five-foot lines south of the Ohio River in 1884, and the Mobile & Ohio followed the next year. The other southern railroads did the same on May 31 and June 1, 1886, when in one well-planned and gigantic operation 13,000 miles of railroad line were narrowed to standard gauge.

While this shift toward a uniform standard gauge was taking place, another movement, in a different direction, became strong. Gauges narrower than the four feet, eight and one-half inch standard had been in use in several countries for some years. In Wales, the Festiniog Railway operated with steam locomotives on a gauge of about two feet, while in Norway several lines laid to a gauge of three feet, six inches (1,067 mm) had been opened between 1862 and 1864 and were very successful. In the wilder and less populated British colonies, narrow-gauge lines now sprang up; Australia, New Zealand, and South Africa used the three-foot six-inch gauge, while, remarkably, India opted for the meter (1,000 mm) gauge. Japan chose the three-foot six-inch gauge, and the Dutch East Indies, after a first line had been laid to standard gauge, did the same.[5] The French colonies mostly used the meter gauge. Cheapness of construction was the most frequent argument for narrow gauges; the resulting lower speeds and smaller loading capacities of rolling stock were taken in stride.

In the United States these developments did not go unnoticed, and the chief protagonists of narrow gauges never tired of boasting of their advantages, chiefly cost. They maintained that savings of forty percent or more could be attained. Starting in 1871 a sizeable network in three-foot gauge was laid down, not only in the mountainous regions of Colorado and New Mexico, where it made sense, but also in the relatively flat terrain of Ohio, Indiana, and Illinois. One of the most comprehensive projects was the Grand Narrow Gauge Trunk, which was to stretch from Toledo, Ohio, to Laredo, Texas—1,642 miles in all.[6] It was never completely finished, but long stretches operated for many years. By 1885 over 11,000 miles in three-foot gauge were in service, but thereafter decline set in. Many lines were abandoned, and others converted to standard gauge, until by 1900 only some 6,700 miles were left.[7] Incompatibility with connecting standard-gauge railroads (necessitating costly transshipment), reduced carrying capacity (which made a difference as traffic grew), and lack of stability at higher speeds all contributed to the decline of the narrow-gauge mileage. Today the three-foot gauge is confined to a few tourist operations in Colorado, New Mexico, and Pennsylvania.

Bridges

Bridging the many rivers and streams for a railroad presented unprecedented challenges. In New England and the states of the Atlantic seaboard, the early railroads often constructed their first bridges of stone. The pioneer Baltimore & Ohio Railroad had many stone viaducts and bridges, some of them so well built that they are still in service today. The New York & Erie constructed its magnificent seventeen-arch Starrucca Viaduct (Pennsylvania) of stone; it too still stands. But most railroad companies found stone too expensive and switched to wood, which was always plentiful. Many engineers—notably Elias Howe, Stephen H. Long, and Thomas Pratt—patented wooden truss bridges, some of which reached respectable spans of 300 feet.[8] Even simpler to construct was the wooden trestle, for crossing dry ravines and the like; they became widely popular and reached enormous proportions, especially in the West, where cheapness of construction was a major factor.

Wooden bridges and trestles alike had, however, the disadvantages of all wooden structures: rapid decay and extreme vulnerability to fire. Iron bridges, of course, had a distinct advantage there, but they were more expensive and needed skilled labor to erect. But once American foundries and rolling mills could supply the necessary iron profiles and structural shapes, iron became the favorite material for railroad bridges. The Pratt truss was adapted to iron, and Squire Whipple, Herman Haupt, and Wendel Bollman all patented designs for iron truss bridges. Steel, lighter and stronger than iron, came into use in the late 1870s and gradually supplanted it as a construction material. Reinforced concrete was first used around 1900 but would really make its mark only in the twentieth century.

Locomotives

Steam as a source of power was, of course, nothing new. In antiquity it had been used as a kind of toy, and since the early eighteenth century Thomas Newcomen's steam-powered pumps had kept tin mines in Cornwall dry. Subsequently James Watt improved the cumbersome, coaleating Newcomen machine into a more generally useful engine, and Richard Trevithick constructed the first high-pressure steam engine running on primitive rails.

In America a steam engine had been used by Robert Fulton in 1807 to propel his boat *Clermont* up the Hudson River all the way to Albany against the current, and since then steamboats had been a fairly common sight on American inland and coastal waters. But steam locomotion on land

was a different matter. Here England again led the way. The steam locomotive as developed by the Stephensons and others embodied all the fundamental design features that would be used to the very end of steam: a
tubular boiler, separate firebox and smokebox, and exhaust up a chim-
ney to provide a strong draft on the fire. American engineers traveled to
Britain to see steam locomotives with their own eyes and order engines
from English firms. In the late 1820s Horatio Allen was sent out by the
Delaware & Hudson Canal Company, and George W. Whistler and Ross
Winans by the Baltimore & Ohio, to study the latest practices, but they
could do little to improve upon the fundamentals.

The first steam engine actually to run in America was the "Stourbridge
Lion," built in England in 1829 for the Delaware & Hudson Canal and Railroad Company, but it turned out to be too heavy for the light track. Other
and more successful engines followed; between 1829 and 1841, when the
last arrived, about 120 locomotives were imported from Great Britain.[9]

These British designs may have been suitable for the relatively heavy,
straight, and level tracks that were common in England at the time, but
they were not well suited to the cheaply constructed light, sinuous, and
undulating tracks of the early American railroads. American engineers set
out to improve the tracking of the locomotive. Most early imported engines were 0-4-0s, with four coupled wheels, or 2-2-0s, with one driven
axle and a carrying axle in front, and their stability left much to be desired. In 1831 John B. Jervis designed for the Mohawk & Hudson Railroad a 4-2-0, with one driven axle behind and a four-wheel truck in front;
this type proved very successful on American rails and was copied by many
builders. A somewhat later development was the 4-4-0, with four coupled
wheels and a truck. It became known as the "American" standard type;
thousands were built until the 1890s.

One of the few early American machine shops, the West Point
Foundry of New York City, turned out some of the first locomotives, and
it was soon followed by others. Baldwin, Norris, and Rogers are some of
the better-known names, but scores of other manufacturers tried their hand
at building locomotives. Most were concentrated in New England, New
York, New Jersey, and Pennsylvania. Virginia had its Tredegar Iron Works
at Richmond, but the rest of the South lacked heavy industry. Cincinnati
had a few builders, but their production was limited. Out west the Union
Iron Works and Vulcan Iron Works, both of San Francisco, turned out a

few engines but never on a significant scale, despite the high shipping charges to bring locomotives from the East around Cape Horn to California. At the end of the nineteenth century the industry was dominated by only six major builders. A great consolidation of eight independent builders, of which Schenectady, Brooks, and Rhode Island were the biggest, took place in 1901 with the incorporation of the American Locomotive Company (ALCO). Rogers, the third-largest builder at the end of the nineteenth century, joined the firm in 1905.[10] In contrast with Great Britain, where most of the railway companies built their own locomotives, the American scene was dominated by the commercial industry. Only the Pennsylvania, the Baltimore & Ohio, the Central Pacific, and a few other railroad companies constructed some of their engines in their own shops.

Remarkably, the price of an average 4-4-0 engine, despite its heavier weight and greater sophistication, remained fairly constant over the whole nineteenth century, at around $8,000. Larger engines, such as "ten-wheelers" (4-6-0s, first introduced in 1847 and the second most popular wheel arrangement in America), "Moguls" (2-6-0s, from 1860), and "Consolidations" (2-8-0s, first built in 1865), were more expensive, at around $15,000.

Most locomotives burned wood, which was plentiful and cheap, at least in the beginning. But after nearby forests were denuded, the price of cordwood went up, and coal was tried as a substitute. Coal burning involved special grates (on which the burning coal would rest in the firebox), however, and it took some time before engineers had figured out how to accomplish this. By 1880 more than ninety percent of the fuel used by the railroads was coal.[11] Petroleum—or "coal oil," as it was called then—was experimented with, but it would come into use as locomotive fuel only in the twentieth century. A familiar sight in the time of the wood-burning locomotive (and later well known from TV and movies) was its enormous conical smokestack with some sort of spark arrestor, to prevent sparks from the engine from starting forest fires. Scores of types were tried and patented, but only a few survived in the harsh railroad world.

American engineers and locomotive builders were a rather conservative group who abhorred experiments. European inventions, such as the Belpaire firebox and the Walschaert valve gear, both Belgian ideas, were only introduced slowly and without much enthusiasm. In the long run, however, when the advantages had been clearly demonstrated, these innovations were adopted. Illustrative is the American experience with one important component of steam locomotive construction, the injector. This instrument, without moving parts and meant to fill the boiler with water, had been invented by the Frenchman Henri J. Giffard in 1858. It was quickly taken up in England and Europe, where it was gladly used to replace the cumbersome and crude crosshead pumps. Despite some initial success in the United States, it was found to be a sensitive and delicate instrument, hated by the enginemen, and quickly dropped as standard equipment. Only after the 1880s did new, improved types of injectors at last replace the crosshead pump in America.

Passenger and Freight Cars

In this field little or no British influence is visible. American engineers simply borrowed stagecoach technology, putting a body of a road coach on a four-wheel truck with flanged wheels. From there it was only a step to lengthening the car by using three compartments, but still on four wheels.[12] These first coaches, not more than twenty feet long, with springs made of leather straps, rolled and swayed dangerously at any speed; the logical solution was to place a longer body on two swiveling four-wheel trucks. Again, the pioneering Baltimore & Ohio led the way, experimenting with double-truck coaches on a considerable scale in the early 1830s. Thus was born the typically American day coach, carrying only one class—as befitted an egalitarian and thoroughly republican society. It was a long wooden box, some forty feet long, with seats on both sides of the aisle, a stove at one end and—sometimes—a lavatory at the other end, access by way of end doors opening onto open platforms, and lighting by means of candles. Over the years many improvements were made: cars became heavier and longer, with more comfortable adjustable seats, sprung and better-riding four or six-wheel trucks, clerestory windows for better ventilation, lighting by means of kerosene or gas lamps, and heating by closed systems instead of the old potbelly stoves. Weights went up too, from 12,000 pounds in the 1830s to around 100,000 pounds for an eighty-foot-long car at the end of the century. With all-wooden construction, a length of seventy feet was about the safe limit, so in the 1890s engineers went over to composite construction, with steel underframes and wooden bodies. All-iron or all-steel construction had been tried out over the years since the 1850s, but without lasting effect. The fundamental aim of that innovation was to eliminate the risk of fire. In accidents the combination of stoves, kerosene lamps, and wooden coaches had often proved fatal. Almost every railroad crash, especially in winter, when the stoves were lit, ended in a major conflagration.[13] The first all-steel cars that were a real success would be built in 1904 for New York's Interborough subway, and from that moment on, all-steel construction became widely accepted.

With the gradual extension of the American railroad network, longer journeys involving night travel became more common. As it was no pleasure to sit up all night in a hard uncomfortable seat, inventors turned their thoughts to devising some sort of sleeping car. Apparently the egalitarian idea was losing part of its charm, as well-heeled travelers no longer wanted to be cooped up all night in cramped surroundings with the lower orders. Experiments with day cars that could be converted into sleeping cars had begun back in the 1830s and 1840s, but the real breakthrough came in the late 1850s, when several sleeping-car companies were founded. T.T. Woodruff & Company dated from 1857, the Wagner Palace Car Company was incorporated the next year, and the most famous of them all, the Pullman Palace Car Company, started operations in 1859. By 1899, when he took over Wagner, Pullman had almost eliminated the competition. By 1900 Pullman operated more than 3,000 cars—sleepers, diners, and parlor cars—on over 158,000 miles of railroad.[14] His name had become a household word all over the world for luxury travel.

The first freight cars were even simpler than the passenger cars of the day. A wooden box on four (later eight) wheels sufficed for most purposes. Soon specialization was necessary for different types of freight.[15] Cattle was first carried in ordinary closed boxcars fitted with slatted doors, but in the late 1860s specialized stock cars were being introduced to accommodate the growing livestock traffic from the West to the stockyards of Chicago, Omaha, and other cities. When the American public objected to the often harsh circumstances in which cattle were transported to market, more elaborate stock cars with troughs for watering and feeding were constructed, and laws were enacted that compelled shippers and railroads to include rests for the animals in their schedules.

In the 1870s, to handle the extensive traffic in meat from the Chicago stockyards to the markets in the East, several meat packers, such as Swift and Armour, developed the refrigerated boxcar in the 1870s. Double walls, tight-fitting doors, and receptacles for blocks of ice made it possible to transport dressed beef to the markets of New York City. Others found uses for these cars in transporting fresh strawberries from Louisiana or citrus fruit from California. Most of the refrigerator cars—by 1900 there were 68,500 of them—were owned not by the railroads but by private shippers.[16] Extensive icing facilities were erected at strategic places to service the solid trains of refrigerator cars.

Other specialized freight cars included gondolas for coal traffic, equipped with bottom or side hoppers for fast discharge of the load. Special equipment also evolved during the nineteenth century for ores, coke, sand, and other such commodities. Petroleum needed yet another sort of specialized car. At first, after Col. Edwin L. Drake struck oil near Titusville, Pennsylvania, in 1859, crude was transported in wooden vats on flatcars, but this turned out to be impractical and dangerous. During the 1860s several inventors and manufacturers patented designs for an iron tank car with a long, horizontal tank, running on two four-wheel trucks, and these were soon in general use. The dimensions were enlarged, and other improvements were introduced over the years, but the design is still essentially the same today.

Another once-familiar sight on the end of every freight train was the caboose, also called a "cabin car" or "way car." The name came from the Dutch word *kombuis,* the galley of a ship or a small kitchen. In the caboose the conductor stored his lanterns, flags, tools, and other equipment and did his paperwork regarding destination bills, switching on the way, etc. Train crews could heat their meals over the stove or take a nap during the sometimes long waits in sidings for other trains to pass on a single track, take a drink from the water cooler, or use the built-in toilet. Out on the road the conductor could supervise the movement of his train from his seat in the high cupola. The first primitive cabooses appeared in the 1850s, mostly converted boxcars, but soon cabooses were built specifically for this service. Four-wheelers were popular for a time, as they added very little unnecessary weight to a freight train, and some railroads stuck to them until the end of the nineteenth century. Other roads, such as the Union Pacific and Santa Fe, operating over vast distances in barren country, had large and comfortable cabooses, sometimes with quarters for as many as ten men. Cupolas or lookouts on the roofs came into use in the late 1860s, but some railroads were slow in adopting them and instead kept bay windows at the sides of the car.

An important element in the freight business was the free interchange of cars between different railroads. At first this happened on a regional scale, but with the extension of the national network and the pressures caused by the Civil War, some form of regulation became necessary. The example here was set by the British Railway Clearing House, which monitored interchange of trucks between all British railways and settled accounts for the use of freight trucks on "foreign" lines. No truly national system was ever evolved, but something similar, under the supervision of the Master Car Builders Association (MCB), was operating in America after the 1860s.[17]

Couplers and Brakes

Chains and iron hooks were the first means to couple cars and engines together. The European system of sprung side buffers with central links was never adopted in America; various forms of link and pin coupler were developed instead. Each car had a heavy iron tube, in which a link was held by a pin dropped from above through a hole. Coupling two cars was done by pushing the cars slowly together, while a brakeman or conductor guided the link of one car into the tube of the other and dropped the pin at the right moment. This was a dangerous practice, of course, especially with long trains, when the engineer on the locomotive could not see very well the cars to be coupled and had to rely on the hand or lantern signals of the conductor. Bad weather and low visibility made things worse, and accidents were all too common. Experienced trainmen could be recognized by their broken or missing fingers.

By 1875, passenger cars, of which there were fewer than freight cars, were equipped with the Miller coupler, an automatic device that allowed coupling to be accomplished by simply pushing the cars together, and separation by means of a lever on the platform, doing away with the dangerous link-and-pin coupler. But by far the most frequent switching involved freight cars, and here no generally accepted automatic coupler was available. Literally thousands of patents were taken out, but none found universal favor.[18] Some states enacted laws requiring the use of some form of automatic coupler, but compliance was slow.

In 1873, a dry-goods clerk in Virginia, Eli H. Janney, took out a patent for an automatic "knuckle" coupler that really worked. Some railroads adopted his design, and with improvements by a Pittsburgh firm of experienced machinist and toolmakers, the mighty Pennsylvania Railroad started to use it for its passenger cars. In trials organized by the MCB in 1885, the Janney coupler came out best, but it still took years before even a small number of cars were so equipped. It was thanks to the activities of Lorenzo S. Coffin, an Iowa farmer, preacher, teacher, and reformer, that at long last Congress took action.[19] Coffin, who had been a commissioner of the Iowa Railroad Commission though not a railroader himself, took up the cause of the many maimed trainmen. Although he was considered a crank by railroad management, his lobbying finally persuaded the authorities that something had to be done. President Benjamin Harrison embraced his cause, and in 1893 the Safety Appliance Act was signed into law. It gave the railroads five years to equip all their rolling stock with some form of automatic coupler; by 1900 all cars not equipped with a version of the MCB or Janney coupler were outlawed.[20]

Brakes were nonexistent at the beginning, and with the low speeds of those days none were deemed necessary. With growing train weights and increased speeds some form of brake became imperative, but at first only passenger cars were equipped—with handbrakes, worked manually from the platform. Accidents involving passengers always generated adverse publicity, so managers were willing to invest in brakes that could prevent such accidents as runaways. But the much more numerous freight stock was another matter, and well into the 1850s some railroads still had no brakes at all on their cars. Trainmen had to rely on the brakes of the locomotive and the handbrake in the caboose. Other lines had better records, but one braked car for every five nonbraked ones seems to have been about the average in the industry.[21] The brakeman's job was not to be envied. Riding on top of the cars, he had to work the brakes on whistle signals from the engine, and in case of sudden obstruction he had to jump over the roofwalks from car to car to work as many brakes as he could. In good weather this was sufficiently dangerous, but in bad weather it meant almost certain death. Many inventors tried to patent some form of self-acting brake, worked by the momentum of the train or the pressure of buffers on the cars. None worked satisfactorily.

Power brakes, worked by steam, vacuum, and water or air pressure, seemed to be the solution. George Westinghouse, although not the actual inventor of the air brake, deserves the credit for working out a practical version. His first brake, patented in 1869, worked well and was adopted by the Pennsylvania Railroad and other lines for their passenger trains. But this brake was not automatic; it worked with air pressure from a pump and storage tank on the locomotive, and when a train parted or a hose connecting two cars broke, the brake became inoperative. Westinghouse reversed the process for his later designs: every car was equipped with an air storage tank of its own, charged from the locomotive through the train line as usual. A new invention, the triple valve, on each car monitored the air pressure and, when all was well, kept the brakes released. Whenever pressure in the train line fell, because of application of the brake by the engineer or a leak somewhere (as from the breaking of a hose), the triple valves automatically set the brakes, releasing them only after the pressure in the train line had been built up again sufficiently.

Here now was the real fail-safe system, and it was gladly adopted by most American railroad companies for their passenger stock. But once again, to equip the tens of thousands of boxcars was another matter. Per car, about $100 was needed for installation, with annual maintenance estimated at $4.50 per car. This price tag was the reason that railroads were very slow in adopting the air brake for all rolling stock, and it took years of heavy lobbying by men like Lorenzo Coffin to get Congress to include in the Safety Appliance Act of 1893 a clause making an automatic brake— together with an automatic coupler, as discussed earlier—mandatory for every car in interstate service. Westinghouse was not the only firm to supply a brake apparatus. Frederick W. Eames had patented a vacuum brake, which was used on a limited scale; it never worked as well as the air brake. In England the vacuum brake did have some success, but on the Continent the air brake reigned supreme. The Eames Vacuum Brake Company ended the production of its vacuum system in 1890, changed its name to New York Air Brake Company, and developed and marketed its own brand of automatic air brake.[22]

Time and Telegraph

At the dawn of the railroad age in America there was no standard, national time scheme. Every town and village had its own time, which could differ substantially from the time kept in the next town. Correct and uniform time was of prime importance, of course, for railroads; they opted for the time of their headquarters or their most important stations. Many, but certainly not all, early New England lines reckoned by the time at the Boston depot; the Pennsylvania RR used Philadelphia time east of

Harrisburg and Pittsburgh time west of there. In 1843 the seven companies that covered the 326 miles between Albany and Buffalo suffered from
a confusion of times. With the formation of the New York Central in 1853
only Albany time was used, although the actual time difference between
Albany and Buffalo was no less than twenty minutes, thirty-two seconds.
In New England an attempt to establish some form of standard time was
frustrated.[23]

Time was important to railroads not only as a basis for scheduling;
safety on the railroads was chiefly dependent on the time-interval system.
No train could depart a station within a fixed number of minutes after the
previous train had left, and "meets" on the mostly-single track lines had
to be fixed in the schedules at certain times and at certain places, where
side tracks were available. Of course, good clocks and trainmen's watches
were the basis of this system, and many accidents of the time can be
ascribed to improper working of timepieces.[24] The exact time of a line's
official, master clock was generally obtained by telegraph from a central
observatory. With the coming of the telegraph, clocks could be set all over
the system to the same time; the New York & Erie had introduced this
technique as early as 1851.

With the coming of long-distance trains, some form of national time
became necessary, but it was many years before the railroad companies
were finally persuaded of its advantages. Back in 1870 a certain Charles
F. Dowd, a schoolteacher from Saratoga Springs, New York, had formu-
lated a plan of four time zones, each one hour different from the next,
covering the United States. But the leading railroads were not interested,
and no more was heard of Dowd's excellent plan for the time being.[25]

But ten years later railroad leaders had changed their minds. Under
the guidance of William F. Allen, editor of the widely used *Travelers'
Official Guide* and secretary of the General Time Convention, a plan along
the line of Dowd's ideas was worked out. Like no one else, Allen knew
the difficulties caused by all the different times used by the railroads,
but he managed to persuade the managers to resolve the problem among
themselves, without waiting for a decision of the government. On Sunday, November 18, 1883, at noon, all railroads set their clocks to the
same time, in four time zones, one hour apart.[26] With minor adjustments
these four time zones were later officially sanctioned by law, and they
are still with us.

The telegraph, invented and patented by Samuel Morse in 1837, had been continually improved by him.[27] Its first practical application, along a stretch of the Baltimore & Ohio, took place in 1844, and it soon came into general use with railroads for the sending of messages over long distances. In 1851 Charles Minot, superintendent of the New York & Erie, became the first to transmit train orders by telegraph to stations and crossing places. Train dispatching by telegraphic order became one of the cornerstones of railroad operating practice during the nineteenth century and for much of the twentieth.

Electricity

Experiments with electricity as a means of propelling cars on rails went on for much of the second and third quarters of the nineteenth century, but with no lasting success. Operators of horse tramways in the cities, especially, were interested in replacing the horse. Large operations had thousands of animals, and after the Great Epizootic of 1872, a disease that killed thousands of horses in a couple of weeks, operators eagerly looked for other form of power. Steam dummies had been used, but in city centers they were considered a nuisance, and they frightened pedestrians and animals. Cable traction was successfully adopted in many cities, but it entailed an enormous investment in power stations, underground cable conduits, and cables. Electric traction promised much, and the experiments of the pioneers were eagerly followed.

The German scientist and inventor Ernst Werner von Siemens was one of the first to put a working electric machine on the rails during an exhibition in Berlin in 1879. He followed this up with a real electric tramway at Lichterfelde two years later. In America, inventors like Charles J. Van Depoele (a Belgian) and Leo Daft had some success with electric streetcars, but the great breakthrough came with Frank J. Sprague's installation of an electric trolley system in Richmond, Virginia, in 1887.[28] After that year electric streetcars proliferated all over the country.

The success of the electric streetcar prompted a new development in the shape of an electric interurban network, and soon the first intercity lines were built. The great boom in interurban construction would come in the early years of the twentieth century, but the first lines were laid down in the late 1890s. Great networks were constructed, especially in such states as Ohio and Indiana, linking major and minor towns, and small villages as well. (The boom would end after World War I, and most lines would be gone by the 1930s.)[29]

With the apparent success of electric traction, the mainline railroads turned their attention to the new form of propulsion. The Pennsylvania Railroad was the first to electrify a minor branch line, in New Jersey in 1895, using Westinghouse electric equipment. The New York, New Haven & Hartford Railroad followed in the same year with a branch line in Massachusetts, using equipment from the General Electric Company.[30] These were minor installations, resembling the contemporary interurban technology, but soon a real mainline followed. The Baltimore & Ohio was constructing a line through the heart of the city of Baltimore to interconnect its operations, and this line included a long tunnel under Howard Street, where steam traction would be undesirable. In 1892, when work on the tunnel started, the B & O contracted with General Electric to electrify the line—an audacious move on the part of both companies, as there was little experience worldwide with this kind of traction. But the results exceeded expectations. At the opening of the line in 1895 electric locomotives easily hauled 500-ton trains, including their nonworking steam locomotives, through the tunnel.[31] In the early years of the twentieth century many more mainline electrifications were to follow, including all lines leading into New York's Grand Central and Pennsylvania Stations. Electric traction had many advantages, but initial cost was high, due to the overhead catenaries and electric substations. Not many American railroads took the plunge, although most suburban operations around the big cities, where pollution by steam and smoke was undesirable, were electrified in due time. No nationwide electrified network, however, such as in Japan and most of Europe, was ever built in America.

Notes

1. For a description of early American railroads and their systems of rails and roadbed see Frederick C. Gamst, ed., *Early American Railroads: Franz Anton Ritter von Gerstner's Die Innern Communicationen (1842–1843)* (Stanford, Calif.: Stanford University Press, 1997).

2. James M. Swank, *History of the Manufacture of Iron in All Ages, and Particularly in the United States from Colonial Times to 1891* (Philadelphia: American Iron and Steel Association, 1892), 410–13.

3. Henry M. Flint, *The Railroads of the United States: Their History and Statistics* (Philadelphia: John E. Potter, 1868); Swank, *History of the Manufacture of Iron*, 415, 440.

4. For a survey of all gauges used in America see George R. Taylor and Irene Neu, *The American Railroad Network 1861–1890* (Cambridge, Mass.: Harvard University Press, 1956); also George W. Hilton, *American Narrow Gauge Railroads* (Stanford, Calif.: Stanford University Press, 1990), 24–47; Douglas J. Puffert, "The Standardization of Track Gauge on North American Railways, 1830–1890," *Journal of Economic History* 60, no. 4 (2000), 933–60.

5. About the narrow gauge in the world see Hilton, *American Narrow Gauge*, 6–23.

6. Ibid., 101–10.

7. Figures from Hilton, *American Narrow Gauge*, 88.

8. Descriptions and drawings of almost all early types of bridges in Gamst, *Early American Railroads*.

9. The best work on the development of the steam locomotive in America in the nineteenth century is John H. White, Jr., *American Locomotives: An Engineering History 1830–1880* (Baltimore: Johns Hopkins University Press, 1997).

10. Survey of all locomotive builders in the United States and their production in Alfred W. Bruce, *The Steam Locomotive in America: Its Development in the Twentieth Century* (New York: Bonanza Books, 1952), 45–62.

11. White, *American Locomotives*, 89.

12. The most exhaustive study of the development of the American passenger coach is John H. White, Jr., *The American Railroad Passenger Car* (Baltimore: Johns Hopkins University Press, 1978); interesting also is August Mencken, *The Railroad Passenger Car* (Baltimore: Johns Hopkins University Press, 1957, repr. 2000). Mencken also prints accounts of contemporary travelers.

13. Robert B. Shaw, *A History of Railroad Accidents, Safety Precautions and Operating Practices* (privately published, 1978), 336.

14. White, *The American Railroad Passenger Car*, 246.

15. An excellent history of the freight truck is John H. White, Jr., *The American Railroad Freight Car* (Baltimore: Johns Hopkins University Press, 1993).

16. Ibid., 270.

17. Ibid., 58–62.

18. Ibid., 498.

19. About Lorenzo Stephen Coffin (1823–1915), see Roger B. Natte, "Lorenzo S. Coffin," in Robert L. Frey, ed. *Railroads in the Nineteenth Century: Encyclopedia of American Business History and Biography* (New York: Facts On File, 1988), 53–57.

20. For the coupler question, White, *The American Railroad Freight Car*, 490–518.

21. Ibid., 528.

22. Robert L. Frey, "Brakes," in *Railroads in the Nineteenth Century*, ed. Frey, 27–32.

23. Ian R. Bartky, *Selling the True Time: Nineteenth Century Timekeeping in America* (Stanford, Calif.: Stanford University Press, 2000), 21–23.

24. Ian R. Bartky, "Running on Time," *Railroad History* 159 (Autumn 1988), 19–38.

25. Bartky, *Selling the True Time*, 97–100.

26. Ibid., 137–46.

27. About Samuel Finley Breese Morse (1791–1872), artist and inventor, see George H. Drury, "Samuel F.B. Morse," in *Railroads in the Nineteenth Century*, ed. Frey, 279–82.

28. William D. Middleton, *The Time of the Trolley* (Milwaukee: Kalmbach, 1967).

29. For an exhaustive survey of the electric interurban, George W. Hilton and John F. Due, *The Electric Interurban Railways in America* (Stanford, Calif.: Stanford University Press, 1960).

30. William D. Middleton, *When the Steam Railroads Electrified* (Milwaukee: Kalmbach, 1974), 25–26.

31. Ibid., 28–34.

CHAPTER 3

FINANCING AMERICA'S RAILROADS

During the nineteenth century, a number of novel ways of financing the American railroad system had to be found. The amount of capital needed for even a fairly simple railroad line was staggering, much larger than anything previously experienced.

The first railroads in the United States were built mostly in New England and New York State, with a few elsewhere in the country. In these states, sufficient capital was generally available, and shares could be sold to the public. The incorporators of these early railroads were local businessmen or lawyers, well respected in their communities, who had little trouble in persuading their fellow citizens to subscribe to the stock of the new companies. Subscribers were invited to pay in installments until the full measure of their subscriptions had been reached. Most of these early lines were quite successful and paid handsome dividends. If more money was needed than originally planned, revenues from operations were often large enough to cover the extra expenses. The cost of bridge construction was often underestimated, while maintenance of the early primitive wooden structures turned out to be much higher than expected. But even so, some of these early lines were amazingly profitable.[1]

On the other hand, not all lines were profitable enough to pay dividends regularly, and capitalists did not feel attracted to companies that did not. The financial crises of 1837 and 1857 tended to aggravate this situation. The result of this tightening of the money market was that a railroad company either had to try to find construction capital from public funds or issue loans to make up deficits.

Shares were initially seen as a safe investment. When fully paid up, they represented a piece of ownership in the company. Holders were entitled to dividends when business was good enough to warrant such payments. As owners of the company in question, shareholders could decide on important matters of policy. On the other hand, when business was disappointing, no dividends could be expected for years to come, which, of course, dampened the enthusiasm of prospective investors. This was especially true of western lines, built out into largely unknown and unsettled country; substantial revenues were to be expected only after civilization caught up. Shareholders of these railroads could expect revenues only in a distant future, if ever.

To address this problem it became customary to issue shares in these railroads but to ask only a token down payment, or none at all. The real construction capital, then, had to be found by floating loans. Sometimes, when a loan could be placed only with difficulty, shares were thrown in as a bonus to attract investors. No one, however, could reasonably expect these shares to yield any dividends, at least not in the near future.

In the course of time, it also became customary to issue preferred stock, giving first right to any dividends earned. Generally, a fixed dividend rate was stipulated, and shareholders in the course of time became accustomed to this rate. If a company saw no way to pay the fixed dividend, it was considered a sure sign of bad financial condition. Market prices of the company's preferred and other stock would plummet, and its securities would become difficult to sell. Hence, railroad directors commonly employed the trick of paying dividends out of capital instead of earnings, to present a picture of stability. The infamous Erie Railway in the 1860s is a well known example of this dubious practice.[2]

Common and preferred stock represented a certain amount of equity, at least in theory. In the course of time, when railroads became more lavish in issuing of common shares, each share represented only a tiny interest in the total property of the company in question. Its par value, therefore, became more or less fictional. This practice of stock "watering" could have several causes. The first and most common was the railroad directors' need to stay in control. Whenever a hostile takeover seemed to threaten their position, the placing of new common or preferred stock in safe hands could secure their majority. Again, the Erie Railway presents a sorry example; the "Erie Wars" of the late 1860s among Jay Gould, Cornelius Vanderbilt, Daniel Drew, and Jim Fisk over control of the company are well known. Gould is reported to have said, "There will be icicles in Hell when Erie common pays a dividend."[3]

If a company was unable to pay dividends, shareholders could do little about it. Only at the annual general meeting could they complain, or, if they could bring a majority together, oust the management and elect another. At reorganizations of a company that had defaulted on its interest payments, shareholders usually came off worst, because of the assumption that they had paid hardly anything for their shares.

When subscribed share capital proved insufficient to finance the construction of a railroad, recourse had to be made to bonds. Early railroad promoters tried to avoid this strategy as much as possible, as bonds carried a fixed interest that had to be paid regularly, generally every six months. When a railroad was in financial difficulties, this could be a heavy burden. Bond issues were generally secured by a mortgage on the property—that is, on the roadbed, rails, and fixed infrastructure, such as depots, freight sheds, and other buildings. A first mortgage constituted a first lien on the property, which made it more secure than second or third mortgages. Only when a company was in great financial trouble did it resort to second mortgages. If a railroad company had acquired a land grant from the U.S. Congress, it could mortgage this land as well. After all, this land constituted a definite value, although its price often depended on the actual building of the railroad.

First-mortgage bond loans were considered safe and sound; they could be easily marketed, especially by companies in good financial standing. After 1873, railroads acquired the bulk of their working capital through loans. By so doing, however, they placed a severe burden on their financial performance. The resulting shift in the relation between share capital and bonded debt illustrates this gradual change. In 1855 the share capital of all American railroads was still 42 percent larger than their total bonded debt. By 1900, 70 percent of the total capitalization of American railroads was in the form of bonded debt, the rest in the form of capital stock.[4]

The first loans floated by railroads carried fairly high rates of interest, usually 8 but even 9 percent. After all, this was a new form of investment, and capitalists had to be lured to place their money in these bonds. Slowly, a gradual decline in interest rates set in, from 6 to 7 percent in the 1870s to between 4 and 5 percent in the late 1880s. Companies in good financial standing could issue loans below 4 percent; railroads with less stable histories often had to go higher than 5 percent.

At the same time, railroads in good standing were able to sell their bonds to the public around par or even slightly above, which meant that the nominal total of the bond issue would flow into the company's coffers. Companies in a less favorable position had to resort to financial intermediaries, who, of course, charged commissions for floating the loans, while the bonds often could be sold only much below par.

When a railroad could not pay the regular interest on its outstanding loans, bondholders could request the court to appoint a receiver, who would run the railroad until a reorganization could take place. In such a reorganization, the first aim was always to bring down fixed charges by scaling down the bonded debt. Outstanding loans could be converted dollar for dollar into new ones at lower rates of interest. Old bonds could also be exchanged for new ones for part of their nominal value, while the rest could be converted into income bonds or even common shares.[5]

Income bonds came in vogue with the reorganizations of the late 1870s of companies that had defaulted during the 1873 crisis. They carried a fixed rate of interest, but only if actually earned; as such, they were a kind of halfway house between shares and mortgage bonds. Because of their unpredictable yield, they were never popular with investors and commanded only low prices on the stock exchanges. Another relatively uncommon form of indebtedness was the convertible bond, used by Jay Gould during the 1860s. It became popular in the early 1900s as an extra incentive for the investing public. Convertible bonds carried fixed rates of interest and could be exchanged for common shares during a certain time, at the owner's pleasure. All this bonded debt, whether secured by mortgages or not, was long-term debt. Loans were issued with stipulated dates for paying off the principal, usually between twenty-five and a hundred years. When a loan fell due, a company generally would try to re-fund the old debt with a new one, preferably at a lower rate of interest; as interest rates declined over the years, this proved a reasonable expectation.

Outside financing remained the most common way for railroads to obtain the necessary capital for extensions and betterments. Well into the late 1880s, at least 98 percent of the capital needed by railroad companies was acquired by the sale of bonds or shares to the public. By 1910 this percentage had dropped to 60; the rest was being generated by the railroads themselves out of traffic revenues.[6]

At first, as we have seen, local capital was generally sufficient to start building a railroad. In New England many merchants had made fortunes in the Asian trade, and money was also available for investment elsewhere. In New York City, the opening of the Erie Canal and the general upswing of trade and commerce meant a steady growth of capital. The same was true for other centers of business, such as Philadelphia and Baltimore. But soon, after people discovered the potential handsome profits, outside sources were attracted to invest in the then-new railroads. In the early years, at least before the crisis of 1837, the Philadelphia stock exchange seems to have been the center of American railroad finance. In the 1840s, however, Boston briefly took over that role.[7] Boston merchants first pioneered regional lines and then shifted their operations to the West, where they took over the Michigan Central from the state of Michigan. Boston banking firms such as Kidder, Peabody & Company and Lee, Higginson & Company continued to play an active role in American railroad finance even after Wall Street developed in the 1850s into the most important source of capital for railroad construction.[8]

Railroads were the nation's first big business, and the sums needed to build them were enormous. Early figures are not easily available, but between 1865 and 1900 the railroads spent five or six billion dollars on construction, development, and equipment.[9]

Not all of this money could be raised in the United States alone; soon assistance from abroad was needed. Foreign investment in the United States was nothing new at the time. French, Dutch, and English capitalists—in chronological order—had already heavily invested in federal bonds, in state bonds, and in land and canal companies. The early canal building in the 1820s and 1830s had been supported by a number of state governments, and these state bonds had been eagerly taken up in Europe, especially in Great Britain and the Netherlands. After several states defaulted on the interest payments in the late 1830s and early 1840s, European investors became wary of new risks in America; after conditions improved, however, English and Dutch investors came back in force. In the railroad field, the English clearly took the lead and remained prominent. The Dutch, however, followed close behind and became an important source of capital for American railroads.[10]

European investors generally were not interested in running the railroads they owned. As long as a company honored its financial obligations and regularly paid its interest and dividends, they did not much care what happened in America. They did have representatives on the boards of directors, however, and American directors of these companies were wise enough to keep in close touch with their European share and bondholders. The Illinois Central, for instance, had a very large foreign investment; in the 1870s, 54 percent of its stock was held in England and 26 percent in Holland. Its president, William H. Osborn, took care to keep the English and Dutch owners of his company in a friendly mood.[11]

The total amount of foreign capital invested in American railroads is hard to establish, because contemporary estimates vary wildly. A U.S. Treasury report of 1853, before the big boom in railroad building really started, listed 3 percent of the stock and 26 percent of the bonds of the 244 American railroad companies then in existence as in foreign hands. In 1873 the total of foreign-held railroad securities was listed as 20 percent, a figure that was to grow to 33 percent by 1890.[12] However undependable and incomplete these figures may be, it is abundantly clear that foreign capital played an important role in the financing of the American railroad network, especially in the boom years between 1865 and 1873, in the eighties until the crisis of 1893, and again in the last few years of the nineteenth century and the early years of the twentieth.

However, contrary to the general belief, not all capital for railroad building came from private sources. Public aid in many forms was important in the growth of the railroad industry.[13] One of the most common was the granting of special rights in charters issued by states. Exemption from taxation in perpetuity or for a certain number of years was frequently given. In Ohio, for instance, all railroads were exempt from property taxes until 1852, which was tantamount to a sizeable subsidy. Other states did much the same to foster the development of the railroads inside their borders. Another form of state aid was the granting of banking privileges to new railroad companies. This form of help was particularly important in Georgia, but in other states it did little good in actually getting the railroads started. Generally such aid led to wildcat banking, to the detriment of the railroad's credit in the long run.[14]

When special privileges were not enough to give a state railroad lines, some states built and operated their own roads. In itself, this was nothing new, as many states, notably New York and Pennsylvania, had built extensive systems of canals. In New York, however, the enormous sums already spent on the Erie Canal and its feeders made lawmakers reluctant to spend on railroads.[15] Other states did more in this respect. Georgia built the Western & Atlantic Railroad, from Atlanta to Chattanooga, Tennessee, as a state railroad; the line was finished in 1851 and became one of the most successful roads in the South. Virginia also built lines of its own; unlike Georgia, it did not operate them as state railroads but leased them to existing private companies.

Michigan had little luck with its state-built railroads. In 1847 both the Michigan Southern and the Michigan Central, not yet completely finished, had to be sold to private investors (as we have seen) at a great loss to the state. In the 1830s Indiana had planned a gigantic scheme of internal improvements, but because of the virtual bankruptcy of the state the only railroad line built, the Madison & Indianapolis Railroad Company, had to be sold.

At least one city built its own railroad. Troy, New York, felt its commerce threatened by Albany, which was favorably situated at the eastern end of the Erie Canal. Not to be outdone by its rival, Troy financed the building of the Schenectady & Troy Railroad by itself, at a cost of some $600,000 in city bonds.[16]

Much more commonly, states and cities helped private companies with subsidies. Apart from the donation of land for roadbeds, depots, and other railroad buildings, millions of dollars were given by individual states and townships in the form of straight cash subsidies or loans. States took up parts of bond loans of railroad companies or issued their own bonds to support the railroads. In the South before the Civil War, more than half of the total construction capital of the railroads came from states or towns. It has been estimated that by 1870 at least ninety million dollars had been borrowed by states to support the railroad industry.[17] Some local and municipal authorities donated even more to foster the construction of railroads in their areas. In states (such as in Iowa, Wisconsin, and, after 1846, New York) in which the law made it impossible for the state government to subsidize railroads, local governments took over, sometimes on a very large scale.

Compared to the largesse exhibited by state and local governments, federal aid was at first small. Straight financial help was considered unconstitutional and therefore impossible. But the U.S. Army Corps of Engineers did a number of the early surveys for roads such as the Baltimore

& Ohio. Because trained engineers were something of a rarity in the country at that time, such help proved invaluable. Federal help, however, in another shape did materially alter the picture. The land grant became the great stimulator for railroad building in virgin territory where no local capital was to be found and in which foreign investors were not interested. After much pressure from western states and long, sometimes acrimonious, discussions, Congress in 1850 finally approved the donation of public land to two planned railroads, the Illinois Central and the Mobile & Ohio, which together linked Chicago to New Orleans.[18] Congress made public land available in alternating sections along the planned railroads, to be given out after the railroad in question was finished. A land grant was not enough in itself to build a railroad, but with a land grant in its pocket a company could issue loans with the land as lien. This was considered very safe, and many eagerly invested.

With the Illinois Central congressional land grant as a precedent, thoughts turned to a true transcontinental railroad. From the outset it was abundantly clear that such a line, running through wild and mostly uninhabited country, could be built only with public aid. The Pacific Railway Bill, signed by President Abraham Lincoln on July 1, 1862, provided for two distinct forms of public aid. First, each company—the Union Pacific building westward from Omaha and the Central Pacific building eastward from Sacramento—was to receive ten alternate sections of land for every mile of railroad constructed. In 1864 this grant was doubled to twenty sections for every mile of track. Second, both companies received loans from the government in the form of thirty-year U.S. bonds for every mile of track constructed. In the easy terrain across the Great Plains the amount was set at $16,000 per mile, while in the relatively difficult terrain between the Rockies and the Sierras the sum per mile was raised to $32,000. In mountainous regions this government aid was raised even further, to $48,000 per mile. Officially this aid was a loan, but repayment of the subsidies was postponed again and again.[19]

Apart from the Union and Central Pacific companies, other railroads in the West received congressional land grants. In 1862 the grandiosely named St. Paul & Pacific Railroad was incorporated in Minnesota, with the same financial structure: the share capital was never fully paid up, and the construction of the railroad was to be financed by loans secured by a mortgage on the property and on the land grant, which was considered safe.[20]

Another transcontinental provided with a land grant was the Northern Pacific Railroad Company, chartered by Congress in 1864. Originally, this company was supposed to issue shares in small denominations to attract small savers, to make it a real "people's railroad." Share capital was set at $100,000,000, but small savers did not come forward in large enough numbers. Only after the company was reorganized and taken over by a consortium led by Philadelphia banker Jay Cooke in 1870 could construction really begin. Cooke sold the NP bonds in domestic and foreign stock markets with great success. Having successfully sold U.S. bonds during the Civil War, he had a network of agents to peddle the Northern Pacific bonds. The land grant allotted to the company was the largest ever, altogether some sixty million acres, reflecting the poor opinion generally held of the quality of the lands on the northern tier traversed by the road.[21]

Not all transcontinental railroads, however, received land grants. Quite a few managed to construct their lines without federal help. The Atchison, Topeka & Santa Fe (1863), building slowly to the West across the Kansas plains, had only a small land grant in Kansas but managed to reach California. The successor to the St. Paul & Pacific, the Great Northern Railway, also managed to reach the Pacific coast on its own, without federal help.

Opposition to squandering so much of the public domain, present from the beginning, grew in strength over the years. Scandals connected with the sale of lands, activities of land speculators, and complaints from homesteaders and veterans did the rest. The policy of giving out federal land grants to railroads was discontinued in 1871, after which railroads had to fend for themselves

In all financial transactions frauds, large and small, will occur. Railroad finance was certainly no exception. Because railroads were the nation's first big business, enormous sums of money changed hands continuously without effective oversight, and swindlers and crooks had golden opportunities for enriching themselves. In an era of somewhat loose business morals, this in itself was nothing to hold the public attention for long. However, because the amount of money involved was truly staggering, these frauds often did attract the attention of the press.

Unscrupulous characters used many methods. Stock speculation was perhaps the mildest and most accepted form of enriching oneself at the expense of other stockholders. Selling securities, with a prospectus describing a line and the land it crossed in glowing terms, of a company that was

hardly viable went one step farther. In the early days that method proved
fairly easy, because American and foreign capitalists hardly ever took the
trouble to inspect the property themselves. After the 1873 crisis this attitude changed, but even then swindles of this kind continued.

Perhaps the most common kind of swindle involved the so-called
construction company. Although not fraudulent per se, a construction
company could easily be used as a vehicle for easy unlawful gains. When
a new railroad company had no ready money in its coffers, a construction company might undertake to finance and build the road in exchange
for shares and bonds. After the road was put into operation and, ideally,
making money, the construction company could sell the securities on the
market for a fair price. So far so good, but railroad promoters could also
set up such a construction company themselves, generally through dummies, and contract with themselves as railroad directors for an inflated sum
in bonds and shares per mile of railroad. They then took care to keep the
market price of the railroad bonds high by paying interest until they had
unloaded their holdings on the market for a good price. This operation
was easy, because they could, as directors of the railroad, pay interest out
of capital instead of earnings with no one knowing. By the time the inevitable crash came, they would have cleared out, leaving the public with
worthless bonds. The infamous Crédit Mobilier of America, the finance
and construction company behind the Union Pacific, is a glaring example,
though in that case bribery of government officials also took place on a
large scale.

There were many more ways to swindle investors, too many to name
them all. In the South after the Civil War, carpetbaggers, helped by corrupt
legislators, managed to lay their hands on millions meant for reconstruction of the railroads and never used them for that purpose. Another trick
was to issue a bonded loan, purportedly secured by a first mortgage on
the property, without telling the investing public that an earlier loan, also
secured by a "first" mortgage had been floated. When the railroad, pre-
dictably, defaulted, the courts had to decide which one was really the first
mortgage; the unfortunate owners of the other bonds lost all of their investments.

Just as gold or silver mines were sometimes "salted" to fool prospective investors, the Rockford, Rock Island & St.Louis Railroad of Illinois
organized a promotional tour for investors to show off the great future of

the road and its "coal lands." Some holes in the ground filled with coal dust were considered enough to make the capitalists believe that this was a good proposition!

Altogether, over the years millions must have ended up in the pockets of unscrupulous businessmen and corrupt politicians instead of in the coffers of the railroad companies. The enormous fortunes amassed by gentlemen like Collis P. Huntington, Jay Gould, and the Vanderbilts simply could not have been acquired by strictly legal means. Toward the end of the nineteenth century, bankers and brokers, both American and foreign, became more cautious and sent out their own men to inspect the railroads in question and supervise the spending of their money. Yet even then they could not always prevent frauds and swindles.

Notes

1. Frederick C. Gamst, ed., *Early American Railroads: Franz Anton von Gerstner's "Die innern Communicationen (1842–1843)"* (Stanford, Calif.: Stanford University Press, 1997), 312–13, 250.

2. Charles F. Adams, Jr., *A Chapter of Erie* (Boston: Fields, Osgood, 1869), and Frederick C. Hicks, *High Finance in the Sixties: Chapters from the Early History of the Erie Railway* (New Haven, Conn.: Yale University Press, 1929).

3. Albro Martin, *Railroads Triumphant: The Growth, Rejection, and Rebirth of a Vital American Force* (New York: Oxford University Press, 1992), 373.

4. Melville J. Ulmer, *Capital in Transportation, Communications, and Public Utilities: Its Formation and Financing* (Princeton, N.J.: Princeton University Press, 1960), 169.

5. Stuart Daggett, *Railroad Reorganizations* (1908; repr. New York: Augustus M. Kelley, 1966).

6. Ulmer, *Capital in Transportation*, 155–57.

7. Alfred D. Chandler, Jr., *Patterns of American Railroad Finance, 1830–1850* (Cambridge, Mass.: MIT Press, 1955), 248–61.

8. Arthur M. Johnson and Barry M. Supple, *Boston Capitalists and Western Railroads: A Study in the Nineteenth-Century Railroad Investment Process* (Cambridge, Mass.: Harvard University Press, 1967).

9. Ulmer, *Capital in Transportation*, 256–59.

10. Mira Wilkins, *The History of Foreign Investment in the United States to 1914* (Cambridge, Mass.: Harvard University Press, 1970); Dorothy R. Adler, *British Investment in American Railways 1838–1898* (Charlottesville: University Press of Virginia, 1970). And see Augustus J. Veenendaal, Jr., *Slow Train to Paradise: How Dutch Investment Helped Build American Railroads* (Stanford, Calif.: Stanford University Press, 1996).

11. Thomas C. Cochran, *Railroad Leaders 1845–1890: The Business Mind in Action* (Cambridge, Mass.: Harvard University Press, 1953), 425.

12. Wilkins, *The History of Foreign Investment*, 76, 198.

13. Carter Goodrich, *Government Promotion of American Canals and Railroads, 1800–1890* (New York: Columbia University Press, 1960).

14. John F. Stover, *The Railroads of the South, 1865–1900: A Study in Finance and Control* (Chapel Hill: University of North Carolina Press, 1955).

15. Harry H. Pierce, *Railroads of New York: A Study of Government Aid 1826–1875* (Cambridge, Mass.: Harvard University Press, 1953).

16. Frank W. Stevens, *The Beginnings of the New York Central Railroad: A History* (New York: Putnam, 1926), 238–48.

17. William Z. Ripley, *Railroads, Rates, and Regulation* (New York: Longmans, Green, 1913), 38–39; George R. Taylor, *The Transportation Revolution, 1815–1860*, vol. 4 of *The Economic History of the United States* (New York: M.E. Sharpe, 1977), 92–94.

18. For the Illinois Central land grant see Brownson, *History of the Illinois Central*, 17–39; for the land-grant policy in general see Lloyd C. Mercer, *Railroads and Land Grant Policy: A Study in Government Intervention* (New York: Academic Press, 1982).

19. John F. Stover, *American Railroads* (Chicago: University of Chicago Press, 1961), 67–76.

20. See Veenendaal, *Slow Train to Paradise*, 130–39; also Augustus J. Veenendaal, Jr., *The Saint Paul & Pacific Railroad: An Empire in the Making, 1862–1879* (De Kalb: Northern Illinois University Press, 1999).

21. Stover, *American Railroads*, 76–78.

CHAPTER 4

RAILROADS IN THE CIVIL WAR

Although the American Civil War (1861–65) was the first armed conflict in which railroads played a major role, military officials in Europe had already noted the capabilities of railroads in transporting large masses of men and equipment over long distances. Especially in the Austro-Hungarian Empire, railroads had already been used in army maneuvers in the 1840s and 1850s, and on a very limited scale in circumstances of a real war in 1848 in northern Italy. The French used their railways when they intervened in the Austro-Sardinian conflict in 1859, but again on a limited scale.[1] The first actual war on a large scale where railroads sometimes played a decisive role was the American Civil War.[2]

The South at the Outbreak of War

The situations at the onset of war in the North and the South were very different. In the eleven states of the Confederacy about 9,000 miles of railroad, less than a third of the American total, had been laid down, but most lines were flimsily constructed and carried only light traffic.[3] Old-fashioned strap rail on wooden stringers was still in use, even on main-lines. More important, some of the few trunk lines in existence in North Carolina and Virginia were constructed in the standard gauge of four feet, eight and one-half inches, while others in those states, and almost all of the rest of the Southern network was chiefly built with a gauge of five feet, making through traffic impossible. Where a number of railroads entered a town from different sides, they were often not interconnected. Connections were in fact expressly forbidden by some town councils; in these places every through passenger had to make his way from one station to the other, and freight had be loaded on horse-drawn wagons and carted across town. This unpleasant situation was the case in such strategic places as Richmond and Petersburg, Virginia, and Augusta and Savannah, Georgia. Only the exigencies of war forced the towns to agree—temporarily—to connecting lines through the city streets.

The total number of railroaders in the Southern states was small, just under 7,000, about the same number as in New York State alone. Some of them were Northerners who left at the outbreak of war. More important, most Southern roads habitually ordered their locomotives and rolling stock from Northern foundries and factories, and only small numbers of locomotives were constructed in the South. Only the Tredegar Iron Works in Richmond, Virginia, produced steam locomotives in some numbers; after the outbreak of war Tredegar switched over to ordnance work for the Confederacy and stopped locomotive building. The Atlanta rolling mills continued to roll rails, but only on a small scale, and Southern roads soon suffered from a lack of iron rails and other hardware. On top of that, the Confederate navy regularly requisitioned rails for armoring its newfangled ironclads. Supplies from England or continental Europe were hampered by the Union blockade of the ports, and railroad managers were soon forced to take up less-used branch lines to keep the mainlines running. The shortage of iron was to take on dramatic proportions during the latter years of the war, when the unusually intensive traffic and lack of maintenance caused heavy wear on the soft iron rails then in general use. Enemy raids, aimed at destruction of railroad property, only worsened matters.

Despite well-meant measures of the Richmond government, no adequate solution was ever found. Proposals to take up rails were met every time by vociferous protests from the individuals who owned the lines and from the affected roads' managers, actively supported by local and regional leaders, who generally put their own interests before those of the Confederacy.[4] Lack of central control played havoc with the good intentions of the government, and numerous military and civilian agencies were soon scouring the country for iron. The price of iron soared to over 1000 percent of prewar prices.

The Confederacy was ill prepared for war. Not only were most railroads regional, not interconnected, and in poor shape, but the jealous guarding of states' rights by the several state governments precluded any real collaboration between the many small railroad companies, which were seen as belonging to the state, not to the common interest. Railroad companies hardly ever operated across states' borders, and their independence was jealously guarded by their state governments. The Confederate government never succeeded in establishing control over the railroads. Hampered by a lack of authority at first and vehemently opposed by many of the state governors, President Jefferson Davis and his cabinet were later reluctant to impose unpopular measures, although many leaders, including the president himself and the commander of the Army of Northern Virginia, Gen. Robert E. Lee, saw the necessity very clearly. A Railroad Bureau to direct government transportation on all railroads was set up in 1862 but without real authority; its chief, William M. Wadley (1815–82), a most capable railroader, could do not much more than recommend and advise. Moreover, Wadley's appointment meant bypassing the office of the quartermaster general (in charge of army supplies, less ammunition), and strained relations with the military resulted. Local officers and government officials continued to meddle in matters of transportation, and railroad directors and managers were only too eager to make use of these bickerings.[5]

At last a law to give the government more power in railroad affairs was introduced in April 1863, but it met with such vehement opposition that it was finally only passed in an emasculated form. On paper it gave the quartermaster general more authority over railroad companies, but in practice things did not work out that way. Moreover Wadley, one of the few really personally disinterested and capable railroad managers, was discharged at the same time. He was succeeded by his chief assistant Frederick W. Sims (1823–75), not a professional railroader like Wadley but a capable, suave, and more diplomatic person. He did not accomplish much more than his predecessor, but at least he managed to organize within the Railroad Bureau an office for finding such sought-after items as locomotive tires, wheels, frames, and other vital ironwork and supplies.[6]

One defect that even Sims, with all his ingenuity, could not solve was the shortage of all material and manpower. Ever more men were being drafted into the army, but it was necessary to keep engineers, machinists, and other skilled workers with the railroads; frequent clashes with the military resulted. Even cordwood, generally used as locomotive fuel, was hard to get in sufficient quantities, not because there were no stands of

timber left but because the woodsmen and farmers who habitually supplied the roads with wood had either been called up for military service
or had drifted into better-paid jobs in government munitions factories.

Railroad rates went up and up again as inflation grew, and the coffers
of the companies were filled with Confederate dollars of little purchasing
power. They paid out big dividends to their shareholders, but only in paper
money of doubtful value. By 1864 the Confederate dollar was down to
five cents in gold! Wages were also going up, but never enough to offset
inflation. Some roads used slave labor for construction or maintenance,
but never in areas close to the Union lines, for fear that the slaves might
run away.

Accomplishments of the Confederate Railroads

Despite all these shortcomings, the Confederacy managed to build
a strategic new line on the standard gauge between Danville, Virginia, and
Greensboro, North Carolina, begun in 1862 and finished after much
trouble in 1864.[7] It was to become a lifeline for the armies in northern
Virginia after both the coast route and the line farther inland by way of
Bristol and Knoxville, Tennessee, had been severed by enemy raids. But
even so, it was handicapped by a break of gauge at Danville, where the
broad-gauge Richmond & Danville formed the connection with the Confederate capital. Even less successful was the attempt to close the gap in
another strategic line, in central Alabama. This connection between
Georgia and Mississippi was of vital importance, especially after the other
east-west line in northern Alabama came under Union control in 1862,
but through lack of iron and manpower this central route was never finished. Even Selma, Alabama, a major supply depot, was not connected to
any eastern railroad.[8] Without a through line in central Alabama, troops
and freight had to be ferried over many miles of undependable rivers or
by a very roundabout way through Mobile, which also involved many
miles of river traffic.

Only at the very end of the war, in March 1865, when the enemy
was hammering at the doors of Richmond, was a Railroad Regulation Bill
passed. It would have given the central government absolute control over
the railroads, but by then it was too late, as there were hardly any railroads left. The failure of the Confederate government to establish a cer-

tain measure of control over its transportation services may be seen as a bureaucratic failure. The Davis administration could not free itself adequately from the pernicious Southern axiom of states' rights, and the several state governments refused to transfer even the smallest amount of power to a central authority. Despite frequent pleas from the military, President Davis never dared to cut through this continous squabbling between the states by placing the railroads under central military control; the ultimate defeat of the Confederacy was materially hastened by the breakdown of its internal transportation system, even before enemy invasions, such as William T. Sherman's march to the sea, wrought havoc with the railroads.[9]

Despite the bad shape of the railroads in the Confederate states, the roads did good work, even miraculous sometimes, in support of the military. The first concentration of troops in northern Virginia in 1861 was possible only by the use of the railroads; it was a somewhat haphazard effort, but most of the troops arrived on time. Again, the battle of Manassas in July 1861 was won by the Confederate armies because their reinforcements could be brought up quickly, thereby turning the fortunes of war decisively. At the battle of Shiloh in April 1862, the Confederate armies were concentrated near Corinth, Mississippi, just in time, despite the bad shape of the railroads in that area; that battle was won by the Union, but railroads had played an important role in bringing up the Southern troops. Even transportation of troops over a really long distance was accomplished, when in September 1863 part of the Army of Northern Virginia was brought over to Tennessee in an attempt to reach a final decision in that theater and throw the Union troops out of Tennessee. Although some brigades did not reach the battlefield of Chickamauga in time, their redeployment was a major feat of transportation. Of the about 20,000 men who were supposed to be entrained, in the end only some 12,000 were actually brought over, but they were enough to ensure a Southern victory in that battle.[10]

On the other hand, the lack of transportation and thus the lack of food and munitions played a major role in the eventual defeat of Lee in Virginia in 1865. His men were undernourished, badly clothed, and in want of almost everything, circumstances that sapped their morale and fighting spirit. The railroads, or what was left of them, were unable to bring in the much-needed food and equipment in sufficient quantities. While

Gen. Ulysses S. Grant strengthened his grip on Richmond every day, helped by an abundance of everything, his opponents were slowly starving to death. Again, the railroads played a decisive role here, albeit in a negative way from the Southern viewpoint.[11]

Running trains under these circumstances became an adventurous and more often than not dangerous occupation. Lack of centralized control, enemy raids, drunken officers and soldiers who attempted to meddle with the operation of the locomotives, the general confusion inherent to warfare, and the bad shape of roadbed and rolling stock all contributed to the dangers of being an engineer or conductor on a railroad in the Confederacy.[12] Yet there was never a real shortage of men willing to operate the trains.

The Railroad Situation in the North

In the North the situation was much different. In practically all fields the North far outstripped the South. Its industrial power far surpassed that of the South. Not only did there exist many foundries and rolling mills where large quantities of rails and other ironwork were made, but scores of locomotive works turned out steam locomotives by the hundreds. Coal and iron ore were plentiful, and imports of strategic materials from Europe had no problem reaching the Northern ports. Heavy industry had been booming and was stimulated even more by the demands of war. In sheer manpower too the North far outstripped the Confederacy, and many more immigrants entered the country even during the war years.

In the North a fairly cohesive network of railroads stretched from the manufacturing centers of New England and New York westward to the new industrial and grain-producing regions of Ohio, Indiana, and Illinois. In the latter state, the Illinois Central RR stretched out from Chicago southward to Cairo at the confluence of the Ohio and Mississippi Rivers. Steam ferries were used to transport freight and passengers to Columbus, Kentucky, where the broad-gauge Southern network began. Very importantly, almost all these Northern lines were constructed more or less on the standard gauge of four feet, eight and one-half inches, and cars could run through over vast distances. Only Ohio had a rail gauge of four feet, ten inches, but this small difference could be overcome by means of wheels with wide tread, certainly not ideal, but workable after a fashion.[13] The New York & Erie, one of the major trunk lines, had a gauge of six feet, and some connecting lines were built to this gauge as well, but laying a third rail was fairly simple. During the war most companies were troubled with unusually heavy traffic, lack of manpower, and high prices of iron and other materials. But unlike the South, they never broke down; they continued to carry the burden, as before.

One railroad that almost straddled the line between Union and Confederacy was the Baltimore & Ohio. Because of its strategic but vulnerable position it was continually fought over. Much damage was done, repeatedly, but under its president John W. Garrett, who remained loyal to the Union, the B & O was quickly restored every time and put back into service.

The U.S. Military Railroads

In the Union, like the Confederacy, no central railroad organization of any kind existed, but the immediate necessity to safeguard the capital and transport troops through a largely hostile Maryland led to the first emergency measures. Thomas W. Scott, vice president of the Pennsylvania RR, assisted by Andrew Carnegie, set up a telegraphic communication between Washington, D.C., and Annapolis, Maryland, and then devised a route by which Union troops could be brought into the capital without having to pass through Baltimore, where mob violence had prevented early troop movements.[14] Scott, who was put in charge of all railroads and telegraphs appropriated for government use, wanted to serve only temporarily, and in September 1861 he was succeeded by Capt. R.N. Morley; Scott, however, stayed on as assistant secretary of war until June of the following year. Morley was succeeded as general manager of U.S. Military Railroads in February 1862 by Daniel C. McCallum.

In 1862 a bill was introduced giving the president of the United States power to requisition any railroad, including buildings, rolling stock, and personnel, when public safety demanded. Opposition in the Senate and the House was fairly easily overcome, and on January 31, 1862, President Lincoln signed the bill. (Provisions for compensating the owners of the railroad were included.) This act formed the foundation of the successful operations of the U.S. Military Railroads under McCallum.[15]

Daniel Craig McCallum (1815–78) was a Scotsman who in 1851 was working as an apprentice carpenter in Rochester, New York, when he invented and patented a type of timber bridge that was to be much used and would make him financially independent.[16] The next year he became superintendent of a division of the New York & Erie RR, and in 1854 general superintendent of that company. In that capacity he designed a rigid pyramidical structure of authority for running a large company such as the New York & Erie; his system was soon adopted by other roads, but oppostion from the ranks cost him his job in 1858. After working in the bridge-building business for some years, he was approached in April 1862 by Secretary of War Edwin Stanton to become director of the U.S. Military Railroads, with far-reaching powers over both military and civilian authorities. Although his rank at first was only colonel, he managed by mediation and persuasion to forge the U.S. Military Railroads into a well-run system that served the Union armies well. He was promoted to brigadier in 1864 and major general in 1865, and toward the end of the conflict he commanded more than 10,000 men and controlled over 2,100 miles of railroad and hundreds of locomotives and other equipment.

McCallum was ably assisted by Capt. Lewis B. Parsons, a former railroad director, who was put in charge of railroads in the Department of the Mississippi and efficiently organized Union transportation on rivers and railroads in that area. Another assistant was Herman Haupt, also a professional railroader. While McCallum was a diplomat, Haupt (1817–1905) was a fairly abrasive personality who frequently clashed with his superiors.[17] Haupt had graduated from West Point in 1835 but had soon left the military service and earned himself a name as a bridge builder. He made a career on the Pennsylvania Railroad and ended up as chief engineer of that prestigious company. A short but unhappy interlude followed when he took charge of the ill-fated Hoosac Tunnel project in Massachusetts in 1856; thereafter he was hired by Stanton to serve under McCallum as engineer of the U.S. Military Railroads in 1862.

While McCallum generally operated from his Washington headquarters, Haupt was in the field supervising the reconstruction of damaged railroads and bridges or developing more efficient means to destroy enemy tracks. His ability to rebuild bridges, using only green lumber and mostly unskilled labor, was phenomenal. President Lincoln once remarked upon seeing one of Haupt's reconstructed bridges in Virginia in 1862, "That man Haupt has built a bridge across Potomac Creek, about 400 feet long . . . , and upon my word, gentlemen, there is nothing in it but bean-poles and cornstalks."[18] Haupt also devised an instrument for destroying enemy rails by twisting them longitudinally, which made it impossible to straighten them out out again. Simply heating and bending them around a tree was not enough, as such rails could be restored almost to normal in a rolling mill. Haupt resigned in September 1863 after a conflict with Stanton about his position; Haupt wanted to stay on as a civilian, but Stanton had commissioned him a brigadier general. By the time he left he had organized the Construction Corps of the U.S. Military Railroads into an efficient unit that could be pressed into service anywhere.

Once organized upon a solid footing in the War Department, the U.S. Military Railroads played an important role in the operations of the Union army. It transported food and equipment to the front, and filled the magazines of supply bases such as the one in Cairo, Illinois; its Construction Corps rebuilt war damage quickly and expertly. The early lack of organization in supplying the armies in Virginia was soon improved by Haupt, although he too was sometimes hindered by officers who did not gladly take orders from a subaltern or civilian. Generally, however, Haupt was adequately supported by his superior McCallum and by army chief of staff Henry W. Halleck, and Gen. George B. McClellan of the Army of the Potomac, both of whom understood the importance of the railroads.[19]

If things in Virginia went fairly smoothly after the initial problems had been overcome, the railroad situation in the West was very different, because of the vast distances involved. In September 1863, after the Union defeat at Chickamauga, it was decided to send part of the Army of the Potomac to Tennessee, 23,000 men and their equipment under the command of Gen. Joseph Hooker. Originally estimates for such a move varied between forty and sixty days, but as organized by McCallum, Scott, and Garrett, it took no longer than fourteen days to cover the 1,233 miles by train and boat without a single accident. It was no mean feat for the railroads, some of them, such as the Louisville & Nashville, being in bad shape.[20]

Notwithstanding this success, the transportation issue in the Mississippi required the personal attention of McCallum early in 1864. Invested with almost absolute power, he had all the lines in the region reorganized and the Nashville & Chattanooga RR completely rebuilt to serve as the lifeline for Sherman's march to Atlanta. To feed and equip an army of 100,000 with only one single-track railroad some 400 miles long was the supreme proof of the dependability of the railroad when properly equipped and run by professionals. Most of the reconstruction of this line was done by E.C. Smeed, an engineer who had served under Haupt in Virginia and who could execute marvels of bridge construction.[21] Under his supervision a large rolling mill, begun by the Confederates, was finished in Chattanooga and operated to roll rails.

Other Uses of the Railroad

Hospital Trains

Hospital cars were soon introduced, first of all by Union commanders on the Louisville & Nashville RR in Kentucky in 1862. The first such cars were improvised from ordinary passenger cars, but at the prompting of Dr. Elisha Harris of the Federal Sanitary Commission, special cars were constructed, with better springs and cushioned draft gear, and better ventilation and lighting. They were equipped to hold twenty-four stretchers suspended by rubber bands; other cars held cooking facilities and surgeon's rooms and equipment. Whole trains of these hospital and ancillary cars could quickly deliver wounded soldiers in relative comfort to the hospitals of New York or New England.[22] After major battles, however, there were never enough hospital cars available, and ordinary passenger cars and highly uncomfortable freight trucks had to be pressed into service. The Confederacy never organized anything comparable to the Union hospital service and habitually pressed everything available into service when needed. Although the Red Cross organization did not yet exist, Union hospital trains were clearly marked, with the words "Hospital Car" in large letters on the sides of the cars. They were generally respected and left unmolested by the enemy.

Artillery on the Rails

During the war both sides used heavy rail-mounted artillery on a limited scale. With the bad roads of the time, the movement of heavy guns was often problematic or even impossible. The first railroad battery, constructed at the prompting of General Lee, seems to have been a thirty-two-pounder naval gun mounted on a railroad flatcar and firing through a screen made of heavy wooden planks on a stout timber frame. Its use was limited, as the gun itself did not traverse; aiming had to be done by turning the whole car on a special curving length of railroad line. It was used on 29 June, 1862, some miles east of Richmond, and must have been the first rail-mounted gun ever used in action anywhere. Another Confederate railroad battery is reported to have been used in Florida after the fall of Jacksonville in March 1863. Union troops used the same kind of railroad batteries, but again with limited results.[23] One of the most effective was the rail-mounted thirteen-inch mortar, nicknamed the "Dictator," used at the siege of Petersburg, Virginia, in 1864. It threw 200-pound exploding shells that did great damage to the Confederate defenses. To protect it from enemy fire, the gun was operated from several well-hidden spurs constructed for the purpose.[24]

Raids

Raids into enemy country with the express purpose of destroying the transportation capacity of the other party became common. As soon as commanders became aware of the criticality of railroads for supplying armies, it became an established tactic to destroy the enemy's roads to force him to withdraw from advanced positions. Confederate generals like Nathan B. Forrest became an expert in such forays, burning bridges and buildings and destroying track, but the Union also developed skills to incapacitate the Southern transportation facilities. With their abundance of men and materials it often did not take the Federals much time to rebuild the destroyed portions, while the scarcity of manpower and materials in the South made it much harder for the Confederacy to reopen lines destroyed by Union raiding parties. The railroads in Virginia, especially those north of Richmond, were much fought over and changed hands often. Of course, the retreating side did its best to destroy as much as it could before having to deliver the road into the enemy's hands. Such railroads as the Orange & Alexandria—running from Alexandria, opposite Washington, D.C., to Gordonsville, Virginia—were in the front line many times and were consequently much damaged.

One of the most famous raids was the so-called Andrews raid of April 1862. A couple of Union soldiers led by James J. Andrews stole a train of the Western & Atlantic near Marietta, Georgia. They uncoupled the locomotive *General* and three boxcars and drove north to Chattanooga with the intention of destroying bridges and depot buildings behind them, so cutting the Confederate connection with the Southern armies in Tennessee. They were pursued and caught, but for some reason this most ineffectual and ill-conceived raid has caught the public fancy and has become one of the best-known feats of the Civil War.[25]

Conclusion

Despite some early misgivings, army commanders in both the North and the South quickly learned one important lesson: without railroads they could not deploy troops as quickly as they wanted, bring up reinforcements when they were most needed, or guarantee regular supply of the armies in the field. To make sure that railroads were adequately equipped and run, it was necessary to have some form of central authority to weld different railroad companies into one strong transportation unit. This last issue was solved by the Federal government with the Act of 1862 and the setting up of the Military Railroads organization. The South never went that far and had to suffer the consequences of its inability to forge a strong central organization.

The lessons of the American Civil War were not lost upon European observers.[26] The Prussians especially made good use of the American experience and in their war with Austria of 1866 used the railroads to move armies quickly in surprise movements. Four years later, in the Franco-Prussian War, the Germans had learned from their own mistakes in 1866 and did even better. Since then railroads and war have been inseparable all over the world.

Notes

1. George E. Turner, *Victory Rode the Rails: The Strategic Place of the Railroads in the Civil War* (Indianapolis: Bobbs-Merrill, 1953), 17.

2. For a general overview of the role of railroads in the conflict see John E. Clark, Jr., *Railroads in the Civil War: The Impact of Management on Victory and Defeat* (Baton Rouge: Louisiana State University Press, 2001).

3. Robert C. Black III, *The Railroads of the Confederacy* (Chapel Hill: University of North Carolina Press, 1952; repr. 1998).

4. Ibid., 200–13.

5. Ibid., 109–23.

6. Ibid., 169.

7. George E. Turner, *Victory Rode the Rails*, 233–37.

8. Black, *Railroads of the Confederacy*, 74; 148–59; 227–29.

9. Ibid., 294.

10. Ibid., 184–91.

11. Turner, *Victory Rode the Rails*, 365–76.

12. Walbrook D. Swank, ed., *Train Running for the Confederacy 1861–1865: An Eyewitness Memoir* (Charlottesville, Va.: Papercraft Printing and Design, 1990);

James A. Ward, ed., *Southern Railroad Man: Conductor N.J. Bell's Recollections of the Civil War Era* (De Kalb: Northern Illinois University Press, 1994), 9–35.

13. George R. Taylor and Irene Neu, *The American Railroad Network 1861–1890* (Cambridge, Mass.: Harvard University Press, 1956).

14. Thomas Weber, *The Northern Railroads in the Civil War 1861–1865* (New York: King's Crown Press, 1952; repr. Bloomington: Indiana University Press, 199), 35–38.

15. Weber, *Northern Railroads*, 103–106.

16. James A. Ward, "Daniel Craig McCallum," in *Railroads in the Nineteenth Century*, ed. Robert L. Frey (New York: Facts On File, 1988), 246–48.

17. Ward, "Herman Haupt," in *Railroads in the Nineteenth Century*, ed. Frey, 165–68.

18. Quoted in George B. Abdill, *Civil War Railroads* (Burbank, Calif.: Superior, 1961), 67.

19. Weber, *Northern Railroads*, 149.

20. Ibid., 181–86; Turner, *Victory Rode the Rails*, 286–96.

21. Weber, *Northern Railroads*, 189–204.

22. Abdill, *Civil War Railroads,* 79; Turner, *Victory Rode the Rails*, 297–309.

23. G. Balfour, *The Armoured Train: Its Development and Usage* (London: B.T. Batsford, 1981), 16–17.

24. Abdill, *Civil War Railroads*, 106.

25. Turner, *Victory Rode the Rails*, 166–77; Abdill, *Civil War Railroads*, 167–72.

26. See for instance: W. Boeheim, "Das Eisenbahn-Corps der vereinigten Staaten: seine Errichtung, Versuche und Leistungen im letzten Kriege," in *Oesterreichische Militärische Zeitschrift,* 1866, vol. 2, 1–27.

A photograph of the first station of the St. Paul & Pacific, forerunner of the giant Great Northern Railway, at Minneapolis, taken in 1873, shows how simple
such structures were. The passenger depot with its planked platform is on the
left behind the locomotive. The freight house in the center and the grain eleva-
tor on the right suggest the more important aspects of the business of this early
railroad company, which helped open Minnesota for settlement. (Great Northern photograph, author's collection)

The laying of track for a transcontinental railroad on the vast prairies was a fairly simple job, requiring only a great deal of manpower and many horse-driven vehicles. This scene depicts the laying of the mainline of the St. Paul, Minneapolis & Manitoba Railroad across the prairies of South Dakota in the early 1880s, but the construction of older transcontinentals, such as the Union Pacific or Kansas Pacific across Nebraska and Kansas, did not differ materially. (Courtesy: James J. Hill Papers, James J. Hill Reference Library, St. Paul, Minnesota)

The station of the Chicago, Burlington & Quincy at Lincoln, Nebraska, in the 1870s. The large building on the left is the Emigrant House, temporary shelter for prospective settlers; the smaller building in the right foreground is the Eating House, important in the days before dining cars were introduced. Behind the Eating House is the passenger depot. All buildings are constructed of wood; water barrels on the roofs testify to the high risk of fire from the wood-burning and spark-emitting locomotives of the time. (Courtesy: Nebraska State Historical Society, Lincoln, Nebraska, Photo RG 2158 PH 0 572)

Jay Gould's sumptuous presidential car No. 200 on the Erie Railway, sometime between 1867 and 1872. Jay Gould himself is said to be one of the men on the rear platform. Such cars, used for official visits and inspections, were usually appointed with all possible luxuries and comforts. Even in these troubled years for the Erie Railway, the directors never gave up these palatial vehicles. (Courtesy: Smithsonian Institution, Chaney photograph 23166)

A typical four-coupled shunting locomotive of the late 1870s of the St. Paul, Minneapolis & Manitoba Railroad, built by Brooks Locomotive Works of Dunkirk, New York, in 1879. This is probably the engine offered by Brooks in Document 16. Such engines hardly ever ventured out on the mainlines; they were used for shunting, or shifting, cars in stations and yards, hence the small tender with the sloping rear to provide a better view for the engineer when coupling up to a car. The large headlight has yet to be fitted by the railroad company. (Author's collection)

Railroad depots in the nineteenth century were the centers of community life in most American towns. They formed the only connection with the outside world in the days before radio, telephone, or television; the telegraph office in the depot was a busy place indeed. This is the elaborate gingerbread depot of the Louisville & Nashville Railroad in Pensacola, Florida, in 1908, with waiting passengers and station hacks. (Courtesy: DeGolyer Library, Southern Methodist University, Photograph Collection, Ag82.264)

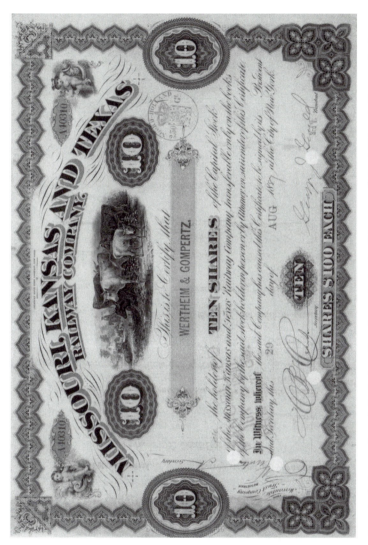

A typical share of an American railroad company, in this case of the Missouri, Kansas & Texas Railway. This certificate of ten shares of $100 each is made out to the Amsterdam firm of Wertheim & Gompertz, which held much stock in the MKT. The revenue stamp of the Dutch province of North Holland, 2,50 guilders, is clearly visible. (Author's collection)

In their timetables and other promotional literature, railroad companies always stressed the travel convenience they offered; through trains and cars were an important selling point. Passengers hated to change trains at unknown stations to make uncertain connections. This is part of the 1886 timetable of the Missouri Pacific Railway. (Author's collection)

To honor the brothers Oliver and Oakes Ames, who played conspicuous roles in the early financial history of the Union Pacific Railroad, the first transcontinental, the UP erected a monument along its mainline east of Laramie, Wyoming. The UP mainline was extensively straightened under Harriman in the early years of the twentieth century, and the monument is now several miles away from the tracks, but it is still impressive on its wind-swept hilltop. (Photograph: Jannie W. Veenendaal)

1127. C. M & St. P. Depot, Missoula, Mont.

The last transcontinental mainline was constructed by the Chicago, Milwaukee & St. Paul Railroad in the early twentieth century. As a triumph of modern technology over nature, it was an impressive achievement, but the company bankrupted itself in the process. Here is the beautiful depot of Missoula, Montana, still standing today, although now used as offices; the railroad has been abandoned and the tracks taken up. (Picture postcard, author's collection)

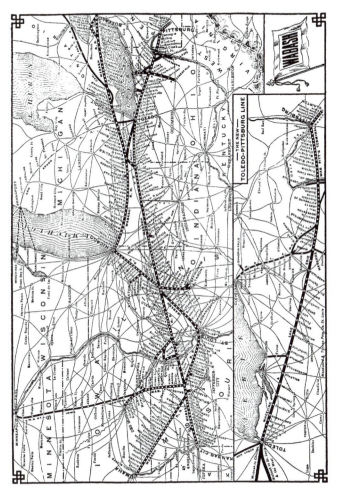

In his attempts to piece together a truly coast-to-coast railroad empire, George Gould, the son of the notorious Jay Gould, leaned heavily on his Wabash Railroad to finance the construction of the ill-starred Wabash Pittsburgh Terminal. Here a somewhat exaggarated map of the Wabash Railroad, with connections, in the early twentieth century. (Author's collection)

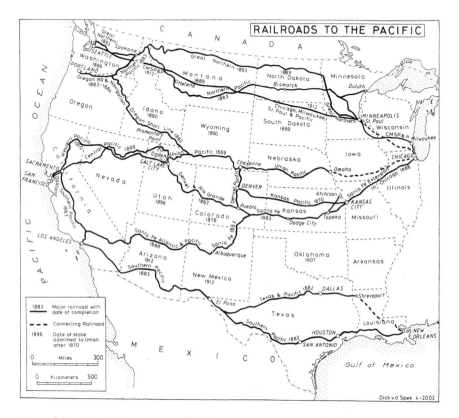

Map of the United States west of the Mississippi River with the transcontinental mainlines and their years of completion. (Drawn by Dick van der Spek, Emmen, the Netherlands)

CHAPTER 5

THE TRANSCONTINENTAL RAILROADS

The idea of a railroad across America is almost as old as the railroad itself. As far back as 1832, just a couple of years after the first steam locomotive was imported into the United States, a Michigan newspaper editor broached the idea of building a railroad from New York to Oregon. At that time the Oregon Territory was still disputed by Great Britain, and California was still under Mexican rule, so this editor was far ahead of his time.

The man who kept this dream alive was Asa Whitney, a New York trader down on his luck who early in 1845 presented a memorial to Congress about the necessity of a transcontinental railroad.[1] His plan envisaged a line from Lake Michigan by way of the South Pass (in present-day Wyoming) to San Francisco, with a branch to the Columbia River. At once a debate started about the best eastern terminus of the proposed line. Some favored Chicago, others St. Louis, while the southern politicians insisted on a line beginning in Memphis, Tennessee, or even farther south. Whitney lobbied extensively, wrote numerous pamphlets and newspaper articles; although he did not participate in the later building of the railroad, he prepared the minds of people for such a gigantic undertaking. The great advantage that a railroad was going to have over the existing means of communication was clear to everyone. The 5,250-mile-long route to the West, first by ship to Panama and then across the isthmus before boarding another ship for San Francisco, took at least thirty-five days. The 13,000-mile sea route via Cape Horn was dangerous and took even longer, while the overland stage from St. Louis to San Francisco, if "only" 2,800 miles and thirty days long, was full of discomfort and danger. Wagon trains for freight were slow, expensive, and not well suited to heavy goods. A railroad seemed the only possible answer.

In the 1850s several surveys for the best route were made by government engineers and surveyors, organized by the secretary of war, Jefferson Davis, the future president of the Confederacy. Four main east-west routes had been studied, plus one north-south line along the Pacific coast. The northernmost route was along the forty-seventh parallel, a central one between the thirty-eighth and forty-first parallel, a more southerly one along the thirty-fifth, and the southernmost one along the thirty-second parallel. It was found that along all four routes a transcontinental railroad would be possible. However, late in the decade the disputes about the course to follow became unavoidably mixed up with the controversy between free and slaveholding states, and nothing could be decided. Another hot item was whether the road was to be constructed by private interests or by government agencies. That private parties would be unable to undertake such as vast enterprise without some form of government aid was clear from the outset, but the shape this aid would have to take was a point of much controversy. Many also envisaged graft and fraud on an enormous scale, but no one really knew how to avoid that.

In April 1860 a bill had been introduced whereby the government would support private parties with a sixty-million-dollar loan in the form of U.S. bonds plus land grants. Many congressmen suspected fraud, and discussions raged for months, but the secession of the Southern states and the coming of war got most of the attention, of course, and matters rested there. On the other hand, the war gave an extra urgency to the idea. California and Nevada were friendly to the Union, and their silver and gold reserves were of the utmost importance, but a quick and safe means of communication was lacking and sorely needed. The withdrawal of the Southern politicians from Congress in 1861 cleared the way for a decision to build along the central route, westward from Omaha; the valley of the Platte River was relatively flat and led in the right direction. Legislation was reintroduced and finally passed by the Senate on June 20, 1862, and by the House of Representatives on June 24. One week later, on July 1, President Lincoln signed bill into law: "An Act to aid in the Construction of a Railroad and Telegraph Line from the Missouri River to the Pacific Ocean, and to secure to the Government the Use of the same for Postal, Military and Other Purposes."

The act stated that the railroad was to be built by two companies: the Central Pacific from Sacramento eastward, and the Union Pacific from

Omaha westward. It was a loosely and ambiguously worded act that gave much opportunity for new discussion, but it did set the machinery in motion. Per mile of track to be constructed, 6,400 acres of land were to be granted to the railroad, plus $16,000 in bonds per mile on the plains, $32,000 on the plateau between the Rockies and the Sierras, and $48,000 per mile in the mountains.[2] But despite this aid, few private capitalists came forward to start the great work. A supplementary act of 1864 enlarged the land grant and allowed the contractor to sell its own bonds, with the government bonds acting as a kind of second mortgage on the property.

Union Pacific–Central Pacific

First in the field was the Central Pacific Railroad, already incorporated in 1861, to build a railroad from Sacramento to the goldfields in the Sierra foothills and beyond. Collis P. Huntington (a hardware dealer), Leland Stanford (grocer and California politician), Mark Hopkins (partner of Huntington), and Charles Crocker (dry-goods dealer) were the founding fathers of the Central Pacific; the chief engineer was Theodore Judah, who had found the passage through the Sierras.

The driving force behind the Union Pacific, incorporated in 1863, was Thomas C. Durant, a medical doctor who had earlier been pushing railroads in Iowa. From the start the Union Pacific was involved in political and financial turmoil, and the prediction that large-scale frauds would be possible came true indeed. Strong support for the Union Pacific came from the brothers Oakes and Oliver Ames, respected hardware manufacturers of Massachusetts, who were induced by Durant to participate. Later they were to be depicted as utterly fraudulent and the villains of the piece; actually they were more foolish or innocent than venal. To finance the building of the railroad a so-called construction company was created, named the "Crédit Mobilier of America," after a French precedent, intended to finance large public works. Under Durant's control as vice president and general manager of the Union Pacific and president of the Crédit Mobilier, a total mix-up of both companies took place, with a strong smell of fraud, sloppy bookkeeping, bribery of politicians on a large scale, illegal profits for insiders, and shady manipulations with contracts for construction. In 1872 the Wilson-Poland Committee, a congressional committee set up to investigate the affairs of the Union Pacific and Crédit Mobilier, opened a veritable cesspool and found almost all parties guilty of some kind of fraud, graft, or wrongdoing.[3] This spectre was to haunt the Union Pacific for decades.

Meanwhile, the actual construction of the UP's track languished. Ground had been broken at Omaha in December of 1863, but the first rails were laid only on July 10, 1865. Progress thereafter was very slow, and by the end of the year Fremont, Nebraska, only some forty miles from Omaha, was the end of line. The year 1866 brought better results. Gen. Grenville M. Dodge, who had been adviser to President Lincoln on problems of the transcontinental projects, was hired as chief engineer, and the brothers Jack and Dan Casement, former Union generals, came in as superintendents of tracklaying. Labor was more plentiful now that the Civil War was over and demobilized soldiers were looking for jobs everywhere. They were hired by the thousands, together with large numbers of Irish, freshly arrived from their impoverished home country. Construction now really took off, and by September 1866 the 100th meridian—between Kearny and North Platte, Nebraska—had been reached, the occasion for grand festivities organized by Durant.

Grading and tracklaying was done mostly by hand, with gangs of graders, their rifles ready to hand, working far in advance of the track-layers. Danger from Indians was all too real. U.S. cavalry troops were detailed to give some protection, but now and then Indian raids dispersed the workers, derailed trains, and slowed progress. Construction camps moved along with the advance of the railroad, and the infamous "Hells on Wheels," with their brothels, bars, and gambling houses, followed the workers closely. Few of these temporary towns survived, and only where the railroad established "division points" did real towns spring up. There locomotives were changed, cleaned, fueled, and repaired, staff were housed, and generally eating places for passengers opened as soon as a line opened for traffic.

Despite bad weather (1867 was one of the worst winters on record), Indian raids, lack of supplies, unfamiliar and rough country, continuous bickering between the road's directors and the politicians in Washington, and financial problems, the Union Pacific rails crept forward, past Cheyenne, which became a division point and site of extensive servicing facilities. Laramie, Wyoming, was reached in May 1868. When the Union

Pacific reached Utah, the Mormon leader Brigham Young offered help with grading and tie cutting, in the hope that the road would pass through Salt Lake City. Chief engineer Dodge, however, wanted the railroad to pass north of the Great Salt Lake; Young, though very disappointed, agreed and later built a branch to the UP mainline.

Rails were laid into Ogden, Utah, on March 8, 1869. The UP graders, far ahead to the west, met the graders of the Central Pacific, working eastward. The result was two parallel competing grades until Congress fixed the official meeting point at Promontory Point, north of the Great Salt Lake. Of course, both companies wanted as many miles as possible because of the government bounty per mile—hence the eagerness of each to build on, in the hope that Congress would determine a meeting point favorable for it.

On Monday, May 10, 1869, the great work was done. Two special trains—one from Sacramento carrying Central Pacific's president, Leland Stanford, and other dignitaries, the other from the east, with Dr. Durant and the chief officers of the Union Pacific on board—slowly met. The last rail was put in place, ceremonial last spikes (gold and silver) hammered in by Stanford and Durant, and the telegraph proclaimed to the rest of the country that the epic struggle had ended. Fireworks and festivities everywhere: the Atlantic and Pacific Oceans had been linked by rail. A new chapter in American history had begun, according to the vice president of the United States, Schuyler Colfax. Altogether the Union Pacific had built 1,038 miles, while the Central Pacific had constructed 742 miles.

The Central Pacific had had much fewer political problems than the Union Pacific. Huntington was the chief lobbyist and purchasing agent in Washington and New York, Stanford directed affairs in California, and Charles Crocker was in charge of supply and construction. Theodore Judah died in November 1863 and was succeeded as engineer by Samuel S. Montague. James H. Strobridge was construction engineer at the railhead.

The first rail was laid in Sacramento on October 26, 1863, but progress was slow for a time. Lack of iron, which had to be shipped around Cape Horn, lack of money to buy materials, and an insufficient supply of labor hampered construction. White workers much preferred to try their hand at gold or silvermining, and it was not until 1865, when Strobridge hired the first local Chinese laborers, that an adequate supply of labor was found. There were strong anti-Chinese sentiments in California, but when these first Chinese workers turned out to be excellent railroad laborers, more and more were brought over from China, until some 14,000 were working for the Central Pacific.[4]

The crossing of the Sierra Nevada over the Donner Pass presented new problems. Many tunnels had to be drilled and blasted through the rock, with hand drills and black powder only. The new explosive nitro-glycerin—the predecessor of dynamite—was tried with some success, but it was dangerous to transport and handle; so many accidents happened that it was banned from the works. In winter, heavy snows in the Sierras made working almost impossible, and strong wooden snowsheds had to be built over the tracks to keep the line open. To speed up construction, men and equipment were hauled over the mountains to begin construction in Nevada even before the track over the Sierras was ready. There the waterless desert caused other problems. Only in March 1868 did the line across the mountains finally open, but from then on the graders and tracklayers made good progress until they met their colleagues—whom they sometimes considered enemies—of the Union Pacific at Promontory Point.

About the time that the Union Pacific was being started in Omaha, the Union Pacific Eastern Division was setting out westward from Kansas City.[5] Despite its name it had no corporate links with the "real" Union Pacific and was soon renamed the Kansas Pacific Railroad, to avoid confusion. Durant rightly considered the Kansas Pacific a possibly dangerous competitor, but it was 1870 before the line had been built over the Kansas prairies all the way to Denver. In Denver the Kansas Pacific connected with the grandly named Denver Pacific Railway and Telegraph Company, which opened a line from Denver to Cheyenne on the Union Pacific mainline in the same year.

When Jay Gould, the renowned financier, started buying into the Union Pacific in 1874, he also secured a stock majority in the by-then bankrupt Kansas Pacific to make sure that the potential competitor would not fall into wrong hands. The Denver Pacific, in receivership since 1878, was a different matter. The courts had placed that road in the hands of the bondholders, represented by a consortium of Dutch bankers, and in 1879 Gould had to travel to Amsterdam in person to buy them out.[6] From that year on both Kansas Pacific and Denver Pacific were parts of the far-flung Union Pacific empire.

Cooperation between Central Pacific and Union Pacific at Ogden did not always go smoothly in the early days, and the UP was soon looking around for an outlet of its own to the Pacific coast. It found this in the Oregon Short Line, which had reached Portland, Oregon, by 1884. Another independent outlet to the Pacific was finally acquired in 1902, in the shape of the Los Angeles & Salt Lake Railroad, opened throughout its length in 1905.

The Southern Pacific Railroad Company

After the festivities at Promontory Point were over, Collis P. Huntington and his associates did not wait for traffic to develop on its own but went aggressively in search of new lines and traffic. The Central Pacific was extended northward into Oregon and westward from Sacramento to San Francisco, and it acquired the Southern Pacific Railroad, which had a line from San Francisco to San Jose. Under this name the "Big Four," as Huntington, Stanford, Hopkins, and Crocker had become known, built south toward Los Angeles and on to El Paso, Texas, which was reached in 1881. Meanwhile, Huntington had been busy acquiring several railroads in Texas and Louisiana, and new construction between El Paso and San Antonio finally forged another transcontinental, a link between the Pacific coast and New Orleans. The first through trains between Los Angeles and New Orleans, along what was to be called the Sunset Route, ran in 1883.[7] Another line to El Paso, this time from Shreveport, Louisiana, had already been opened by an independent company, the Texas & Pacific, in 1882. For through traffic beyond El Paso it had to cooperate with the Southern Pacific.

The corporate structure of the Southern Pacific and its associated companies had by then become so complicated that a new Southern Pacific Railroad Company was incorporated under a Kentucky charter in 1884; all its associated roads, including the Central Pacific, were leased to the new giant. Huntington's dream of creating a truly coast-to-coast transcontinental by using his Chesapeake & Ohio and other southeastern lines to link New Orleans with the Atlantic coast came to nothing. Only in the 1990s would Amtrak, putting in a through Sunset Limited train from Los Angeles to Miami, Florida, by way of New Orleans, finally realize the dream cherished by many.

In the closing years of the nineteenth century, Edward H. Harriman, already in control of the Union Pacific, began buying into the Southern Pacific, and after the death of Collis P. Huntington he managed to acquire a controlling interest in the company. As he had done with the Union Pacific, Harriman ordered a large rehabilitation program for the somewhat decrepit Central Pacific and Southern Pacific. One of the most spectacular items of this program was the Lucin Cut-Off, a new line including a giant trestle across the Great Salt Lake, which abolished the roundabout way along the north shore of the lake. The old line past Promontory Point became superfluous, and despite its monumental importance for the history of railroad transportation in America, it was finally abandoned and lifted. (Recently the National Park Service established a museum at the original meeting point, where the old grades are still visible.) Harriman's giant combine of Union and Southern Pacific came to be seen as a threatening monopoly, and in an age of antitrust laws this could not be tolerated. In 1912, the Union Pacific was ordered to divest itself of its Southern Pacific stock. Harriman was dead by then, but in the last decade of the twentieth century the Union Pacific would again acquire the Southern Pacific and its subsidiaries, thus creating an even larger empire than Harriman had ever contemplated.

The Northern Pacific Railroad Company

Even after the choice of the middle route to be followed by the Union Pacific had been made, the northern route still had many protagonists, and in 1864 Isaac Stevens, former governor of Washington Territory and now a representative in Washington, D.C., obtained legislation whereby the Northern Pacific Railroad Company was created. President Lincoln signed the bill on July 1864. The largest land grant ever, amounting to nearly sixty million acres, was given to the young company by Congress to facilitate the construction of a line from Duluth, on Lake Superior, to the Pacific coast. Yet despite this liberal policy, no private parties came forward to risk their capital until 1869, when the project really got started. The Philadelphia banking house of Jay Cooke & Company, famous because of its successful sales of U.S. bonds in the United States and Europe during the Civil War, put its weight behind the Northern Pacific, and by 1873 the company had reached as far as Bismarck, North Dakota, by new construction and by leasing an existing railroad.[8] Cooke started an aggressive press campaign to market the bonds of the Northern Pacific; he described in glowing words the boundless fertility of the country to be traversed by the line, earning the Northern Pacific country the nickname, "Jay Cooke's Banana Belt."

But even with Cooke's support the NP was in trouble. Bond sales were slow, and construction costs high, and Cooke had to advance money to the company to cover the deficits. Even the solid house of Jay Cooke & Company could not continue this costly procedure for long, and in 1873 it had to close its doors, precipitating a general economic and financial crisis in the country. With the downfall of Cooke & Company the Northern Pacific went under too. All construction ended until the reorganization of the company in 1878 by an eastern consortium under Frederick Billings. A German investor, Henry Villard, with backing from Europe, acquired a majority in the new company and finally managed to finish the line, 1,675 miles between Duluth and Tacoma, Washington. On September 8, 1883, the last spike was driven near Gold Creek, Montana, amid great rejoicings and flocks of dignitaries from America and Europe.

But overextension, a high debt load, and lack of traffic caused the NP to default again in 1893, when the crisis of that year hit, and a new reorganization had to follow, which lasted until 1896. Meanwhile, the great competitor James J. Hill of the Great Northern had been quietly buying NP stock; he was in control by 1901. Together with the banker John Pierpont Morgan he then formed the Northern Securities Company, which also included the Chicago, Burlington & Quincy Railroad, and which gave both northern transcontinentals a direct link to Chicago. This combination had to be dissolved in 1904 as a result of the antitrust laws passed during President Theodore Roosevelt's administration, but the Great Northern and Northern Pacific continued to live peacefully side by side. Today both, with the CB & Q, are part of the giant Burlington Northern–Santa Fe system.

The Atchison, Topeka & Santa Fe Railroad Company

The AT & SF, better known as the Santa Fe Railroad, was the brainchild of Cyrus K. Holliday, a lawyer and politician of Topeka, Kansas, and was intended to tap the lucrative trade along the Santa Fe Trail. The company was incorporated in 1859, and Holliday managed to obtain a congressional land grant of some three million acres in Kansas Territory. Construction was delayed by the Civil War, but in 1868 the first rails were laid from Atchison to Topeka. By 1872 the Colorado border had been reached, just before the land grant was to expire. Pueblo, Colorado, was connected in 1876, and that same year a line to Kansas City was acquired.[9]

Construction into New Mexico was resumed in 1878, and the vital Raton Pass, where only one line of rails could be laid, was occupied just before the track gangs of the rival Denver & Rio Grande arrived on the spot. Albuquerque was reached in 1880, El Paso and a connection with the Southern Pacific at Deming, New Mexico, in 1881. The town of Santa Fe was connected to the mainline with a branch only, as the final goal was now no longer that sleepy town but the Pacific coast. A connection with Los Angeles over the rails of the Southern Pacific was not enough; the Santa Fe teamed up with the St. Louis & San Francisco Railroad ("the Frisco") to acquire the rights and the land grant of the already existing Atlantic & Pacific Railroad and to construct its Western Division from Albuquerque to the California border at Needles, where the Southern Pacific line from Mojave was met in 1883. Again a connection over the rails of a competitor was considered inadequate. After the A & P–Santa Fe threatened to build its own line from Needles westward, the SP sold its line to the A & P in 1884, finally giving the Santa Fe access to Los Angeles over its own rails. Earlier, in 1885, San Diego had been reached over the subsidiary California Southern, and another subsidiary, the Gulf, Colorado & Santa Fe, carried the Santa Fe trains to Houston and the Gulf coast. In 1887 a line from Kansas City to Chicago had been opened, and Denver was reached from the south, making the Santa Fe a well-rounded-off transcontinental system, tapping all important traffic-generating regions.

Unfortunately, this rapid expansion had strained the financial resources of the company too severely, and the ill-considered purchase of both the St. Louis & San Francisco and Colorado Midland companies, together with faulty bookkeeping, made bankruptcy unavoidable. The line went into receivership in 1893; an American-British-Dutch reorganization committee managed to get the company on its feet again in 1895, without the Frisco and the Colorado Midland but retaining the A & P. Just before the end of the nineteenth century a line from Mojave to San Francisco through the fertile San Joaquin Valley was acquired, giving the company access to new sources of traffic—fruit and vegetables foremost. From that moment on the Santa Fe was one of the most successful and well-managed transcontinentals, and a sound financial performer.

In the 1880s the Santa Fe company actively searched for immigrants to settle on its lands, and it was successful in attracting thousands of Russian Mennonites, who were persecuted in their own country and willing to settle in Kansas. They brought with them their particular variety of red wheat and with it they produced bumper harvests in Kansas.

Another special feature of the Santa Fe was its connection with Fred Harvey, an Englishman who in 1876 had leased the operation of the dining room at the Topeka depot. He insisted on good food in clean surroundings, served by well-trained and respectable waitresses; this concept turned out to be so successful that the Santa Fe asked him to operate other dining rooms and dining cars as well. Harvey Houses became popular all over the Southwest, and the Harvey Girls, apart fom being skilled waitresses, became much-sought-after marriage partners for the local males in an area where respectable women were scarce.

Great Northern Railway Company

A latecomer among transcontinentals was the Great Northern Railway, which reached Puget Sound in 1893. It had started inauspiciously as the St. Paul & Pacific Railroad, which never built any farther than the Minnesota-Dakota border before it defaulted in 1873. James J. Hill bought the property from the Dutch bondholders and incorporated it anew as the St. Paul, Minneapolis & Manitoba Railroad in 1878.[10] As the name implied, Manitoba was the goal, and the young railroad did very well in bringing in construction materials for the Canadian Pacific, then being built from Winnipeg to the West. But as soon as that line was completed all the way from Montreal to Vancouver, it no longer needed the Manitoba road as a feeder, and Hill turned his attention westward. His St.PM & M started construction from Breckenridge west across the fertile Dakota farmlands and reached Helena, Montana, in 1887. In 1889 he changed the name of his railroad into the more resounding Great Northern Railway. Seattle was chosen as the terminal, and the Great Northern opened its line to that port in 1893, without ceremony.

By following a more northerly route, Hill's engineers managed to find a better route across the Rockies than his competitor nearby, the Northern Pacific, and generally the GN was shorter, better constructed, and better operated. Jim Hill proved to be a master railroader, and he managed his properties better than most of his contemporaries. Moreover his Pacific coast terminal, Seattle, was more promising than Tacoma of the NP. The Great Northern never enjoyed any government subsidy, never had a land grant except for a very early one given to the St. Paul & Pacific, and yet managed to weather all the financial storms that brought many of its subsidized competitors to their knees. It not only never failed but always paid good dividends, making it a blue-chip investment on Wall Street and in London and Amsterdam. The close cooperation after 1901 with an old competitor, the Northern Pacific, and its link with Chicago by way of the Chicago, Burlington & Quincy RR have already been discussed.[11]

The Last Transcontinentals

This survey does not cover all transcontinental railroad lines, as two more were finished in the early years of the twentieth century. For the sake of completeness, these two will be described here.

The first one was the Western Pacific, the brainchild of George Gould, Jay Gould's son, who had inherited his father's railroad empire but not his business acumen. Gould was already in control of the Missouri Pacific and the Denver & Rio Grande and thus had a through line from St. Louis to Pueblo, Colorado, and beyond through the Rockies to Salt Lake City. In 1903 the Western Pacific Railway was incorporated to construct a line from Salt Lake City across the Sierras to Oakland. Gould himself did not yet appear as being behind the scheme, probably to mislead Harriman, who was in control of the competing Union Pacific and Southern Pacific. Soon Gould's position and intentions became known, though, and Harriman did his utmost to keep the new competitor at bay. He was successfull, as it turned out; construction of the line proved to be much more expensive than planned, and the Rio Grande and Missouri Pacific had to come forward with large loans when the sale of bonds of the Western Pacific itself remained slow. The line was finally finished in 1909, but revenues were disappointing and the company entered receivership in 1914. Reorganization followed in 1916, but the company failed again in 1935.[12]

The Western Pacific was part of George Gould's dream, which he shared with such giants as his father or Collis Huntington, a truly transcontinental railroad from coast to coast. Apart from his Missouri Pacific, Denver & Rio Grande, and Western Pacific, he was already in control of the Western Maryland, the Wabash, and the Wheeling & Lake Erie, and together these roads almost formed the transcontinental Gould was dreaming of. He overextended himself, though, his empire collapsed in 1907, and he lost control.[13] Today the Western Pacific, with the Denver & Rio Grande and the Missouri Pacific, is part of the Union Pacific empire, its old adversary.

The last of the transcontinentals was the Chicago, Milwaukee, and St. Paul Railroad, a prosperous and well-managed Granger railroad that reached from Chicago to the Twin Cities and westward all the way to Evarts, South Dakota. Afraid of being crushed between the Hill lines—the Great Northern, Northern Pacific, and Burlington—on one side, and the Harriman lines—Union Pacific and Southern Pacific—on the other, its management decided late in 1905 to construct a 1,400-mile line of its own to the Pacific coast with the intention of getting a fair share of the booming trade of Seattle with the Orient. Construction costs were estimated at some sixty million dollars, but crossing the Rockies and the Cascades was more difficult than expected, and costs soared to an unbelievable $256 million. The line was well built and even included some 600 miles of electrified track in the mountains, but the funded debt of the company became so high that servicing it proved impossible. The expected boom in the traffic from the Northwest never materialized, and in 1925, after many years of deficits, the Milwaukee entered receivership.[14] Today most of the Pacific extension is abandoned and lifted; the company itself was dissolved in 1977. What was left of the network was taken over by the Soo Line.

Notes

1. About Asa Whitney (1797–1872) see W. Thomas White, "Asa Whitney," in *Railroads in the Nineteenth Century*, ed. Robert L. Frey, *Encyclopedia of American Business and Biography* (New York: Facts On File, 1988), 436–38.

2. Details in Maury Klein, *Union Pacific: The Birth of a Railroad 1862–1893* (New York: Doubleday, 1987), 13–16.

3. The most recent history of the Union Pacific is Maury Klein, *Union*

Pacific. The Birth of a Railroad 1862–1893. Klein's careful coverage of the Crédit Mobilier scandal is on 285–305. A second volume, *Union Pacific: The Rebirth 1894–1969* (New York: Doubleday, 1989), continues the story.

4. There is no real history of the Central Pacific available, but Wesley S. Griswold, *A Work of Giants. Building the First Transcontinental Railroad* (London: Frederick Muller, 1963) is useful.

5. George L. Anderson, *Kansas West* (San Marino, Calif.: Golden West Books, 1963).

6. See Augustus J. Veenendaal, Jr., *Slow Train to Paradise. How Dutch Investment Helped Build American Railroads* (Stanford, Calif.: Stanford University Press, 1996), 100–102.

7. There is no serious history of the Southern Pacific in the nineteenth century, but Don L. Hofsommer, *The Southern Pacific, 1901–1985* (College Station: Texas A & M University Press, 1986), gives a good deal of early history in his first chapters.

8. The early history of the Northern Pacific is in Eugene V. Smalley, *History of the Northern Pacific Railroad* (New York: Putnam's, 1883). The later history is in Louis T. Renz, *The History of the Northern Pacific Railroad* (Fairfield, Wash.: Ye Galleon, 1980).

9. History of the Santa Fe is in Keith L. Bryant, *History of the Atchison, Topeka and Santa Fe Railway* (New York: Macmillan, 1974).

10. See Augustus J. Veenendaal, Jr., *The Saint Paul & Pacific Railroad: An Empire in the Making, 1862–1879* (De Kalb: Northern Illinois University Press, 1999).

11. Ralph W. Hidy, Muriel E. Hidy, Roy V. Scott, with Don L. Hofsommer, *The Great Northern Railway. A History* (Boston: Harvard Business School Press, 1988).

12. Don DeNevi, *The Western Pacific* (Seattle: Superior, 1978).

13. James L. Larson, "Wheeling & Lake Erie," in *Railroad History* 185 (Autumn 2001), 67–69.

14. August Derleth, *The Milwaukee Road: Its First Hundred Years* (New York: Creative Age Press, 1948), 171–95.

CHAPTER 6

MERGER, MONOPOLY, AND REGULATION

The first railroads were local, or at best regional, railroads, without any physical connection to others. But with the steady growth of the railroad network, railroads began to touch each other in places, and connections were made—that is, as long as the gauges of the roads in question were compatible. A good example is the series of railroads that eventually formed an iron link between Albany and Buffalo in New York State. The first, the Mohawk & Hudson, ran from Albany to Schenectady and made contact there with the Utica & Schenectady. Other roads followed, and finally in 1842, with the opening of the Attica & Buffalo, a string of seven separate railroads stretched all the way from New York's capital to Lake Erie, almost duplicating the Erie Canal.

The Tycoons

Erastus Corning, a successful proprietor of an iron works at Albany and New York politician, was director of several of these independent companies.[1] Upon completion of several other competing railroads, such as the New York & Erie, linking the Hudson River with Lake Erie, he came to the conclusion that these seven roads could survive only if they acted together. In 1851 he began lobbying the state legislature to permit the merger of the seven companies, and after two years of hard work in Albany he managed to get the politicians to approve that move. The New York Central Railroad was born, the first great railroad merger in America. Corning became its first president.

The necessary connection of the new New York Central at Albany was the Hudson River Railroad, since 1865 securely under control of

"Commodore" Cornelius Vanderbilt, who had made a fortune in shipping and who had already bought into the New York & Harlem Railroad. Vanderbilt did not want to rely on another railroad for his western connection, so he started to buy into the NYC until in 1867 he was in control. In 1869 all Vanderbilt's roads were merged into a new New York Central & Hudson River Railroad, with Vanderbilt and his sons in charge. Among his other and later acquisitions were the Lake Shore & Michigan Southern and the Michigan Central, which gave the Vanderbilt lines access to Chicago.[2] These lines formed the nucleus of a mighty Vanderbilt railroad empire that would stretch from New England and New York City all the way to Chicago and St. Louis.

Of course, the New York Central was not the only railroad to merge and to buy up connecting lines. Other big companies did the same and gobbled up possible competitors or allies. In an era when business morals were loose anyhow, the morals of railroad tycoons may have been unusually bad. An infamous episode was the so-called Erie War over control of the Erie Railway, just reorganized in 1860 from the earlier New York & Erie, which had gone bankrupt. The Erie was a serious competitor of Vanderbilt's New York Central, and to eliminate the competition Vanderbilt decided to buy control. Helped by the shady financier Daniel Drew, he got a seat on the Erie board, but the slippery Drew shifted position and teamed up with Jay Gould and Jim Fisk to oust Vanderbilt again. Every trick of the trade was used by Gould and his allies: buying judges, corrupting politicians in Albany, watering the Erie stock by printing thousands of new shares, physical violence, even flight by night from Manhattan to New Jersey to get out of the reach of New York law. These machinations earned the Erie the nickname "Scarlet Woman of Wall Street." By 1868 Vanderbilt had to admit defeat and managed to maneuver himself out of the Erie without too much loss. The real losers, of course, were the common-stock and bond holders in America and Europe over whose heads the fight had been raging but who would not see any dividends or interest for many years to come. Not for nothing did the cynical Gould say, as we have seen, "There will be icicles in Hell when Erie common pays a dividend." Burdened by a heavy funded debt and overcapitalized, the Erie Railway went under again in 1875, to be reorganized in 1878 as the New York, Lake Erie & Western Railroad. It remained a weak sister among its competitors.[3]

Jay Gould came out of the Erie Wars with a greatly enhanced reputation as a financial predator to be reckoned with but never trusted. Feared
and despised, he went his own way and continued to build up his railroad empire. Although Gould was generally seen by his contemporaries
as a wrecker of railroads, his tenure on the board of the Union Pacific did
much to improve that property. When Gould obtained control in 1874 it
was a run-down and badly managed railroad, with a large funded debt
and competitors on all sides. Gould disentangled its finances, bought up
competing lines, such as the Kansas Pacific and Denver & Pacific, and set
the UP on its feet again. But Gould did not confine his attention to the
UP; he also bought up roads in the Southwest and created a new empire,
with the Missouri Pacific as its center and the Texas & Pacific, the Missouri, Kansas & Texas, and others as its feeders. In the East he was in
control of the Wabash, the Lackawanna, and several other roads; by 1880
his railroad empire was said to total over 8,000 miles. But many people
rejoiced when his empire seemed to collapse in 1884. He managed to
survive, however, and in 1890 even got hold again of the Union Pacific,
which he had relinquished earlier, shortly before his death. His son George
took over his business interests, but with markedly less success.

Of course, Gould was not the only railroad tycoon who amassed a
fortune through his holdings of railroad stock. The last quarter of the nineteenth century is one long story of consolidations, mergers, takeovers, and
buyouts. Gould and Vanderbilt may have caught the public fancy during
the Erie Wars, but they were certainly not the only such figures. Collis P.
Huntington and his associates, collectively the "Big Four," with their
Central and Southern Pacific holdings, built an empire in California by
means both legal and illegal, by which they held the state, its economy,
and its politicians in a stranglehold. Frank Norris's 1901 novel *The Octopus*
may have been an exaggeration, but there was certainly much truth in his
accusations.[4]

In the Northwest, James Jerome (Jim) Hill did what his nickname
"The Empire Builder" implied. But he was not only a collector of railroads
and an amasser of a fortune for himself but also a superb railroader, who
from modest beginnings in St. Paul, Minnesota, constructed a network of
railroads all over the Northwest. His Great Northern Railway was one of
the great names of Wall Street. It always paid good dividends, never defaulted, even in times of general financial panic such as 1893 or 1907, and

it gave superb service to the traveler and the shipper. Apart from his own Great Northern, his empire also came to include the Northern Pacific, the second of the great transcontinentals, and the Chicago, Burlington & Quincy, which gave him access to Chicago.

It seemed to be the same everywhere, even if the managers of the railroads in question did not seek the limelight in the way Vanderbilt, Gould, and Hill did for a time. The Pennsylvania Railroad, led by Thomas A. Scott (1823–81), extended its network far beyond its home state, sometimes by way of seemingly independent lines, such as the Pittsburgh, Fort Wayne & Chicago, sometimes by taking over smaller roads or by new construction. In the South, Henry B. Plant (1819–99) built up a railroad system that became the forerunner of the Atlantic Coast Line, which in turn came to control the venerable Louisville & Nashville through stock ownership. The great competitor of the Atlantic Coast Line was the Seaboard Air Line Railway, which paralleled it almost everywhere. The Seaboard was pieced together by two banking houses of Richmond and Baltimore, and by 1900 it stretched all the way from Richmond to Miami, with other lines far into Alabama. In the West, the Atchison, Topeka & Santa Fe developed into a major player, a worthy foe of the Southern Pacific, after it took hold of the California Southern, the Atlantic & Pacific, and several smaller lines. So it went almost everywhere, smaller lines being gobbled up by larger neighbors, or new systems being created out of a large number of small roads, with new construction to connect the pieces. It was a question not only of economies of scale but of territory and the exclusion of others. Competition and control became familiar bywords in the world of railroads.

One way of eliminating competition was the formation of "pools," wherein several railroads that served more or less the same region or had the same interests pooled their equipment, charged the same rates, divided the available traffic, and split the revenue between them. Such pools were often kept secret and lasted only as long as all participating railroads obeyed the rules. As soon as one road started undercutting the others, the pool fell apart and became a free-for-all. One of the most lasting was the Trunk Line Pooling Association of 1877, formed originally by the New York Central, the Erie, the Baltimore & Ohio and the Pennsylvania but soon embracing almost forty railroads north of the Ohio River and east of the Missisippi. Albert Fink (1827–97), an engineer of German extraction and a former director of the Louisville & Nashville, was its director; he managed to keep the pool alive until his retirement in 1889.[5] Another pool, but somewhat less successful and less enduring, was the "Iowa Pool," formed by three Granger railroads—the Burlington, the Rock Island, and the Chicago & North Western. Other Granger roads did not participate, and in some cases it proved almost impossible to keep these roads, with their many conflicting interests, together.[6]

Another element that deserves attention in this shady world of railroad business was the so-called nuisance railroad, meant not to provide real transportation of any kind but just to siphon off business from a big competitor. A prime example was the New York, West Shore & Buffalo, built simply to hinder the New York Central on the other bank of the Hudson River. George Pullman, said to be annoyed by the fact that Vanderbilt's New York Central did not use his sleeping and parlor cars, was behind the New York, West Shore & Buffalo, and so was Thomas Scott of the Pennsylvania. But Vanderbilt retaliated by organizing the Southern Pennsylvania Railroad, just a little to the south of Scott's Pennsylvania Railroad. All this was sheer folly, of course, wasteful of money, men, and materials. Bankers like the redoubtable John Pierpont Morgan (1837–1913) saw that it simply had to stop; and in 1885 Morgan brought leaders of the Pennsylvania and New York Central together on his yacht *Corsair* and kept them there long enough, steaming up and down New York Harbor, to agree to end the fight. The NYC acquired the West Shore, the Pennsylvania got the (still unfinished) Southern Pennsylvania; Morgan pocketed a large fee for his services, rumored to be as high as three million dollars. Another nuisance railroad was the "Nickel Plate," officially the New York, Chicago & St. Louis, incorporated in 1881 by two somewhat shady financiers, George I. Seney and Calvin S. Brice. With a line from Buffalo to Cleveland and farther west, it invaded territory that was already well served by other roads, notably Vanderbilt's Lake Shore & Michigan and Gould's Wabash. It was built to high standards, hence its nickname, but it never made money and was practically bankrupt when Vanderbilt bought it in 1883; he thought its price too high, but he was willing to pay to get rid of the competition.[7]

The role of bankers like Morgan in railroad consolidation was important. The House of Morgan had in the 1880s grown from an old-fashioned bank into an institute that provided capital to corporations in industry and transportation in exchange for a large measure of control of those corporations by Morgan and his henchmen. He reorganized a large number of railroads, starting with the bankrupt Philadelphia & Reading in 1886 and the Chesapeake & Ohio the next year. One of the key elements in his handling of reorganizations was the scaling down of the funded debt of the companies in question, enabling them to start new lives with smaller interest payments. Existing shareholders usually had to give up most, if not all, of their holdings or pay cash to obtain new shares, while bondholders had to be content with lower-renting bonds. New shares were generally placed for a number of years in a voting trust, where Morgan and his henchmen had absolute control. One of his greatest successes was the formation in 1893–94 of the Southern Railway out of some thirty companies, of which the bankrupt Richmond Terminal was the largest. The debt load was scaled down, and a voting trust for five years assured Morgan that the manager he put in, Samuel Spencer (1847–1906), would remain in charge. The new Southern became one of the best-run railroads in the country.

But Morgan was not in control everywhere. His attempt to reorganize the Union Pacific after its default in 1893 ended in defeat, and in the end the then still relatively unknown Edward H. Harriman, assisted by Rockefeller's Standard Oil, the National City Bank of New York, and Kuhn, Loeb & Company, in conjunction with the many German and Dutch bondholders, reorganized the property successfully. On a much more positive note for Morgan, the reorganization of the Northern Pacific was achieved by James J. Hill of the Great Northern, together with Morgan; they practically took over the NP. One of the key members of Morgan's team was Charles Henry Coster (1852–1900), who held directorships in scores of railroad and other companies and was involved in most if not all of Morgan's consolidations—"Morganization" as it was jokingly called.[8]

Not all of Morgan's operations, as we have seen, ended successfully. The New York, New Haven & Hartford, a prosperous New England road, was selected by Morgan to form the nucleus of a transportation empire in the area. He put one of his men, Charles S. Mellen (1851–1927), in charge with orders to embark on an ambitious scheme of expansion. Mellen bought everything in sight, steamboat lines, trolley networks, and other railroad companies, generally at exorbitant prices. In doing so he ran afoul of a Massachusetts law, but when ordered to divest himself of the shares of other roads, he brazenly sold them to dummies and henchmen while retaining control himself. In ten years between 1903 and 1913 the capitalization of the New Haven rose from a modest ninety-three million dollars to no less than $417 million—far too much for the company, of course. For many years it was unable to pay any dividends at all; it resumed dividends only in 1928, just before the Great Crash, when the whole American economy broke down.[9]

Morgan did not confine himself to railroads. In 1901 he was an important factor in the incorporation of United States Steel, then the largest joint-stock corporation in the world, and he also helped finance new conglomerates, such as General Electric, and firms as diverse as International Harvester, Western Union, and AT&T. Around 1906, when most railroads had been consolidated into larger groups, the Morgan-Hill lines totaled some 39,000 miles; the Vanderbilt lines 22,500; the Pennsylvania system 20,000; the Gould lines 17,000; Harriman's Union–Southern Pacific combination another 21,000; and the Rock Island system, soon to fall apart, some 15,000 miles.

This enormous concentration of power in the hands of a few was eyed suspiciously by the public, the press, and the government alike. The ostentatious display of dazzling wealth by some of these men did not help either. Their sumptuous "cottages" at Newport, the glamorous townhouses on Park Avenue in New York City and on San Francisco's Nob Hill, and such palaces as "Biltmore" near Asheville, North Carolina, modeled after a French castle, were seen as rewards of fraud, embezzlement, or even open theft. By 1900 the time was ripe for measures to curb the power of these few families.

Complaints and Regulation

One of the most vociferous of organizations critical of railroads was the Grange, or the National Grange of Patrons of Husbandry, as it was known officially. Founded in 1867 by Oliver Kelly as a secret fraternal organization, it had grown by 1875 into a political force, with over 850,000 members, concentrated in the Midwest. Farmers there were not doing badly in general, but they were unhappy with falling wheat and corn prices, competition from other countries, such as Argentina and Russia, and from their dependence on a market in Europe, over which they had no control. In times when demand for their product had been high, they had extended farmland into marginal areas, where droughts and other cyclical meteorological phenomena made farming hazardous at best.[10] The Grangers demanded regulation of the railroads, the banks, and the big corporations, which were seen as the enemies of the free "Jeffersonian" farmer—who had never existed in the Midwest, of course, but who was still seen as the ideal type of American citizen, the cornerstone of American democracy. As the railroad was nearby, it was the first to be attacked. Farmers forgot that they had clamored loudest for more railroads to be able to transport their harvest to the markets, and they also forgot that since 1870 railroad freight rates per ton-mile had been falling almost as fast as farm prices. Transatlantic freight rates had even fallen by two-thirds—a positive factor for American farmers, of course, as a sizeable portion of their wheat was exported to Europe.

On the other hand, there were indeed many abuses. When a railroad company held a practical monopoly in a certain region, it could dictate freight rates. Terminal facilities for the storage of grain and elevators along the line were often in the hands of the railroads themselves. Where more than one railroad served the same community, secret pooling often made competition meaningless. Many complaints concerned the difference between long-haul and short-haul rates, as the latter were generally higher. It was often cheaper to get a carload of wheat from Minneapolis to Chicago than from the Minnesota hinterland to Minneapolis. Other charges were that some large preferred shippers got special low rates or rebates and that free passes were given liberally to congressmen, local politicians, judges, and other officials in return for a favorable treatment in the courts and legislatures.

Grangers demanded regulation of rates, and some state governments indeed passed legislation in this respect. Illinois was the first in 1871, followed by Iowa and Wisconsin in 1874 and Nebraska, Kansas, and Missouri in the late 1870s. This legislation established a degree of regulation of rates and of other debated points, initially for intrastate traffic but later also for interstate shipments. Even non-Granger states enacted some measures in this respect, Georgia in 1879 and California later in the same year. Naturally the railroads opposed these laws as much as possible, used tactics of obstruction, and complied only with much foot-dragging when really forced to do so. They also took their case to court, but initially without much success, as even the Supreme Court of the United States upheld the state laws, in a series of decisions in 1876. In the first case, *Munn v. Illinois,* the Court upheld a law of 1871 whereby the state of Illinois had established maximum rates for the storage of grain. Two other cases, *Peik v. Chicago & North Western R.R.* and *Chicago, Burlington & Quincy R.R. v. Iowa,* also were decided against the railroads, on the grounds that in the absence of national legislation states could establish rates not only for intrastate but for interstate commerce as well.

With these successes in view, more and more people sought some form of national legislation, as the problem went beyond individual states and was indeed nationwide. In Washington, John H. Reagan, congressman from Texas, in 1878 managed to get a proposal for regulation on the national level through the House, but it stalled there. However, politicians had by now become aware that there really was a railroad problem; President Chester Arthur, in his 1883 State of the Union message, urged Congress to do something about it. Three years later a Senate committee led by Shelby M. Cullom published a report enumerating all the familiar and just complaints and abuses, from secret rebates, free passes, and discrimination to stock-watering and malfeasance on the level of the directorates. The Cullom committee strongly recommended federal regulation.

Later in that same year, 1886, the Supreme Court decided in the highly controversial case of *Wabash, St. Louis and Pacific Railway v. Illinois* that state regulations could not be applied to traffic passing beyond its borders—a complete reversal of earlier decisions. Interstate commerce could be regulated only by the federal government, and so federal action seemed to be called for. The Reagan and Cullom bills were now combined into the Interstate Commerce Act and were passed by Senate and House. It was signed into law by President Grover Cleveland on February 4, 1887. It was a victory for the regulators, but a hollow one, as it soon turned out. It set up the five-member Interstate Commerce Commission to see that railroads charged "just and resonable" rates; that secret rebates, drawbacks, and pools were abolished; that every discrimination between shippers and localities was ended; that freight rates were published and filed with the government; and that short-haul rates were never higher than long-haul. But the act failed to give the ICC the necessary powers to establish rates and enforce them if necessary. It could only recommend, taking action only through the federal courts in cases where a railroad refused to comply.[11]

In any case, what were "just and reasonable" rates, and who was to decide that? The ICC, the members of which were capable and respected men with wide railroad experience, headed by Thomas M. Cooley, could do little. The problem was that court action could drag on endlessly; an average case took four years! Of the sixteen cases between a railroad company and the ICC before the Supreme Court between 1887 and 1905, only one was decided in favor of the ICC. It was clear that the ICC had to have more powers to prescribe or suspend rates and to enforce them.

Two more court decisions in 1897 and one in 1901 clearly established the fact that the ICC had no right to establish either short or long-haul rates. This hastened the political process to strengthen the powers of the commission. In a political climate where the Progressive movement, which was strongly against monopoly, was gaining strength, the time seemed right to act. The Sherman Antitrust Act of 1890 had been as toothless as the act that set up the ICC, but the new president, Theodore Roosevelt, wanted to act. His first big case against monopoly was the suit against the Northern Securities Company, the holding company set up by Morgan and Jim Hill to keep Harriman of the Union Pacific out of the Pacific Northwest. The case dragged on for years, but in 1904 the Supreme Court finally ordered the NSC dissolved (although in reality not much changed in the actual ownership of the railroads involved).

More was to come. The Elkins Act of 1903 again prohibited the practice of giving rebates to favored shippers and made railroad officials liable to prosecution. In Roosevelt's second term in office he stressed the need for more regulation, and in 1906 a new law was finally passed, with overwhelming majorities in both houses. This Hepburn Act at last gave the now seven-member ICC the power to establish "just and reasonable" rates, if need be against the will of railroad companies. The much-maligned system of free passes and certain other abuses were also outlawed. Roosevelt's successor, William H. Taft, went even farther. He was prejudiced against the small group of men who ran the railroads and other big businesses, and was prepared to fight them. The Mann-Elkins Act of 1910 cleared up all misunderstanding about the short-haul–long-haul question, set up a Commerce Court to hear appeals of rate decisions by the ICC, and permitted the ICC to suspend for as long as ten months new rates established by a railroad. The authority of the ICC was extended to telephone and cable companies; pipelines and sleeping-car operations had already been brought under its jurisdiction by the Hepburn Act. Finally, in 1913, the

Railroad Valuation Act required the ICC to establish the true value of every railroad company, its capital structure in comparison to the real value of its infrastructure and rolling stock, thus showing abuses such as stock-watering or other forms of overcapitalization by which railroads had based their rates to obtain "fair" returns on the invested capital.

By 1914 the railroads were bound hand and foot, with every movement regulated by federal laws and with little room left for maneuvering on the part of the management. Some critics said, with force of argument, that the railroads were now overregulated, unable to earn a decent return on invested capital or to run their business as they should. In comparison with the trucking business, which grew strongly after World War I, the railroads were indeed in a unfavorable position. They had to pay for their own infrastructure, were heavily taxed for every square foot of property they owned and for every dollar they earned, were bound by all kinds of regulations, and had to maintain services that had become superfluous, while the truckers paid little or nothing for the highways they used, were hardly regulated or not at all, and had no obligation to maintain unprofitable services and schedules.[12] Only new legislation in the 1980s would finally put an end to this inequitable state of affairs.

But the railroads themselves had called down this enmity upon them. In an age when they were practically free of competition from other modes of transportation, they had abused their position of monopoly to such an extent that was to be long before the general public and the politicians forgot the long years of ill will and abuse. While there were quite a few honest and competent railroad managers and directors, there had been far too many of the robber-baron type, the sharks who were out primarily for their own profit and cared little or nothing for the public they were supposed to serve, or for the shareholders of their companies.

Notes

1. Daniel Larkin, "Erastus Corning, 1794-1872," in *Railroads in the Nineteenth Century,* ed. Robert L. Frey (New York: Facts On File, 1988), 64–69.

2. Alvin F. Harlow, *The Road of the Century: The Story of the New York Central* (New York: Creative Age Press, 1947).

3. John Steele Gordon, *The Scarlet Woman of Wall Street: Jay Gould, Cornelius Vanderbilt, the Erie Railway Wars, and the Birth of Wall Street* (New York: Weidenfeld and Nicolson, 1988).

4. Frank Norris, *The Octopus: A Story of California* (1901; repr. New York: Airmont, 1969).

5. E. Dale Odom, "Albert Fink," in *Railroads in the Nineteenth Century*, ed. Frey, 120–22.

6. Julius Grodinsky, *The Iowa Pool: A Study in Railroad Competition, 1870–1884* (Chicago: University of Chicago Press, 1950).

7. John F. Stover, *The Routledge Historical Atlas of the American Railroads* (New York: Routledge, 1999), 114–15.

8. Albro Martin, "Charles Henry Coster," in *Railroads in the Nineteenth Century*, ed. Frey, 70–76.

9. Alvin F. Harlow, *Steelways of New England* (New York: Creative Age Press, 1947), 331–36.

10. Jeremy Atack, Fred Bateman, and William N. Parker, "The Farm, the Farmer, and the Market," in *The Cambridge Economic History of the United States*, ed. Stanley L. Engerman and Robert E. Gallman (Cambridge: Cambridge University Press, 2000), vol. 2, 245–84.

11. Gabriel Kolko, *Railroads and Regulation: 1877–1916* (New York: W. W. Norton, 1965).

12. Albro Martin, *Enterprise Denied: Origins of the Decline of American Railroads, 1897–1971* (New York: Columbia University Press, 1971).

CHAPTER 7

RAILROADS AND THE AMERICAN ECONOMY

The first railroads were generally built either to complement existing canals and waterways or to provide transportation where canals were impractical. Soon they also competed directly with rivers and canals. The South Carolina Railroad, for instance, was intended to direct from upstate South Carolina toward Charleston traffic that would otherwise have used the Savannah River all the way to Savannah, Georgia. The Western Railroad of Massachusetts was clearly meant to keep at least part of the western trade for Boston, in direct competition with New York City and its Erie Canal and Hudson River. With the success of these early railroads, it became clear that railroads provided smooth all-weather transportation. Canals froze over for three months or more every year, but the railroad remained in operation through snow, ice, or rain. Freight charges had already fallen dramatically with the opening of the first canals, but they were to fall even lower with the coming of the railroad. The rate for carrying a ton of freight from Buffalo to New York City before the opening of the Erie Canal had been around $100; after the opening it fell to around $8.50 and even lower in the 1850s.[1] Competition from the railroads was the chief cause here.

Speeds were low, however. Wagons on the turnpikes and canal boats drawn by horses or mules made about two miles an hour at best. Steamboats were much faster, of course, and made ten miles per hour on average, with the Hudson River steamers the fastest, at just under twenty miles an hour. Freight trains on the railroads were not much faster in those days, but they generally had the advantage of more direct routes. From Cincinnati to Pittsburgh it was 470 miles by river but only 311 by railroad. It had taken fifty days to ship freight from Cincinnati to New York by a succession of boats and wagons; by rail it took only six to eight days. No wonder that the railroads soon carried most of the freight offered. Only heavy, low-value goods, such as coal or ores, continued to be shipped by water well into the twentieth century.

When in a hurry, travelers took the stagecoach, which was fast; it was also expensive and uncomfortable, but there was no alternative when there was no canal or navigable river available. Coaches made more than ten miles an hour but charged between five and nine cents per mile. Canal boats were more comfortable but much slower and cheaper—from 1.5 to two cents a mile, maybe 2.5 for the fastest boats (but even these did not average more than between three and four miles an hour). Steamboats on the rivers and on the coastal runs were speedier, of course, and a bit more expensive. But fares on the Hudson River between New York City and Albany dropped from seven dollars in the 1820s to fifty cents by 1850. Coastal shipping between New York and ports in Massachusetts remained popular well into the nineteenth century. Fast and sumptuous ships could compete with the railroads, because of their greater comfort and low fares.

Almost everywhere else the railroad killed off most of the steamboat, by virtue of greater speed and all-weather availability. The railroad's fares may have been higher, between three and five cents per mile, but even so the traveling public and shippers adopted them warmly. Most lines had at first only one class, but soon special extra-fare parlor cars were introduced on some lines. At the other end of the scale, special fares, as low as one cent per mile, were charged for poor immigrants; the accommodation offered was spartan at best. Only the Erie Canal managed to keep part of the immigrant traffic to the West, because of its low fares. On all other canals passenger traffic fell off dramatically as soon as competing railroads opened for traffic. By 1860 most canals were dead, except for slow-moving, low-value freight. Steamboat trade on the western rivers survived longer, but it declined sharply on the upper reaches of the Missouri and Mississippi, where ice in winter and low water and sandbanks in summer impeded navigation. Railroads soon penetrated areas formerly dependent on the steamboat and took away most of the trade. For instance, steamboat arrivals in St. Paul, Minnesota, the end of Mississippi navigation, fell from an all-time high of 1,068 in 1858 to 777 by 1866, and even lower to a paltry 218 in 1874, after the railroad had reached the Minnesota capital.[2] In most places on the upper Missouri River, even harder to navigate than the Mississippi, it was much the same.

Because of the availability of cheap and dependable transportation, the pattern of agriculture changed profoundly. From the small-scale subsistence farming of the early decades of the nineteenth century a shift toward market-oriented production is visible. Especially in the "old Northwest," where land prices had been low because of the lack of transportation, the coming of the railroad had a profound effect on the value of land. Settlers moved in in large numbers from the stony fields of New England to the rich arable lands of Ohio, Indiana, and Illinois, driving farm prices up. New immigrants, generally not people of substance, moved even farther west, where prices still were much lower.

The pattern of industrialization of the country changed too. Formerly, most textiles and metalworking industries had been situated in areas where water power was available and distances were small. With the growing network of canals and railroads, coal as fuel became a real alternative to water power, and railroads provided transportation of the finished products of the mills. Industry moved west, into Pennsylvania and Ohio first, and into Illinois in the 1850s. After the Civil War, which brought a temporary stop in many respects, the westward movement of population and industry went on at ever higher levels. Railroads played a vital role here; without them the empty spaces could not have been filled up so quickly.

The Civil War was a kind of watershed: after Appomattox, the forces that had been used for warfare were available for more peaceful pursuits again. Railroad construction was resumed on an ever larger scale, although the crisis of 1873 and its aftermath meant a temporary setback, driving many railroad companies into receivership. By 1879 the situation was back to normal, with almost 40,000 miles of new construction between that year and 1883, when the next crisis struck. Most of this new mileage was built with a clear profit motive, not ahead of demand, as has so often been charged. Even a railroad like the Union Pacific, built into the vast unknown west, was profitable in itself. Only the fraudulent overcapitalization of many companies prevented a fair return on the investment. It was overbuilding, especially in the 1880s and 1890s, and construction of lines without viable economic expectations, only to keep out a competitor, that produced lines never expected to become paying propositions. On the other hand, the more solid railroads, and there were many of them, did make money, and domestic and foreign shareholders did indeed get handsome dividends.

Railroads represented investments of a magnitude previously unknown. Even in the early period of 1828–43, $137 million was invested in infrastructure and rolling stock, and by 1850 total investment in railroads was more than that in turnpikes and canals combined. In the last decade before the Civil War the sum spent on railroads reached a staggering $737 million.[3] Most of this money came from American sources, 25 percent from public funding, the rest from private investors. The average return on capital in railroads has been estimated at around 6 percent, not spectacular but sufficient to attract more capital, especially from Europe, where interest rates tended to be lower. Between 1865 and 1900 an estimated $2.5 billion in American securities were bought by European investors—not all railroad securities, of course, but an overwhelming majority. American railroad securities commanded high prices on European markets and were eagerly sought, but with ups and downs, under the influence of the general business cycles. English capital was abundant, and London had the largest share in this buying spree, followed at a distance by the Netherlands, Germany, and France.

Another important source of investment, apart from the Wall Street market, was the capital invested by the railroads themselves out of their surplus revenues, to improve property and build feeders to generate more traffic. Return on this type of investment may have been modest in strictly financial terms, but it was high from the viewpoint of the company itself. Total investment in railroads—infrastructure and equipment—had been growing at a fast rate after 1865 and reached a high point of more than four billion dollars in the decade 1880–89, and an all-time high of almost five billion between 1900 and 1909.[4]

The technological advances in railroad construction and the actual running of trains—steel rails, heavier locomotives capable of hauling longer trains, automatic airbrakes, and such—meant lower costs per ton-mile. Between 1870 and 1910 average freight rates fell from 2.2 cents per ton-mile to 0.75 cents; passenger rates from 2.8 to 1.9 cents per passenger-mile during the same period, somewhat in excess of the average fall in general price level of about 25 percent.[5] Yet complaints about high rates and discrimination between large and small shippers and different locations were numerous; in reply, the railroads maintained that such discriminatory rates were necessary. They could not easily adjust to changing circumstances, because of their costly infrastructure, which could not be adapted quickly. External circumstances that affected crop prices, such as bad harvests, overproduction, or falling prices on the world markets, were not the railroads' fault, of course. Despite the low rates, well-managed railroads continued to give an average return on invested capital of around 6 percent well into the first decade of the twentieth century. Generally rising prices thereafter and the unwillingness of the Interstate Commerce Commission to allow increases of rates to compensate for higher costs brought the return on capital down to around 4 percent by 1914. Other industries, oil or electrotechnics, were yielding higher averages by then.

The railroads themselves were big business, of course. The complicated machinery of railroad service over vast distances, involving thousands of men in many capacities, called for a new form of organization, wherein the managers, not the actual proprietors, played the crucial role.[6] In this respect the railroads were the forerunners of today's incorporated companies, where the stakeholders have little to say in day-to-day operations.

Railroads were also large users of steel, for rails and bridges and such. But before 1860 only about one-fifth of the total pig-iron output in the country was used by the railroads; the rest went into stoves and nails. More iron was imported from Europe, until prohibitive tariff barriers were erected. After the Civil War, railroad construction was resumed at a fast pace. Domestic steel and iron output was then chiefly taken up by the railroads—between 1867 and 1880 more than 80 percent of all steel production went into rails, and even as late as 1889, 29 percent of all domestic rolled iron and steel was used for railroad rails.

The first American machine shops did not really specialize but just constructed everything for which a demand existed. Here, the railroads did not make their mark as clearly as they did in the case of steel-rolling mills. Building of boilers and engines for steamboats continued to play an important role, and later the construction of machinery for textile mills and other industries always employed more hands than the steam-locomotive and railroad car–building industries. But the railroads did influence the spread of skilled metalworkers through their own maintenance shops, which were situated all over the country. Altoona, Pennsylvania, and Cheyenne, Wyoming, grew chiefly because of the large shops established there by the Pennsylvania and Union Pacific Railroads, respectively. There are many other examples to be found of centers of heavy industry fostered by the railroads.

Railroads were large users of coal, of course, but only after the 1860s or 1870s. Before that time cordwood was the preferred fuel; only the denuding of eastern forests and the falling price of suitable locomotive coal persuaded railroad managers to switch to coal. It is significant that of the two locomotives that touched pilots at Promontory Point on May 10, 1869, the Union Pacific's *Nr. 119* was a coal burner, while Central Pacific's *Jupiter* was a wood burner. On the treeless prairies of Nebraska and the hills of Wyoming, wood was an expensive item, while in the Sierras firewood was abundant. Carrying coal from Iowa mines over long distances was more efficient than carrying cordwood, so Union Pacific's choice was understandable. For railroads in general, coal was for a long time more important as freight and a source of revenue than as fuel. Between 1880 and 1910 railroads consumed only about one-fifth of the total output of coal in America; the rest was used for heating, export, and in the domestic industry.[7]

Contemporaries did not hesitate to name the railroads as the single most influential force in transportation. Without an adequate rail network the transformation of the United States from a predominantly agrarian and preindustrial society into the world's largest and most powerful industrial nation would not have taken place, at least not as quickly as it did, between 1865 and 1916. Recent research of econometrists and economic historians has only partly altered this view, despite the ground-breaking work of one scholar.[8] The general consensus now seems to be that the railroads did indeed play a vital role in the transformation of America, although other factors are now taken into consideration as well. Without railroads the development would have taken place at a slower pace and probably differently in respect of regions and products.

The year 1916, the end of the period covered in this book, was a record year for the railroads in many respects: they carried about 98 percent of all intercity passenger business (a billion passengers) and 77 percent of all intercity freight (366,000,000,000 ton-miles). Revenue from passenger traffic was about a fifth of total earnings of the average railroad. Exceptions to that average, of course, were companies whose locations had made passengers their chief business, such as the Long Island RR of New York. Total railroad mileage in the United States peaked in that year at 254,037, only to decline from then. The number of employees stood at 1,701,000 in 1916, up from 1,018,000 in 1900—5 percent of the total American labor force in that year—largely as the result of the introduction of the eight-hour day in 1916. The future looked bright for the railroad, but there were clouds on the horizon. The financial outlook was not very good, for although revenues had reached an all-time high, the funded debt of all companies had risen to an almost unmanagable sum of just under ten billion dollars. Indeed, many railroads, the Rock Island and the St. Louis & San Francisco among them, were on the verge of bankruptcy or already in the hands of receivers. Even more threatening for the future was the emergence of the automobile. In 1916 three million registered motor vehicles were already on the roads, and by the next year there were two million more. Road transportation would cut deeply into the revenues of the railroads after the end of the war, a process that would go on unabated well into the 1970s.

Notes

1. Figures from George R. Taylor, *The Transportation Revolution 1815–1860* (New York: M.E. Sharpe, 1977), 136–52.
2. Figures from Augustus J. Veenendaal, Jr., *The Saint Paul & Pacific Railroad: An Empire in the Making, 1862–1879* (De Kalb: Northern Illinois University Press, 1999), 20.
3. Figures from Albert Fishlow, "Internal Transportation in the 19th and early 20th Centuries," in Stanley L. Engerman and Robert F. Gallman, eds., *The Long Nineteenth Century,* vol 2 of *The Cambridge Economic History of the United States* (Cambridge: Cambridge University Press, 2000), 543–642.
4. Ibid., 590.
5. Ibid., 596.
6. Alfred D. Chandler, Jr., *The Visible Hand: The Managerial Revolution in American Business* (Cambridge, Mass.: Harvard University Press, 1977).
7. Most figures given here from Fishlow, "Internal Transportation," 607–16.
8. Robert W. Fogel, *Railroads and American Economic Growth* (Baltimore: Johns Hopkins University Press, 1964).

BIOGRAPHIES:
THE PERSONALITIES BEHIND
THE AMERICAN RAILROADS

Matthias William Baldwin (1795–1866)

Matthias W. Baldwin was born in Elizabethtown, New Jersey, where his father was a well-to-do carriagemaker. After the father's death, however, the financial position of the family became so desperate that Matthias had to leave school. At age sixteen Baldwin was apprenticed to a jeweler not far from Philadelphia, and by 1817 he was a journeyman jeweler for a Philadelphia firm. Three years later he set up his own (ultimately successful) jewelry business.

Apparently, despite commercial success, Baldwin was not content. More interested in mechanical devices and machines than jewelry, together with a partner, Peter Mason, he set up a shop in Philadelphia for making bookbinding tools. Machines for calico printing, which revolutionized the cotton-printing industry, soon followed. The workshop was powered by a steam engine, but because of its frequent breakdowns Baldwin decided to build a better one himself and subsequently for outside customers as well. From fixed steam engines it was only a small step to steam locomotives. In 1830 he was asked to build a small steam locomotive for the Philadelphia Museum for demonstration purposes; it drew large crowds as it puffed around a circular track on the museum grounds. Heartened by this useful experience, he then agreed to assemble a full-scale steam locomotive, imported from England, for the Newcastle and Frenchtown RR in 1832. Now thoroughly at home in the new world of steam locomotion, that same year he ventured to construct his first full-scale steam locomotive, called "Old Ironsides," for the Philadelphia, Germantown & Norristown RR. More orders followed soon.

In 1837, having built ten machines, Baldwin moved to larger premises in Philadelphia, but the depression of that year brought him to the verge of bankruptcy. It took him five years to pay off his debts, but he weathered the storm and never looked back. His factory grew into one of the biggest locomotive factories of the world; at the time of his death Baldwin's had constructed some 1,500 steam locomotives, most of them of the well-established and popular 4-2-0, 4-4-0, and 4-6-0 types. Although a number of patents were taken out in his name, it does not appear that Baldwin himself had much to do with them; it is not quite clear how many of new ideas originated with him and how many were contributed by others. Most of the inventions probably came from men in his employ. One of these, Matthew Baird, the works foreman and a mechanical genius, later became partner in the firm. Baldwin's own special contribution (as he claimed) to the locomotive world was the flexible-beam engine, generally of an 0-6-0 or 0-8-0 wheel arrangement. This type, while having its total weight available for adhesion, could traverse fairly tight curves because of a clever arrangement of sliding axles. After his death the works were continued under the name of the Baldwin Locomotive Works, M. Baird & Co., and later with Burnham, Parry, and Williams as partners. Prior to 1901 over 18,000 engines were constructed by Baldwin.

Baldwin was not a great engineer or skilled inventor himself, but by good management, care for detail, and excellent workmanship he became one of the largest builders of steam locomotives of conservative design. As most master mechanics of American railroads of his time wanted nothing unorthodox or untried, his products became popular all over the United States and in some export markets as well. A well-known and respected citizen, Baldwin was active in public affairs in Philadelphia but was particularly involved in founding churches in his hometown. He personally funded the construction of no less than five churches there.

Grenville Mellen Dodge (1831–1916)

Grenville M. Dodge was born into an old and established Massachusetts middle-class family and graduated from Norwich University in 1850 with a degree in engineering. He became interested in the still fairly new technology of railroads and in 1852 obtained an appointment as surveyor with the Illinois Central RR. He served in similar positions with other railroads and farmed for a time near Omaha but returned to railroad work in 1855. During this time he met Abraham Lincoln and discussed with the future president the possibility of a transcontinental railroad.

He joined the Union army at the outbreak of the Civil War and served with distinction as an engineer, rebuilding railroads destroyed by the enemy. In 1863 he was summoned to the White House by President Lincoln to discuss the transcontinental railroad, and he recommended his favorite route, by way of Council Bluffs and up the Platte Valley. When later this route was indeed finally chosen, the president of the Union Pacific RR, Thomas Durant, asked Dodge in 1866 to become chief engineer of the company. Dodge, by then a brigadier general, resigned from the army and took charge of construction of the UP, which was badly managed and in very bad financial shape at the time.

He reorganized operations completely, brought in new contractors, like the Casement brothers, and pushed construction vigorously ahead. Despite lack of supplies, Indian raids, and financial problems that Durant could or would not solve adequately, the UP tracks crept westward. However, relations with Durant soured to such an extent that in 1868 Dodge was on the verge of resigning, but mediation by Gen. Ulysses S. Grant and others was successful, and Dodge remained with the UP. He was instrumental in inducing Collis P. Huntington of the Central Pacific, who was building eastward from California, to agree to fix the meeting point of the two railroads at Promontory Point, Utah.

In 1870 Dodge finally resigned as chief engineer but joined the board of the UP the next year. He was not directly involved in the Crédit Mobilier scandal that rocked the UP, or in other company matters, although he remained on the board. Instead he was active in railroad building in the Southwest with Tom Scott, of the Texas & Pacific RR, and Jay Gould, of the Missouri, Kansas & Texas, and other railroads. Working closely with Gould, Dodge formed a better opinion of the financier than did most of his contemporaries. In 1883 Dodge was brought back into the UP fold and managed to extend the road to the Pacific coast in Oregon and Washington State. He remained active in the company until Edward Harriman took over its management in 1897. After that year Dodge, although officially retired, interested himself in railroads in Cuba and South America until ill health forced him to slow down.

Dodge was a railroad builder, not a financier, and he developed a remarkable skill in locating railroad lines in difficult and unknown terrain, which stood him in good stead during the construction of the Union Pacific. His good relations with Presidents Lincoln and Grant made him a much-sought-after and successful lobbyist in railroad matters.

Jay Gould (1836–1892)

A farmer's son born in a small town in New York State, Jay was a sickly child, not fit for the harsh farm life, but highly intelligent and a quick pupil. As a young man he entered the tanning business; through circumstances largely out of his control he lost a lot of money, but he gained much experience. He then spent some years mastering the intricacies of high finance while serving in minor positions on Wall Street. In 1867 he suddenly gained a place on the board of the Erie Railway, nicknamed "the Scarlet Woman of Wall Street" as a result of the machinations of the notorious Daniel Drew. To keep Cornelius Vanderbilt from taking over the Erie, Drew teamed up with Gould and another shady financier, Jim Fisk. After the smoke of the "Erie War" had cleared, Gould and Fisk were securely in control of a looted Erie, but their reputations had been much damaged. Gould's reputation would suffer even more from his attempt in 1869 to corner the nation's gold supply—the infamous "Gold Ring," which resulted in Black Friday, September 24, which paralyzed the country's financial institutions for days.

After these episodes, Gould returned to Wall Street, where he made significant gains and further strengthened his image as a shrewd speculator. In 1874 he got hold of the Union Pacific RR, then scandal ridden and on the brink of bankruptcy. Distrusted at first by his fellow directors, Gould turned out to be an excellent manager of the property. He straightened out its finances, found new sources of traffic, and generally put the house in order. By constructing or buying branch lines into Idaho and Montana, he greatly enlarged his Union Pacific empire. Then in 1878 Gould was caught in a speculative scheme; to cover his losses he sold off most of his UP stock. He then bought into the Missouri Pacific RR and built up a new empire in the Southwest by adding lines such as the Missouri, Kansas & Texas, the Texas & Pacific, and a few others. At the same time he was also active in the Midwest and East, with the Wabash and the Lackawanna roads as his main properties. By 1880 his railroad empire amounted to some 8,100 miles of track. He also entered the telegraph field and in 1881 ended up with control of Western Union, giving him a practical monopoly of the long-distance telegraph business. Next came the New York Elevated system, which he acquired in 1881; here again a strong smell of fraud and bribery, although never proven, hung around Gould's actions.

By 1884 it became clear that Gould had bitten off more than he could swallow, and he had trouble protecting his interests and investments. He left Wall Street but continued to expand his Missouri Pacific system in the Southwest, although at the expense of some of his holdings, such as the Missouri, Kansas & Texas, which he had to cast off in dilapidated shape. With his health failing, he managed unexpectedly in 1890 to recapture the Union Pacific with the stated intention of upgrading the property and stabilizing rates by reaching agreements with the other transcontinental systems. His death from tuberculosis prevented him from accomplishing this lofty goal.

One of the most controversial of all railroad tycoons and one of the most hated men of his age, Gould is best known as a financial pirate, a shark, working only for his personal interests and leaving a long trail of wrecked railroads and destroyed competitors. Yet by careful management Gould also tried to resurrect properties that he had bought cheaply. By his aggressive policies he forced others to follow him in order to protect their own interests, and in this way he shaped the railroad system of the United States. He preferred to remain in the background and let others steal the glory. His relations with the press were always strained, contributing greatly to his bad reputation. The empire created by him was left to his son George Jay Gould, who, while not able to emulate his father, succeeded in piecing together a truly transcontinental system for a very short time, before the inevitable crash.

Edward Henry Harriman (1848–1909)

The son of an Episcopalian minister in Jersey City, Edward Harriman received an excellent education until 1862, when he entered the commercial world as an office boy. His advance was so rapid that he was able to buy a seat on New York's Stock Exchange in 1870. There he worked chiefly in the commission business, earned a great deal of money, and befriended some of Wall Street's greats. Soon he was himself seen as a great name there. His first experience with railroads came in 1880, when he became director of the ailing Lake Ontario Southern. He reorganized the road and sold it to the Pennsylvania RR at a profit.

Greater things came in 1883, when he was elected to the board of the Illinois Central RR as representative of its Dutch shareholders. Here he learned the practical sides of railroading, the real business of the transportation of freight and passengers, and the construction and maintenance of the physical plant. As director, however, he collided with the grand old man of the IC, Stuyvesant Fish, and he had to be content with a very subordinate role in the company. He more than compensated for this setback with his role in the rebuilding of the Union Pacific RR. This company, bankrupt in 1893 and in the hands of receivers, had to be reorganized, but no one knew how it could be done. Harriman, at first working against, later with, Jacob H. Schiff of the banking house of Kuhn, Loeb & Company, and backed by the credit of James Stillman's National City Bank and the Illinois Central, managed to reorganize the railroad and become its undisputed leader. He then set out to rebuild the physical plant of the road from the ground up. Millions were spent, and the result was a spectacular upswing in traffic and income. Other roads, such as the Kansas City, Pittsburg & Gulf, and the Chicago & Alton, were also reorganized by Harriman, although in the latter case there was a strong suspicion of fraud, probably not justified.

With the Union Pacific on its feet again, Harriman turned his attention to its western connection, the Central Pacific RR, owned by the Southern Pacific and still controlled by its old leader Collis P. Huntington. When Huntington died in 1900 Harriman's UP purchased a controlling interest in the SP. Again he spent millions to upgrade his new acquisition.

Until then, Harriman's career had been one of almost continuous successes. In 1900, however, he experienced a major setback in his attempt to acquire control of the Chicago, Burlington & Quincy RR. Here he clashed directly with James J. Hill of the Great Northern and Northern Pacific, whose bid was found more acceptable by the CB & Q owners. In a countermove Harriman tried to wrest the Northern Pacific from Hill by buying a controlling interest on the stock market. In an epic struggle the Hill-Morgan group narrowly managed to keep a majority of NP stock, although Harriman and his UP made a fortune out of the final settlement with Hill and Morgan.

Under pressure from the antimonopoly movement, which was gaining strength in the early 1900s, the Interstate Commerce Commission in 1906 investigated the Harriman roads and found that competition had been curtailed by the "unofficial" merger of the Union and Southern Pacific companies. As a result the UP had to divest itself of its holdings of SP stock, leaving Harriman an embittered man. What stung Harriman even more was the growing feud with his old friend President Theodore Roosevelt, who now championed attacks on big business for political reasons.

Harriman moved in other circles as well. He became early interested in social work among boys on New York's poor East Side. The Tompkins Square Boys' Club in New York City opened in 1876, largely financed by Harriman personally, who never ceased giving it direction and financial support. It became a huge success. When in 1899 he was advised by his doctors to take a long vacation, he used this forced absence from work to fit out an extensive scientific expedition to Alaska's wilderness. Scientists, artists, and photographers joined him in a prolonged cruise to the North that resulted in the discovery of many new species and the mapping of areas until then largely unknown.

Harriman's name as master railroader was made by his rebuilding of the Union and Central/Southern Pacific Railroads after his takeover, but his complicated financial dealings also earned him a reputation, probably undeserved, of being a shady financier. His masterful character and abrasive personality did not help to make him a popular figure, although he later managed to improve his relationships with his antagonists in the transportation business and with the press.

James Jerome Hill (1838–1916)

Born in a Canadian farming community near Guelph, Ontario, of Scots-Irish stock, young Jim had poor schooling until age fourteen, but with a love of literature and some religiosity were implanted in him by one of his teachers. Untroubled by the loss of vision in one eye as a result of a boyhood accident, Jim Hill in 1856 set out into the world. After some rambling through New York State and along the Atlantic coast, he settled in St. Paul, Minnesota, where he started as a shipping clerk, then moved into the fuel business, and next, with Norman Kittson as partner, into the Red River trade into Canada. In so doing he acquired a thorough knowledge of the transportation business in fast-developing Minnesota.

By this time the first railroad had been opened between St. Paul and Minneapolis, with plans for lines to the west and northwest. This line, backed by Dutch capital, soon drew his attention. He became the forwarding agent of the railroad, and when it defaulted in 1873 he conceived the idea of buying the road and starting his own. Lacking capital, he and two other Canadians, George Stephen and Donald A. Smith, managed to buy the railroad, chiefly on credit, from the Dutch owners. In 1878 he formed the St. Paul, Minneapolis & Manitoba Railroad, which became the nucleus of his vast railroad empire.

Initially, Hill envisaged his line running into Canada as a feeder to the Canadian Pacific, then being built (and in which he consequently interested himself). But when the CP started building a line from Winnipeg eastward, cutting out his Manitoba road, Hill changed course and decided to build westward on his own. In direct competition with the (American) Northern Pacific, he set out to construct his own line all the way to the Pacific, without any kind of public support, and he managed to find a better route than his heavily subsidized competitor. Hill's Manitoba road, renamed the Great Northern Railway in 1890, finally reached the Pacific at Seattle in 1893.

Hill, although without experience in this field, turned out to be a master railroader. He had an eye for detail and paid personal attention to every aspect of his railroad. A hard worker himself, he drove his men hard, becoming feared but at the same time respected by his subordinates. His Great Northern became one of the great North American railroads, an example for others. Not only was its service impeccable but its financial performance made it into one of the cherished blue-chip investments on the stock exchanges of New York, London, and Amsterdam.

To foster the trade of his railroad Hill took a hand in developing the country it traversed. He interested himself in agriculture and stock raising, organized evening classes for farmers, staged traveling exhibitions of new products and improved farm implements, and personally inspected farms and businesses within reach of his railroad. To crown his achievements he managed to seize control of his old competitor, the Northern Pacific. In this operation, which earned him the nickname of "Empire Builder," he was supported by the Morgan banking interests of New York. When, however, Hill and Morgan also tried to acquire the Chicago, Burlington & Quincy, to extend the network he controlled as far as Texas and the Gulf coast, they ran into a conflict of epic proportions with Edward Harriman of the Union Pacific and the Rockefeller group. In the end Hill and Morgan triumphed, but the cost was high, and public opinion turned strongly against them. To control their holdings Hill and Morgan in 1901 formed the Northern Securities Company—which, however, soon brought them into conflict with antitrust laws, vigorously promoted by President Theodore Roosevelt. The company had to be dissolved, although Hill remained in control of both the NP and CB & Q. Despite these late disappointments, Hill's contribution to railroading and to the development of the Northwest was substantial and lasting.

Collis Potter Huntington (1822–1900)

Collis P. Huntington was born to a poor family in a small Connecticut town and received hardly any formal education. At age fourteen he moved to New York and started a career as traveling salesman in watches and cheap jewelry. He did well enough to open, with one of his brothers, his own hardware shop in Oneonta, New York. In 1849 he led a group of emigrants from his hometown to California by way of the Isthmus of Panama, but after arrival in the goldfields he quickly found out that he was not suited for mining. Instead he opened a dry-goods store in Sacramento, which prospered. In 1853 he entered into a partnership with Mark Hopkins in a very successful hardware company, supplying the miners with tools and equipment. At the same time he became active in politics and was one of the founders of the California Republican Party.

Around 1860 the plans for a transcontinental railroad became known, and together with Hopkins, Charles Crocker, and Leland Stanford, he founded the Central Pacific Railroad Company in 1861 to form the western part of the proposed transcontinental. Using a survey for a route made by Theodore D. Judah, the CP slowly crept forward from Sacramento toward the Sierra Nevada. Huntington spent most of his time in Washington, D.C., lobbying Congress and procuring the necessary construction capital. By means legal and quasi-legal he managed to obtain more government aid than strictly warranted by actual mileage of track laid down. On May 10, 1869, the CP construction crews met those of the Union Pacific building west at Promontory Point, Utah.

After reaching this goal, Huntington started to build a railroad empire in the West, by taking over existing lines and constructing new ones. To consolidate these acquisitions Huntington and his partners had in 1865 incorporated the Southern Pacific Railroad Company, which by 1883 had reached New Orleans from the west. With this new railroad, the "Big Four," as the four incorporators became known, completed their stranglehold on California. As Stanford slowly stepped away from the forefront, it was Huntington, much hated and abused, who drew the ire of his opponents.

Meanwhile, Huntington had also been busy on the other side of the continent, where he headed a syndicate that took over the ailing Virginia Central and Covington & Ohio, reorganizing the property as the Chesapeake & Ohio RR. Despite a temporary setback as a result of the 1873 panic, Huntington managed to extend the C & O to Memphis, Tennessee. As an extension of his activities in the C & O he developed the port of Newport News, Virginia, and incorporated a shipyard company there that later became famous as the Newport News Shipyard & Dry Docks Company. The dream of a truly coast-to-coast railroad seemed to come true when Huntington incorporated, again with Crocker and Stanford, a new company that was to continue from Memphis to New Orleans. By the time that line was finished in 1884, however, he had lost control of the C & O again, never to regain it.

Huntington was a tightfisted businessman, hard to deal with and hard to please. He had no use for charities or philanthropy, and after his death his estate ended up in the hands of his second wife, Arabella Duval, and his nephew Henry E. Huntington. Henry Huntington later married his uncle's widow, sold most of his uncle's Southern Pacific holdings, and founded an electric railway and trolley empire in southern California. At his death he left a famous art gallery and library in San Marino, California.

John Bloomfield Jervis (1795–1885)

John Jervis was a farmer's son from near Rome, New York, who at age fifteen left school to tend the family farm and sawmill. In 1817 he was hired by the chief engineer of the Erie Canal, Benjamin Wright, a friend of the family, to help with the first surveys for the canal. He soon learned the trade of a surveyor and did so well that he was quickly promoted to resident engineer; in 1823 he was appointed engineering superintendent of a fifty-mile section of the canal. Here he had not only to use his engineering skills but also learn how to manage a large public work and how to handle contractors, workmen, and politicians.

After the opening of the Erie Canal in 1825 Wright took Jervis with him as assistant to the Delaware and Hudson Canal project. Jervis made the initial surveys for the canal, and when Wright resigned in 1827 Jervis succeeded him as engineer. In that position Jervis not only had to construct the canal itself, which was difficult enough, but also to tackle the stretch from Honesdale, the end of the canal, to the coal mines at Carbondale, sixteen miles away and in a country where it was impossible to dig a canal. Jervis instead designed a railroad, partly on inclines—where the trains were hauled up by fixed steam engines—and partly on a more level course with steam locomotives. As there was at that time practically no experience with railroads in America, Jervis had to develop the new technology almost from scratch, with help only from a few British books. He sent his chief assistant, Horatio Allen, to England to study railway building and to order locomotives. The result of this journey was one of the first steam locomotives in the United States, the "Stourbridge Lion," built by an English firm. The locomotive was a technical success, but it was too heavy for the light strap rail of the railroad and had to be set aside.

In 1830, when the Delaware & Hudson Canal project was finished, Jervis became engineer of the Mohawk & Hudson Railroad, the first line in New York State. Undeterred by the fate of the "Stourbridge Lion," which had been built for this line, he ordered from the West Point Foundry one of the first steam locomotives constructed in the United States. This engine, named "DeWitt Clinton," was a complete success and helped to persuade railroad directors of the advantages of steam locomotion. For a branch of the M & H to Saratoga Springs with many sharp curves, Jervis designed an engine, named "Experiment," with a swiveling truck in front and one driven axle behind, the 4-2-0 type. This type became the most common passenger engine in America for many years; the four-wheel front truck as invented by Jervis became a standard in American locomotive practice and was the first American contribution to the new technology.

After these years of railroad construction Jervis returned to canals again, widening and deepening the Erie Canal, among other jobs. Next came the Croton Dam and Aquaduct to supply drinking water to New York City, a major project, finished in 1846, that established Jervis's fame beyond doubt. In that year he came back into the railroad world as chief engineer of the Hudson River Railroad; he served in the same position from 1850 to 1851 on the Michigan Southern & Northern Indiana and from 1851 to 1858 on the Chicago & Rock Island, where he was more active as manager than engineer; lastly, he was until 1864 general superintendent of the Pittsburgh, Fort Wayne & Chicago, which he turned from a bankrupt line into one of the most prosperous in the country.

John B. Jervis was one of the railroad pioneers of America, whose lasting contribution is the four-wheel swiveling truck and whose unwavering support of the new technology did much to spread the popularity of steam locomotion in America. Apart from his engineering works, he was also successful in other fields, such as banking and land speculation in his home state.

William Henry Osborn (1820–1894)

Born of Massachusetts farmer's stock in Salem, Massachusetts, young Osborn attended school only until he reached thirteen and then went to work for an East India trading house in Boston. At sixteen he was representing his firm in Manila, in the then Spanish Philippine Islands, where he soon set up his successful own import and export firm. He returned to America in 1853 and married the daughter of an influential New York merchant, Jonathan Sturges, who in 1851 had been one of the original incorporators of the Illinois Central Railroad. Through his father-in-law he became involved in the IC and was elected a director in 1854. In the next year he climbed still higher when he was chosen as president of the company.

At that time, the Illinois Central faced significant problems. The 705-mile line was not yet finished, traffic was disappointing, and capital scarce despite a valuable congressional land grant. But under Osborn's expert guidance the road was finished in 1856, and even the nationwide depression of 1857 did not materially affect the health of the company. The Civil War brought an unbelievable upsurge in traffic for the road, as its southern terminus at the confluence of the Ohio and Mississippi Rivers at Cairo, Illinois, became the starting point of Gen. Grant's Tennessee campaign. Dividends climbed steadily to 10 percent in 1865, making the company more popular with foreign and American investors than ever. To foster agriculture on the land along the road and boost sales of company land, Osborn set up a model farm near Chatsworth, where visitors could see the possibilities of the fertile Illinois soil.

In 1865 Osborn stepped down as president but retained his seat on the board, in which capacity he was instrumental in extending the IC southward to the Gulf. After the Civil War Osborn urged his company to offer financial assistance to two struggling southern roads that were trying to make a connection with the IC at Cairo. After completion of this link the depression of 1873 forced the southern roads into bankruptcy, and Osborn in 1877 quickly snapped up both companies. The IC merged them into the Chicago, St. Louis & New Orleans, with Osborn as president and a majority of the board appointed by the parent company. He remained in charge of the southern extension of the Illinois Central until 1882, when he retired to New York and devoted himself to philanthropy.

Although Osborn had begun his railroad career with little or no experience in this field, he turned out to be a fast learner, soon mastering almost every detail of the complicated railroad world. However, he made his greatest mark in field of finance. He knew that some 75 percent of the IC shares were held in England and Holland, and, unlike some of his contemporaries, he was very careful to establish good relations with the representatives of these foreign bond and stock holders. Under his guidance the Illinois Central grew into a prosperous north-south trunkline, popular with shippers and investors alike. He was not an easygoing man, and at times he was difficult for colleagues and subordinates to work with. But it was always clear that he alone was in charge.

William Jackson Palmer (1836–1909)

Born into a Quaker family of Delaware, Palmer had a fairly good education and then entered the engineering business, helping lay out a small railroad in Pennsylvania. In 1855 he sailed for England, where he studied railways and mines for a year. While visiting Wales, he examined the successful narrow-gauge Ffestiniog Railway, which carried slate from the mines to a Welsh port. Back in the United States in 1856, he first worked for a coal mining company and then was hired by John Edgar Thomson of the mighty Pennsylvania Railroad as his private secretary. At the outbreak of the Civil War, he joined the Union army, having overcome his religious scruples as a Quaker. He organized a troop of light cavalry and then a complete regiment of Pennsylvania volunteers, of which he was appointed colonel. He and his men became well known for daring actions, and as a reward he was promoted to brigadier general in 1864, just twenty-eight years old.

After Appomattox Palmer returned to his old love, the railroad, and joined the Union Pacific, Eastern Branch, later called the Kansas Pacific, as treasurer and after 1869 as a director. Under his guidance the line was finished to Denver in 1870. Not content to stop there, he formed a new company, the Denver & Rio Grande Railway, to build a line from Denver southward to El Paso and into Mexico. Finding the necessary capital for his new venture in England and Holland, Palmer began construction southward to the infant town of Colorado Springs, which soon developed into a spa for wealthy patrons. In view of the mountainous terrain the gauge chosen for the railroad was made three feet, instead of the usual four feet, eight and one-half inches, to cut construction costs. The depression of 1873 slowed the progress of the little road, and a competitor, the Atchison, Topeka & Santa Fe, blocked further construction toward El Paso. Palmer then decided to build westward across the Continental Divide to Salt Lake City and Ogden. For legal reasons he had to incorporate a new company, the Denver, Rio Grande & Western, to build into Utah. In 1883 the line between Denver and Ogden, 770 miles long, was opened. At the same time the original DRG developed a dense network of narrow-gauge lines to open up the mineral riches of Colorado. However, internal dissension among several financial groups on the DRG board led to Palmer's resignation as director in 1884.

Meanwhile Palmer had also been active, often with English and Dutch associates, in land companies in Colorado and New Mexico. The coal and iron ore deposits on those lands led to the incorporation of the Colorado Coal & Iron Company in Pueblo. Its blast furnaces and steelworks opened in 1881–82. But Palmer was soon ousted from the board by the same New York interests that had driven him from the DRG. He remained in control of the DRGW until 1901, when he sold out to the Gould interests.

William Palmer, after a notable military career, turned out to be as successful as a railroad engineer and as a promoter. Through his English associates, especially Dr. William A. Bell, he gained access to the European capital markets to fund his Colorado railroads and mining ventures. Without his Denver & Rio Grande Railroad, the development of Colorado and its mineral resources would not have been so meteoric. Although he was bitter at the shabby treatment meted out to him by competing financial interests, Palmer never lost interest in the development of his beloved Colorado Springs.

Charles Elliott Perkins (1840–1907)

Charles Perkins was born in Cincinnati the son of a poor preacher, but he had rich and powerful relatives in Boston. He received a fairly good education and then served as a clerk for a fruit wholesale company in Cincinnati. But this job did not satisfy him long, and through one of his Boston cousins, John Murray Forbes, he got a position as a clerk in the land office of the Burlington & Missouri RR, financed by Forbes and partners. He soon rose to be land agent of that road, and when the Chicago, Burlington & Quincy, also financed by the Forbes group, supported the B & M and extended it into Nebraska and a junction with the Union Pacific, he climbed even higher. He was appointed vice president of the B & M, and when the CB & Q absorbed his road, he became vice president and general manager of the Burlington's western lines. Perkins viewed the internal strife he saw among the members of the Burlington's board about what strategy to adopt as wasteful. He always advocated a strictly east-west road with feeders as the best policy for the Burlington, and Forbes agreed with him. Finally Forbes, supported by Perkins, got the upper hand on the board, and in 1881 Perkins became president of the Burlington.

The junction with the UP had never generated much traffic, because of opposition from the UP, now led by Jay Gould, so Forbes and Perkins decided on a bold stroke, a line of their own all the way to Denver; it opened in 1882. Three years later a line to St. Paul was opened, and with the acquisition of the Hannibal & St. Joseph, the Burlington stretched from Chicago to Denver, with branches to Kansas City and St. Paul—in Perkins's opinion the ideal railroad. The Burlington under his leadership never missed a dividend, and while competitors went down in the depression following the panic of 1893, his road survived unscathed. He toyed with the idea of buying competitors, such as the Northern Pacific, but his directors hesitated to commit themselves. In the end, Perkins closed a deal with James J. Hill of the Great Northern, which had already swallowed the Northern Pacific. In 1901 Hill's Northern Securities Company bought the outstanding stock of the Burlington for $200 per share. Although the three railroads closely cooperated, they continued to operate under their own names.

Perkins was seen as the ideal railroad manager, who cut costs where possible, maximized earnings, and adopted sound business methods.

Devoted to only one railroad all his life, righteous and straightforward, he was the opposite of men like Jay Gould. But he had no use for trade unions other than for social or educational purposes, maintaining that management should never bow to collective bargaining by workers. He never tired of writing letters and treatises on the best way to run a railroad. His ready wit and generosity were valued by everyone who met him in business or private life.

George Mortimer Pullman (1831–1897)

George M. Pullman was born into a family of modest means and was forced to leave school at age fourteen and begin his career as a clerk in a country store. For a time he joined his elder brother in a cabinetmaking business, before setting out on his own in the house-moving business, where he became quite successful. Moving to Chicago in 1857, he contracted to raise several buildings and streets above the level of Lake Michigan, making a substantial profit.

Being a general contractor was not Pullman's ideal, and he looked about for other fields. Together with a partner, Benjamin C. Field, he entered the sleeping-car business and remodelled two cars for the Chicago & Alton RR in 1858. Several other railroads ordered sleeping cars from the new company, but obtaining a fair market share in competition with older, established companies, such as Mann & Woodruff and Wagner, turned out to be difficult. Pullman himself wandered about the country, even engaging in mining and land speculation in Colorado, while Field tended the sleeping-car business, but by 1865 Pullman had decided to concentrate on sleeping cars.

The Pullman Palace Car Company was founded in 1867, with the help of prominent Chicago businessmen, such as Marshall Field, and Pullman set to eliminate the competition. Despite acute business methods it took him until 1899 to acquire the last, the Wagner company. But in these years the name Pullman became a byword for luxury travel on rails, for elegance, comfort, and good service. Pullman established his own car-building facility in Detroit in 1870, but even then he had to turn to outside builders because of the great demand for his products. His company not only built sleeping, dining, and parlor cars but also ran and serviced them on a majority of U.S. railroads. He also branched out to England, Italy, and India, although he never succeeded in breaking into the European mainland, where the Belgian Compagnie Internationale des Wagons Lits et des Grands Express Européens had a practical monopoly.

Flushed by his success, Pullman in 1879 decided to build a new model factory and car shop south of Chicago, complete with housing for the workers, hotels, churches, schools, shops, and parks. He was inordinately proud of the town of Pullman, which was completed in 1881 and housed 12,000 people. But it was not only the town itself that was planned; the lives of its inhabitants were also controlled by Pullman. Discontent was fanned by a decision to lay off workers and cut wages as a result of the 1893 depression. A violent strike broke out in 1894 and soon spread to the railroads around Chicago; police and federal troops had to be called out, and they suppressed the strike with excessive force. It was one of the nastiest large-scale railroad strikes in the country and it left a lasting impression. Pullman never quite understood why "his" men had walked out on him, but neither could he ever adequately explain why he did not lower rents in his town after he cut wages. He died soon after these turmoils, an embittered and broken man.

Pullman was not an engineer or a mechanic, and neither was he the inventor of the sleeping car or of luxury traffic in general, but he was a good businessman who sensed the opportunities and the market potential of his cars and who knew how to hire craftsmen and engineers. He managed to secure a practical monopoly of the sleeping car business on U.S. railroads and founded a great car-building enterprise that continued to florish after his death. After antitrust laws finally ended the Pullman monopoly of the sleeping-car business in 1944, the cars were sold to the participating railroads in 1947; thereafter the Pullman company restricted itself to car building only.

Arthur Edward Stilwell (1859–1928)

Arthur E. Stilwell was born in Rochester, New York, the sickly son of a small businessman who had failed and ended up as a clerk in the city administration. At age fourteen Arthur ran away from home and went to St.Louis, but he returned after having achieved no success there. Back in Rochester he severed all ties with his family and became a salesman for a stationery shop. He next sold advertising space in railroad timetables, in which he did well. Stilwell moved on to Kansas City, and then Chicago, where he held various jobs, the last as agent for an insurance company.

But Stilwell was not happy with his relative success as an insurance salesman, and his ambition drove him on. In 1886 he moved back to Kansas City and entered the burgeoning real estate market. He soon branched out into railroads. Kansas City was served by a number of railroads and with a couple of associates Stilwell in 1889 organized the Kansas City Suburban Belt Railroad to connect some of them; next came the Kansas City & Independence Air Line and the Union Terminal Railroad. Meanwhile, Stilwell had larger dreams. The idea of a line from Kansas City to the Gulf of Mexico was not his, as he would later claim, but he made it come true. His Kansas City, Pittsburg & Gulf was incorporated in 1892; slowly the line crept south, by buying up existing roads and by new construction. Until this point Stilwell financed his enterprises locally and with help from Philadelphia bankers, as he wanted to avoid the world of "Haute Finance" of Wall Street—the "Cannibals of Finance" as he used to call them. But in 1893, in the midst of a severe worldwide depression, he needed a great deal of new capital for his KCPG. He had met a rich Dutch coffee merchant, Jan de Goeijen, on a voyage to Europe, and together Stilwell and De Goeijen raised millions in Holland for the extension of the line. In 1897 the road reached the Gulf at a new harbor, Port Arthur, Texas. Traffic boomed, but the road was badly constructed and lacked an adequate supply of rolling stock, for which no capital was available. The Dutch investors hesitated to invest more, and in 1899 the KCPG entered receivership. Stilwell was ousted, and the company was reorganized as the Kansas City Southern, still with a large Dutch interest.

Undaunted by the loss of his brainchild, Stilwell formed plans for an even more grandiose railroad empire, a 1,600-mile line from Kansas City to the Mexican port of Topolobampo, connecting with shipping lines to China and Japan. In 1900 he incorporated the Kansas City, Mexico & Orient Railroad for this purpose, and construction started soon after. Capital came chiefly from England, but never enough to finish the line. Civil war in Mexico halted construction there completely, and World War I dried up the trickle of money from England. In 1912 the KCM & O entered receivership, followed by a second receivership in 1917; the American parts of the line were sold in 1928. By then the "promoter with a hunch," as he had called himself, was dead.

Stilwell, an active Christian Scientist, always maintained that he acted on hunches, or dreams, in which his future was visible. He was no railroad manager and no financier but an expert promoter and salesman of stocks and bonds who managed to find millions for his railroad schemes while avoiding the established channels of Wall Street. His enthusiasm and optimism was contagious, and he had little difficulty in raising capital in Holland and elsewhere, although in the end he had to surrender to those same cannibals, losing his railroad empires. The way of financing his companies by a system of collateral trust bonds, wherein bonds of one company secure the bonds of another, and so on, was not his invention, but he used it to advantage. His brainchild the Kansas City Southern eventually developed into a healthy trunkline, and Port Arthur, although largely through the unforeseen discovery of a major oilfield, later became a major port for petroleum and chemicals.

John Edgar Thomson (1808–1874)

Born not far from Philadelphia in a Quaker family, young Edgar Thomson had little formal schooling and learned most of his engineering skills from his father, who was an engineer in his own right. In 1827 young Thomson got his first job helping in the survey of a railroad or canal between Philadelphia and Columbia. Because of his superior skills he soon advanced through the ranks as engineer of several early railroads in Pennsylvania. He spent time in Britain to observe railway building. In 1834, after his return he was appointed chief engineer of the newly incorporated Georgia Railroad. By 1845 he had finished the line from Augusta to the nascent town of Marthasville, soon renamed Atlanta at his prompting. In Georgia he learned the importance of being on friendly terms with the directors of the company and the politicians in power, skills he needed desperately in his later career.

In 1847 he was recalled to Pennsylvania to become chief engineer of the new Pennsylvania Railroad Company, which strove to cross the Alleghenies, a stupendous undertaking for the time. He mastered all problems with superior technology and finished the 355-mile Harrisburg-Pittsburgh line in 1855. However, clashes, chiefly about finance, with the board of the company became ever more violent; Thomson was supported by a majority of the stockholders, who favored him over the cautious directors. These disputes led in 1851 to the ouster of most directors and the election of Thomson to the presidency of the PRR. He still supervised the construction of the railroad, designing the famed Horseshoe Curve near Altoona, one of his most famous works.

But as president he had other responsibilities as well, foremost of which was the provision of sufficient capital to finance construction. He traveled to Europe several times in the 1850s and 1860s to promote the sale of bonds on the London market. He had little success, however, through no fault of his; the European money markets were depressed for reasons that had little to do with the Pennsylvania Railroad itself. Another matter that commanded his full attention was the westward extension of the PRR. Competing roads, such as the Baltimore & Ohio, the Erie, and the New York Central, were vigorously pushing lines or buying up and leasing existing roads to reach Chicago and St. Louis. In a direct conflict with Erie's Jay Gould Thomson managed to lease the Pittsburgh, Fort Wayne & Chicago and some other roads in 1869, thus providing his PRR with the necessary connections to the West. At the other end of his Pennsylvania Railroad, he also obtained access to New York City over leased or purchased lines on the New Jersey shore. By 1874 the mileage of his company stood at almost 1,600, for the time a sizeable railroad empire.

By now the company covered such vast distances that management encountered problems in overseeing the whole. Inspired by Daniel McCallum's reorganization of the Erie, Thomson introduced the divisional structure on the PRR to create the first line-and-staff managerial oganization in American corporate history. The general crisis of 1873 hit the Pennsylvania hard, partly through unwise overinvestment of some of its directors in several western railroads, and Thomson had to use his own private capital to bolster the road's finances. Weakened by pulmonary problems and heart trouble, Thomson died amid general mourning and was buried in Philadelphia. His lasting work was the Pennsylvania Railroad, one of the truly great American railroad systems, the "standard" railroad of the country.

Cornelius Vanderbilt (1794–1877)

Cornelius Vanderbilt was born on Staten Island, opposite Manhattan, in an old-established Dutch family of farmers. As a young man Cornelius, already fed up with life on the farm, set up a ferry service to New York with a small boat of his own. The War of 1812 with Great Britain brought more traffic, and Vanderbilt exploited this opportunity to the utmost, even acquiring government contracts for the conveyance of men and materiel to the forts around New York Harbor. He expanded his services, switched over to steamboats when these became practical, and evaded the monopoly of steam navigation on New York State waters held by the Fulton-Livingston combine. Vanderbilt branched out into the Hudson River traffic, and when bought out there by the competition he opened shipping lines on Long Island Sound. Shrewd management, superior service, and low fares ensured his success. As a result of his widespread activities he became known as "Commodore" Vanderbilt.

The California gold rush of 1848 offered new opportunities to Vanderbilt, who opened a transportation line to San Francisco by way of Nicaragua, again with great success. He also tried his hand at a transatlantic line, but here he found that it was hard to compete with the established lines, which were subsidized with lucrative mail contracts.

By 1865, when he was already seventy-one, the commodore decided to step into the railroad business on a grand scale. He had already invested in the New York & Harlem Railroad, which he reorganized, and in 1865 he became president of the Hudson River Railroad, running from New York City to Albany. West of Albany a combination of several smaller lines had been forged into the New York Central, under the guidance of Erastus Corning. But the New York Central relied on the Hudson River RR and the Hudson River shipping line for its connections, and both were under control of the commodore. The almost inevitable result was that Vanderbilt was made president of the NYC, and in 1869 he combined his lines into the New York Central & Hudson River Railroad, the first railroad merger on a large scale. To give the new road better visibility in New York, he had the magnificent Grand Central Station built; it opened in 1871. Thus far almost everything that Vanderbilt had touched had been successful, but he was to be defeated in a struggle for the New York & Erie RR by Jay Gould, Jim Fisk, and Daniel Drew, who used every means, legal or illegal, to win the "Erie War." To leave behind this nasty episode, Vanderbilt set about to extend his railroad westward to Chicago, buying up such smaller lines as the Buffalo & Erie, the Lake Shore, and the Michigan Southern & Northern Indiana, which were all combined under the name of Lake Shore & Michigan Southern, with Vanderbilt as its president. Other lines followed, making the NYC & HR one of the powers in the land.

Despite his age Commodore Vanderbilt remained active until the end, but he left much of the actual work to his son William Henry Vanderbilt (1821–85), who had been involved in his father's railroads since 1864.

William assumed responsibility for most of the mergers and acquisitions, always subject to his father's approval. Thanks to the son's practical leadership the 1877 strikes, which crippled neigboring roads, left the NYC & HR undamaged. Vanderbilt, Jr., paid his men well and truly cared about their well-being.

The elder Vanderbilt was an astute businessman with an almost golden touch. A hard worker himself, he expected the same from his subordinates, but never unreasonably. His success was based on providing service superior to that of the competition, higher speed, and lower fares. The expression "the public be damned," attributed to him, is probably apocryphal, as he knew very well that the opinion of passengers and shippers mattered. But only under the guidance of his son William did the public image of the NYC & HR improve materially. Commodore Vanderbilt had always been a tight-fisted man, but his second wife induced him to give money to charities, churches, and a school that was later named after him, Vanderbilt University in Nashville, Tennessee. But even so at his death his estate was valued at over $100 million, mostly left to William, who managed to double it in a few years after his father's death.

George Westinghouse (1846–1914)

George Westinghouse was the eighth of ten children of a small mechanic and maker of farm implements in a minor New York State town. Without much schooling, he enlisted in the Union army; after the conflict he went back to his father's shop, by now in Schenectady, and started his lifelong work perfecting machinery. His first product was a stationary steam engine, but next came more marketable inventions: a device to rerail railroad cars, and a cast-steel "frog" for railroad switches. In 1868 he moved to Pittsburgh and continued his successful business.

Railroad brakes of the day were primitive; the braking power of trains largely depended on brakemen on top of the cars, who applied the brakes upon whistle signals of the engineer on the locomotive. Passenger trains were getting heavier and faster, and a better and more dependable brake was needed. Many inventors in England and America had tried to design systems that could be operated from the locomotive, using steam, chains, or air as a medium, but without lasting success. It is unclear what Westinghouse knew about the work of his predecessors, but he was certainly not the inventor of the air brake. Nonetheless, he patented in 1869 an air brake that, if primitive, was workable. Not everybody believed his claims for it; Commodore Vanderbilt of the New York Central is reported to have said to him, "Young man, do you want to tell me that you can stop trains with wind?" Fortunately for Westinghouse, the mighty Pennsylvania Railroad was willing to try out his brake; it was a success, and by 1870 eight railroads were installing air brakes on their passenger trains.

However, there was one great problem to be solved. When a hose parted or when a train broke in two, the brake, which depended on air pressure from the locomotive, became inoperative. Westinghouse accordingly reversed the working of his system—the brakes would no longer actuated by air pressure but by a *reduction* of pressure. Every car was equipped with an air reservoir, pressurized by the locomotive, and a triple valve, an ingenious pressure-sensitive device. The engineer on the locomotive actuated the brakes of the train by reducing the air pressure in the main air line. Whenever a train broke in two or the air line parted, causing loss of pressure, the brakes would set automatically, thus creating a fail-safe system. This was the final breakthrough of the Westinghouse automatic air brake in the railroad world. A factory was opened in London to supply brake systems to European railways; after 1881 the factory was under the direction of Albert Kapteyn, a Dutch engineer, who contributed materially to the success of the Westinghouse brake in Europe and improved the essential part of the system, the triple valve, to make it fool-proof in the harsh railroad environment. Other factories followed, and the Westinghouse brake became a household word all over the world. The original Pittsburgh plant became too small, and a new large factory was opened in Wilmerding, east of Pittsburgh, with a model town built around it.

From air brakes it was only a small step to railway signaling and power interlocking and switching systems, and from there to electric power. Westinghouse bought the American rights to the high-speed turbine as invented by Charles Parsons and used it to power large generating stations. He advocated the use of high-tension alternating current (AC) as opposed to Thomas A. Edison's low-voltage direct current (DC); his Westinghouse Electric Company of 1886 slowly overcame the opposition of the Edison interests until AC became the common approach to generating and transporting electric power for industrial and domestic purposes.

Westinghouse was the archetype of an inventor—he had 361 American patents to his name—but also a sound businessman who could see opportunities for entering new markets for his inventions. His relations with labor differed greatly from those of his contemporaries. He paid good wages, introduced paid vacations, and generally was interested in the welfare of his employees. No ugly labor trouble like the Pullman strike marred his record. He was greatly disturbed by the loss of his factories in the 1907 financial panic and the ensuing reorganizations, although personally he remained financially comfortable.

Primary Documents Related to the American Railroads

Document 1
The First Locomotive Headlight, 1832

Early railroads operated only during daylight hours, but soon it was found necessary to run trains at night as well. Horatio Allen, engineer of the South Carolina Railroad, fashioned the first primitive headlight for use on that road. Gradually all American locomotives were equipped with headlights, burning rape oil, coal oil, or kerosene; they were later adapted to electricity.

That the locomotive was to be used in the night, and during the whole night, was plainly to be anticipated. It was thought well to make trial of such running by night, that it might be known what it was necessary to provide. For such trial two platform cars were placed in front of the locomotive. On the forward platform was placed an inclosure of sand, and on the sand a structure of iron rods somewhat of an urn shape. In this structure was to be kept up a fire of pine-wood knots. Suitable signals as to the rate of speed, etc., were provided. The day preceding the evening of the trial closed in with as heavy a fog as I have ever seen, and I have seen a first-class London fog. But the fog did not prevent the trial when the appointed time came.

The country to be run through was a dead level, and on the surface rested this heavy fog; but just before we were ready to start, the fog began to lift and continued to rise slowly and as uniformly as ever curtain left surface of stage, until about eighteen feet high; there it remained stationary, with an under surface as uniform as the surface it had risen from. This under surface was lit up with radiating lines in all directions with prismatic colors, presenting a scene of remarkable brilliancy and beauty.

Under this canopy, lit on its under surface, the locomotive moved onward with a clearly illuminated road before it; the run was continued for some five miles, with no untoward occurrence, and I had reason to exclaim, "The very atmosphere of Carolina says, 'Welcome to the locomotive.'"

Source: Horatio Allen, *The Railroad Era, First Five Years of Its Development* (New York, 1884), 28–29.

Document 2
Description of the Pontchartrain Railroad, 1839

Railroads sprang up in America in the 1830s in the most improbable places—not only in New England, New York, or Pennsylvania but also in Louisiana, only recently acquired by the United States. As a matter of fact, the Pontchartrain Railroad in New Orleans is one of the oldest of the country. We owe a description of this very early but out of the way railroad to an Austrian engineer, Franz Anton, Ritter (knight) von Gerstner, who had built the pioneer Budweis-Linz railway in the Austrian empire and the first railway in Russia. Together with his young bride, Von Gerstner toured America between late 1838 and July 1839 at the request of the czarist Russian government. In his report, titled *Die innern Communicationen*, published in two volumes in German in 1842–43, Von Gerstner described meticulously all canals, roads, and railroads in the young country, published operating figures, technical details, and drawings of bridges, depot buildings, and such. It was the first comprehensive description of American railroads by an expert and as such is invaluable, as his observations are shrewd and very much to the point.

Before construction was begun on the canal from New Orleans to Lake Pontchartrain, a project was conceived to lay a railroad along that same route. This was primarily to serve passengers arriving via steamboat from Mobile, allowing them to be transported from the lakeside to New Orleans and in the opposite direction as well. The original idea for this came from lawyer M.W. Hoffmann, who sought in a brochure made public in 1829 to demonstrate the advantages of this railroad as well as the feasibility of building it. At that time, almost no one believed that it was possible to build a railroad through the swamp lying between New Orleans and the lake. This place had always been thought to be impassable. Work began in March 1830 to hack through the cypress forests. But even when, in spite of all objections and hindrances, this cutting work was completed in April 1831, many still feared that the first locomotive would sink with its train into the swampy depths.

Construction of the road. The Pontchartrain Railroad is only 4½ miles long, and it measures 5 miles from the end of the lake wharf to the Mississippi River. It goes from the lake to the city of New Orleans in a completely straight line. Within the city it has been extended along Canal Street to the Mississippi. To that end, the company purchased for $25,000 the old Market Canal, which had run along that street, and filled it in. The aggregate drop in elevation of this railroad from the lake to the bank of the Mississippi is only 16 inches. As it was first built, the line was single track. After the trees were cut down along the right of way, and their stumps and roots removed, a ditch was dug on both sides of it. The dirt was piled up on an embankment to a height of 2 or 3 feet. Although this in time settled by 1 to 2 feet, it nonetheless formed a sufficiently compact base for the track. Onto the earthen embankment were placed longitudinal ground timbers, crossties, and then more longitudinal timbers, onto which rolled rails were secured by spikes driven in through openings in the base, spaced every 3 feet throughout. . . . Their weight per yard was 24 lbs.

In 1838, a second track was laid in the following way. Cypress logs having a length of 15 to 20 feet and a diameter of 10 inches were driven in two rows 5 feet apart and then sawed off 2 feet above ground level. Onto these logs, 9-foot-long, 8-by-10-inch crossties were laid and joined. Recesses were cut into them, and they admitted 20- to 25-foot-long, 8-inch-square longitudinal stringers. The rails for the new track weigh 56 lbs. per yard. . . . The ramming in of the logs was done using Captain Smith Cram's steam pile driver, which is mentioned in the description of the Syracuse & Utica Railroad. The space between the timbers was filled in with mud that had been excavated by steam dredges used to make the harbor deeper.

Buildings, etc. Rolling stock. At the station in New Orleans, a large roofed structure is found. At the other end of the line, in addition to sheds, numerous storehouses exist, plus 2 hotels and 4 bath houses. In addition, a harbor was created at an expense of $230,000, so that steamboats and other ships could have a calm, secure landing place by the railroad.

This road's rolling stock, in 1839, consisted of 4 locomotives brought from England; one of these weighs 7½ tons, the others only 5½. Also, there are 28 4-wheeled passenger coaches and 48 freight cars. In 1836, the company offered a prize of $5,000 for the best spark catcher and spent between $3,000 and $4,000 on tests of the many designs that were submitted. The device developed by a Mr. Turner was adopted. Installed in the smoke chamber beneath the stack, it forces the smoke through spaces in which the air is rarified, and the small glowing coals are precipitated. This device appears to suit its purpose exactly, for hay and cotton are now hauled in completely open cars, and under the blazing sun at 30 degrees north latitude, without having to fear that the materials transported will ignite. A disadvantage of this invention is that it requires a smoke chamber almost twice as high as is usually present in such machines. This makes it necessary that they undergo a significant and expensive alteration, if attention is not given to the need to attach the device when the locomotive is being built.

Construction costs. Up to December 1, 1838, the company's expenditures were as follows: for the original single track, the rolling stock, station buildings, and the harbor, $491,448; for building sites, 2 hotels, and bathing facilities, $42,000; for 22 Negro slaves, $23,581; for the second track, $87,573; and for a steam dredge to deepen the harbor, $8,436. The total was $653,038..

The actual railroad in its double track configuration, plus everything pertaining to it but excluding the $230,000 for the harbor, cost $349,021. But when the second track is fully complete, the costs will have reached $360,000, or an average of $72,000 per mile. Some $500,000 was paid in on 2,500 shares by the stockholders, but only $115 per share in ready cash. The remaining $85 was withheld from dividends.

As great as the costs of this road relative to its length may have appeared to be, it nonetheless is among the most lucrative public enterprises in the United States. During the seven years since the line was opened—that is, until May 1838—some $338,444 was distributed in dividends, or $19.33 per share every year.

Operation of the road. Passengers pay 37½ cents to ride. For each ton of freight, $1 is charged: 75 cents for transport and 25 cents for on- and off-loading. Traffic on this railroad is significant. In the summer, trains depart every hour from each end, beginning at 4:30 A.M. and continuing until 9:30 P.M. In the winter the same frequency of service is maintained between 6:30 A.M. and 7:30 P.M. On Sundays, extra trips are also made.

In the evenings, trips are made once or twice using horses. The 4½ mile stretch is covered by locomotives with passenger trains in 15 minutes, and by horses in 30 to 40 minutes. . . .

The number of passengers includes 3,000 to 4,000 persons who ride free each year because they are stockholders or lessees, and also an average of 12,000 children who pay only half fare. . . .

Source: Frederick C. Gamst, ed., *Early American Railroads. Franz Anton Ritter von Gerstner's Die innern Communicationen (1842–1843)*, trans. David J. Diephouse and John C. Decker (Stanford, Calif.: Stanford University Press, 1997), 747–50. Copyright © 1997 by the Board of Trustees of the Leland Stanford Jr. University, by permission of the publishers.

Document 3
An Englishman Travels by Train, 1842

The English novelist Charles Dickens (1812–70), already famous in America, in 1842 visited the United States and Canada, where he was enthusiastically received. He traveled extensively by stagecoach, steamboat, and railroad and left vivid descriptions of his adventures in his *American Notes for General Circulation*, first published in 1842. His first impressions were generally favorable, but later he became disillusioned with some aspects of life in America and did not hesitate to write negatively about those he disliked, which impaired his popularity somewhat.

Before leaving Boston, I devoted one day to an excursion to Lowell. I assign a separate chapter to this visit; not because I am about to describe it at any great length, but because I remember it as a thing by itself, and am desirous that my readers should do the same. I made acquaintance with an American railroad on this occasion, for the first time. As these works are pretty much alike all through the States, their general characteristics are easily described.

There are no first and second class carriages as with us; but there is a gentlemen's car and a ladies' car: the main distinction between which is, that in the first everybody smokes; and in the second, nobody does. As a black man never travels with a white one, there is also a negro car; which is a great, blundering, clumsy chest, such as Gulliver put to sea in from the kingdom of Brobdingnag. There is great deal of jolting, a great deal of noise, a great deal of wall, not much window, a locomotive engine, a shriek, and a bell.

The cars are like shabby omnibuses, but larger: holding thirty, forty, fifty people. The seats, instead of stretching from end to end, are placed crosswise. Each seat holds two persons. There is a long row of them on each side of the caravan, a narrow passage up the middle, and a door at both ends. In the centre of the carriage there is usually a stove, fed with charcoal or anthracite coal; which is for the most part red-hot. It is unsufferably close; and you see the hot air fluttering between yourself and any other object you may happen to look at, like the ghost of smoke.

In the ladies' car there are many gentlemen who have ladies with them. There are also a great many ladies who have nobody with them: for any lady may travel alone, from one end of the United States to the other, and be certain of the most courteous and considerate treatment everywhere. The conductor, or check-taker or guard, or whatever he may be, wears no uniform. He walks up and down the car, and in and out of it, as his fancy dictates; leans against the door with his hands in his pockets, and stares at you, if you chance to be a stranger; or enters into conversation with the passengers about him. A great many newspapers are pulled out, and a few of them are read. Everybody talks to you, or to anybody else who hits his fancy. . . .

Except when a branch road joins the main one, there is seldom more than one track of rails; so that the road is very narrow, and the view, where there is a deep cutting, by no means extensive. When there is not, the character of the scenery is always the same. . . .

The train calls at stations in the woods, where the wild impossibility of anybody having the smallest reason to get out is only equalled by the apparently desperate hopelessness of there being anybody to get in. It rushes across the turnpike road, where there is no gate, no policeman, no signal: nothing but a rough wooden arch, on which is painted "When the bell rings, look out for the locomotive." On it whirls headlong, dives through the woods again, emerges in the light, clatters over frail arches, rumbles upon the heavy ground, shoots beneath a wooden bridge which intercepts the light for a second like a wink, suddenly awakens all the slumbering echoes in the main street of a large town, and dashes on haphazard, pell-mell, neck or nothing, down the middle of the road. There—with mechanics working at their trades, and people leaning from their doors and windows, and boys flying kites and playing marbles, and men smoking, and women talking, and children crawling, and pigs burrowing, and unaccustomed horses plunging and rearing, close to the very rails—there—on, on, on tears the mad dragon of an engine with its train of cars; scattering in all directions a shower of burning sparks from its wood fire; screeching, hissing, yelling, panting, until at last the thirsty monster stops beneath a covered way to drink, the people cluster round, and you have time to breathe again. . . .

I returned at night by the same railroad, and in the same kind of car. . . . But glancing all the way out of the window from the corners of my eyes, I found abundance of entertainment for the rest of the ride in watching the effects of the wood fire, which had been invisble in the morning, but were now brought out in full relief by the darkness: for we were travelling in a whirlwind of bright sparks, which showered around us like a storm of fiery snow.

Source: Charles Dickens, *American Notes for General Circulation* (first published London, 1842; repr. London: Chapman and Hall, 1895), 29–33.

Document 4
Asa Whitney's Proposal for a Transcontinental Railroad, 1845

Whitney (1797-1872), a New York merchant who had lost his fortune in the depression of 1837, started a new career as agent of several American mercantile houses in China, where he amassed a new fortune. On his return from China he first aired his bold plan for a transcontinental railroad and continued for some years to lobby for his grand scheme. His press campaigns had no direct results but helped prepare the way for the Pacific Railroad Act of 1862. Many elements of Whitney's original proposal to Congress would appear in that act. From his proposal it becomes clear that he not only thought of the economic advantages of a transcontinental railroad but that he was also aware of the political and military implications of his scheme.

Memorial of Asa Whitney, of New York City, relative to the construction of a railroad from lake Michigan to the Pacific Ocean, January 28, 1845.

Your memorialist begs respectfully to represent to your honorable body [House of Representatives], that by rivers, railroads, and canals, all the States east and north of the Potomac connect directly with the waters of the great lakes. That there is a chain of railroads in projection and being built from New York to the southern shores of lake Michigan, crossing all the veins of communication to the ocean, through all the States south and east of the Ohio river, producing commercial, political, and national results and benefits which must be seen and felt through all our vast confederacy.

Your memorialist would further represent to your honorable body, that he has devoted much time and attention to the subject of a railroad from lake Michigan, through the Rocky mountains, to the Pacific ocean; and that he finds such a route practicable—the results from which would be incalculable, far beyond the imagination of man to estimate. To the interior of our vast and widely spread country, it would be as the heart to the human body; it would, when all completed, cross all the mighty rivers and streams which wend their way to the ocean through our vast and rich valleys from Oregon to Maine, a distance of more than three thousand miles.

The incalculable importance of such a chain of roads will readily be seen and appreciated by your honorable body. It would enable us, in the short space of eight days, and perhaps less, to concentrate all the forces of our vast country at any point from Maine to Oregon, in the interior, or on the coast. Such easy and rapid communication, with such facilities for exchanging the different products of the different parts, would bring all our immensely wide-spread population together as one vast city; the moral and social effects of which must harmonize all together as one familiy, with but one interest—the general good of all.

Your memorialist respectfully represents further to your honorable body, that the roads from New York to lake Michigan (a distance of 840 miles) will no doubt be completed by the States through which they pass, or by individuals; that from lake Michigan to the mouth of the Columbia river is 2,160 miles, making from New York to the Pacific 3,000 miles, and can be performed in eight days; from the Columbia river to the Sandwich islands is 2,100 miles, making from New York to the Sandwich islands 5,100 miles; from the Columbia river to Japan is 5,600 miles, making from New York to Japan 8,600 miles; from Columbia river to Amoy, in China, (the port nearest to the tea and silk provinces) is 6,200 miles, making from New York to Amoy only 9,200 miles; which, with a railroad to the Pacific, thence to China by steam, can be performed in 30 days; now being a sailing distance of nearly 17,000 miles, requiring from 100 to 150 days for its performance. Then the drills and sheetings of Connecticut, Rhode Island, and Massachusetts, can be transported to China in 30 days; and the teas and rich silks of China, in exchange, come back to New Orleans, to Charleston, to Washington, to Baltimore, to Philadelphia, to New York, and to Boston, in 30 days more. Comment is unnecessary. Your honorable body will readily see the revolution by this to be wrought in the entire commerce of the world; and that this must inevitably be its channel, when the rich freights from the waters of the Mississippi and the Hudson will fill to overflowing with the products of all the earth the storehouses of New York and New Orleans, the great marts dividing the commerce of the world; while each State, and every town in our vast confederacy, would receive its just proportion of influence and benefits, compared with its vicinity to, or facility to communicate with, any of the rivers, canals, or railroads crossed by this great road.

Your memorialist would respectfully represent to your honorable body its political importance; that, affording a communication from Washington to the Columbia river in less than eight days, a naval depot, with a comparatively small navy, would command the Pacific, the South Atlantic, and Indian oceans, and the China seas.

Your memorialist begs respectfully further to your honorable body, that he can see no way or means by which this great and important work can be accomplished for ages to come, except by a grant of a sufficient quantity of the public domain; and your memorialist believes, that, from the proceeds of such a grant, he will be enabled to complete said road in a reasonable time, and at the same time settle the country through which it passes, so far as the lands may be found suited to cultivation, with an industrious and frugal people; and thus, in a comparatively short space of time, accomplish what will otherwise require ages, and thus at once giving us the power of dictation to those who will not long remain satisfied without an attempt to dictate to us. Our system of free government works so well, diffusing so much intelligence, dispensing equal justice, and securing safety to all, and producing so much general comfort and prosperity, that its influence must, like a mighty flood, sweep away all other systems. Then let us not flatter ourselves that this overwhelming current is not to meet resistance; for to us directly will that resistance be applied, and your memorialist believes that we must yet meet that desperate and final struggle which shall perpetuate our system, and religious and civil liberty.

Your honorable body are aware of the over-population of Europe; and your memorialist would respectfully represent, that by the application of machinery, and its substitution for manual labor, the latter no longer receives its just or sufficient reward, and thousands in the fear of starvation at home are driven to our shores, hoping from our wide-spread and fertile soil to find a rich reward for their labor. Most of them ignorant, and all inexperienced, having been herded together in large numbers at home, they dread separation—they fear the wilderness or prairie—refuse to separate from their associates, or to leave the city; their small means soon exhausted, they see abundance around them, almost without price, but that small price they can no longer pay; necessity plunges them into vice, and often crime, and they become burdensome to our citizens, and which evil is increasing to an alarming extent; and your memorialist believes it must increase, unless there can be some great and important point in our interior to which they can be attracted immediately on their landing; where their little means, with their labor, can purchase lands; where they will escape the tempting vices of our cities, and where they will have a home with their associates, and where their labor from their own soil will not only produce their daily bread, but, in time, an affluence of which they could never have dreamed in their native land…

Your memorialist would further respectfully represent to your honorable body, that from an estimate (as near accurate as can be made, short of an actual survey) the cost of said road, to be built in a safe, good, and substantial manner, will be about $50,000,000; and as the road cannot (from the situation of the uninhabited country through which it will pass) earn anything, or but little, before its completion, therefore a further sum will be required to keep it in operation, repair &c., of $15,000,000; making the total estimated cost of said road, when completed, $65,000,000. It may require some years before the earnings of said road (at the low rate of tolls necessary for its complete success) can be much, if anything, beyond its current expenses for repairs, &c.; but after a period of—years, and at the very lowest possible rate of tolls, it must earn more than ample for its repairs and expenses. . . .

Your memorialist respectfully further represents to your honorable body, that, from the knowledge he can procure of them, he finds that the lands for a long distance east of the mountains are bad—of little or no value for culture; that through, and for some distance beyond the mountains, would also be of but very little, if any, value; therefore your memorialist is satisfied that it will require an entire tract of 60 miles in width, from as near to lake Michigan as the unappropriated lands commence, to the Pacific ocean. Therefore, in view of all the important considerations here set forth, your memorialist is induced to pray that your honorable body will grant to himself, his heirs, and assigns, such tract of land, the proceeds of which to be strictly and faithfully applied to the building and completing the said road—always with such checks and guarantees to your honorable body as shall secure a faithful performance of all the obligations and duties of your memorialist; and that after the faithful completion of this great work, should any lands remain unsold, or any moneys due for lands, or any balance of moneys received for lands sold, and which have not been required for the building of the said road, then all and every of them shall belong to your memorialist, his heirs, and assigns, forever.

Your memorialist further prays that your honorable body will order a survey of said route, to commence at some point to be fixed upon as most desirable on the shore of lake Michigan, between the 42d and 45th degree of north latitude; thence west to the gap or pass in the mountains; and thence by the most practicable route to the Pacific ocean.

Your memorialist would respectfully represent one further consideration to your honorable body: that, in his opinion, Oregon must fast fill up with an industrious, enterprising people from our States; that they will soon attract and draw to them large numbers from the states of Europe, all expecting to share in the benefits of our free government, claiming its care and protection. But the difficulty of access to them, either by land or water, will forbid such a hope; and your memorialist believes that the time is not far distant when Oregon will become a State of such magnitude and importance, as to compel the establishment of a separate government—a separate nation—which will have cities, ports, and harbors, all free— inviting all the nations of the earth to a free trade with them; when they will control and monopolize the valuable fisheries of the Pacific; control the coast trade of Mexico and South America, of the Sandwich islands, Japan, and China; and be our most dangerous and successful rival in the commerce of the world. But your memorialist believes that this road will unite them to us; enabling them to receive the protecting care of our government; sharing in its blessings, benefits, and prosperity, and imparting to us our share of the great benefits from their local position, enterprise, and industry. But your honorable body will see this, and more. . . .

Asa Whitney.

Source: Congressional Papers, 28th Congress, 2nd session, House of Representatives, Document no. 72.

Document 5
Open Letter from Abraham Lincoln to the People of Sangamon County, 1847

Many early railroads started as local or regional affairs, and local construction capital was eagerly sought. In many cases where the local population was thinly spread, outside capital had to be found as well. To show outside financiers that the local people really cared about the construction of their railway, it was deemed necessary to raise at least some capital locally. The future president Abraham Lincoln, then a young lawyer in Springfield, Illinois, was an enthusiastic supporter of railroads in his home state, hence his optimistic plea for subscriptions to the stock of the Springfield & Alton RR (later part of the Chicago & Alton).

June 30, 1847.

To the People of Sangamon County,

An effort is being made to build a Railroad from Springfield to Alton. A charter has been granted by the Legislature, and books are now open for subscriptions to the stock. The *chief* reliance for taking the stock must be on Eastern capitalists; yet, as an inducement to them, we here, must do something. We must stake something of our own in the enterprise, to convince them that we believe it will succeed, and to place ourselves between them and subsequent unfavorable legislation, which, it is supposed, they very much dread. The whole is a matter of pecuniary interest; and the proper question for us is, whether, with reference to the present and the future, and to direct and indirect results, it is our *interest* to subscribe. If it can be shown that it is, we hope few will refuse.

The shares in the stock are one hundred dollars each. Whoever takes a share is required to advance five dollars on it, which will be returned to him, unless the whole stock is taken, so that the work may certainly go on. If the whole shall be taken, the fund created by the five dollar advances will be used to begin the work; and as it progresses, additional calls will be made until it is finished. It is believed it can be completed in about three years. Up to its completion, the shareholders will have lost the *use* of their money, from the times of the respective advances. The questions occur, "What will the road be *worth* when completed?" "How will it pay for the use of the money—how return the principal?" Many who have already subscribed, and who therefore, if they deceive others also deceive themselves, are satisfied that the road can be built for something less than seven hundred thousand dollars. No actual survey has been made; but a good engineer, well acquainted with the route, and the subject, estimates it at this. Now, if the nett income shall be seven or eight—say eight—per cent. per annum upon this sum, in the aggregate $56,000, the stock will be *very* good; and the shareholder who does not wish to have money out at eight per cent. interest, can readily sell at par, or above it, and so have a return of his principal.

But will the road nett $56,000 a year? Will it make repairs, bear expenses, and still leave this much? These are questions which no one can, beforehand, answer with precise accuracy. The more difficult it is to make a road at first, the more difficult it is to keep in repair, and *vice versa*; so that the expenses and cost of repairs of railroads, have been found very nearly uniform at about ten per cent. per annum on the capital expended in building them. This, on our road, would be $70,000 a year. Now, if we can insure a gross income of the $56,000 and the $70,000 together; that is, $126,000—all is safe.

This gross income must, of course, depend upon the amount of business done upon the road. We suppose it is quite fair to assume that all the transportation now done, directly and indirectly, between Saint Louis and Springfield, together with its increase, will be done upon the road when completed. We learn it as an unquestionable fact, that the merchants of Springfield now pay, annually, for carrying goods *from* Saint Louis *to* Springfield, something more than $22,000. This being so, how much does the country produce, that pays for these goods, cost in carriage *from* Springfield *to* Saint Louis? Certainly *more*, in the same proportion as the produce *weighs* more than the goods. But what is this proportion? One of our largest dealers, who has, at our request, made an estimate, and has taken some pains to be accurate, assures us that the average of country produce is *five* times as heavy as the average of the articles in his business, in proportion to value. His business, too, is exclusively of *dry goods*, between which and produce the difference in weight, in proportion to value, is still greater. Another merchant tells us that a barrel of flour is quite equal in weight to a hundred dollars' worth of average dry goods articles. We suppose, then, we are far within bounds, in estimating that the transportation of produce from here to St. Louis costs *five* times as much as the transportation of goods from there here. This gives us $132,000 as the present annual cost of transportation of goods and produce between St. Louis and Springfield. And this does not include the trade of the villages of the county, nor of the counties above and adjoining; nor of the intermediate country; nor anything for the mail, nor for passengers. These must, on a moderate estimate, double the amount, swelling it to $264,000! Assuming this as the gross income, and it makes repairs, pays expenses, and leaves a nett sum of $194,000; being nearly 28 per cent. on the capital. This sum, however, is arrived at as the assumption that transportation is to remain as *dear* as it now is; while the chief reason for desiring the road is that transportation may be *cheapened*. Reduce, then, the cost of carriage to one third its present rates, and it still leaves more than nine per cent. as the profits of the stockholders. This the *distant* holder will be abundantly satisfied with; while the resident will have the same, and more than as much additional, in the cheapening what he buys, enhancing what he sells, and greatly increasing the value of his real property.

Another important matter, already alluded to, is the certain and large increase of business which must occur on the line of the road; and this, whether the road shall or shall not be built; greater, however, if it shall. Increase of business would naturally follow the building of a good road in any country; and this applies especially to this road, by the facts that the country of its line is unequalled in natural agricultural resources, is new, and only yet very partially brought into cultivation. Not one tenth of the land fitted for the plough has yet been subjected to it. Add the *new* fact, that the use of Indian corn has, at length, been successfully introduced into Europe, under circumstances that warrant the hope of its continuance, and the amount of means of transportation which the people of this county must need, is beyond calculation.

Again: at no distant day, a railroad, connecting the Eastern cities with some point on the Mississippi, will surely be built. If we lie by till this be done, it may pass us in such a way as to do us harm rather than good; while, if we complete, or even begin, our road first, it will attract the other, and so become, not merely a local improvement, but a link in one of a great national character, retaining all its local benefits, and superadding many from its general connection.

In view of the foregoing considerations, briefly stated, is it not the interest of us all to *act*, and to act *now*; in this matter?

It is encouraging, in a double aspect, to know that near a hundred thousand dollars of the stock has already been taken, by some four hundred farmers, mechanics, merchants, and members of all classes, resident in the counties of Madison, Jersey, Macoupin, Morgan, and Sangamon. It is encouraging, in the *amount* taken, and also in the evidence of *confidence* in the success of the undertaking, entertained by so great a number of men, well acquainted with the country through which the road is to pass.

Committee:

A. Lincoln,	John T. Stuart,
J.N. Brown,	William Pickrell,
John Calhoun,	J. Bunn,
B.C. Webster	John Williams,
P.P. Enos,	S.B. Opdycke.

Springfield, June 30, 1847.

Source: Sangamon Journal, July 6, 1847. Also printed in Roy P. Basler, ed., *The Collected Works of Abraham Lincoln* (New Brunswick, 1953), 1, 395–98.

Document 6
The First Use of the Telegraph for Train Dispatching, 1851

On single-track railroads with passing loops at stations only, as was the case with most early American roads, the capacity of a road was severely limited by the inability of a dispatcher to communicate with train and station crews out on the line. Whenever some mishap occurred that made the fixed schedules of the timetable untenable, chaos prevailed. Use of the telegraph began in 1844, and gradually the wires went up along almost every railroad track. Charles Minot, superintendent of the New York & Erie Railroad, was the first to adapt the telegraph to the running of trains.

To Charles Minot belongs the honor of having made the first practical application of the telegraph to railroading, either in this or any other country, by his adopting it in the early autumn of 1851, as near as the date can now be fixed, to the running of a train by telegraphic order, which led to a system that was adopted by railroads throughout the world, and remained the standard signal and reporting system on railroads until the block system began to take its place. Up to the time of Minot's initial experiment with telegraph orders, trains on the railroad were run on what was called the "time interval system." The rule was that a ruling train had right of one hour against the opposing train of the same class. Trainmen were anxious to get through. As an instance of this, once Conductor Ayers had lost his hour at Pond Eddy, he took the switch, and after waiting ten minutes, as was the rule, and the opposing train not being in sight or hearing, he started a brakeman with a red flag, and giving him twenty minutes start, he followed with his train. A little west of Shohola he caught the flagman, who had stopped on enough straight line to make it safe. The exhausted man was taken aboard the train and a fresh man started on with the flag, which operation was repeated until the train expected was met at Callicoon, 34 miles from Pond Eddy. Captain Ayers used to say that he had flagged the entire length of the Delaware Division more than once.

W.H. Stewart was running the west-bound express on the day when Superintendent Minot made his astounding innovation in railroading, he happening to be going over the road on that train. The train, under the rule then existing, was to wait for an east-bound express to pass it at Turner's, 47 miles from New York. That train had not arrived, and the west-bound train would be unable to proceed until an hour had expired, unless the tardy east-bound train arrived at Turner's within that time. There was a telegraph office at Turner's, and Superintendent Minot telegraphed to the operator at Goshen, fourteen miles further on, and asked him whether the east-bound train had left that station. The reply was that the train had not yet arrived at Goshen, showing that it was much behind its time. Then, according to the narrative of the late W.H. Stewart, given to the author in 1896, Superintendent Minot telegraphed as follows, as nearly as Stewart could recollect:

To Agent and Operator at Goshen:
> Hold the train for further orders.
>
> Chas. Minot, Superintendent

He then wrote this order, and handed it to Conductor Stewart:

To Conductor and Engineer, Day Express:
> Run to Goshen regardless of opposing train.
>
> Chas. Minot, Superintendent

"I took the order," sais Mr. Stewart, relating the incident, "showing it to the engineer, Isaac Lewis, and told him to go ahead. The surprised engineer read the order, and handing it back to me, exclaimed:

"Do you take me for a d—d fool? I won't run by that thing!"

"I reported to the Superintendent, who went forward and used his verbal authority on the engineer, but without effect. Minot then climbed the engine and took charge of it himself. Engineer Lewis jumped off and got in the rear seat of the rear car. The Superintendent ran the train to Goshen. The east-bound train had not yet reached that station. He telegraphed to Middletown. The train had not arrived there. The west-bound train was run on a similar order to Middletown, and from there to Port Jervis, where it entered the yard from the East as the other train came into it from the West."

An hour and more in time had been saved to the west-bound train, and the question of running trains on the Erie by telegraph was at once and forever settled.

Source: Edward H. Mott, *Between the Ocean and the Lakes: The Story of Erie* (New York: John S. Collins, 1899), 420.

Document 7
Abraham Lincoln's Defense of the Railroad Interest in the Rock Island Bridge Case, 1857

On April 22, 1856, the first railroad bridge across the Mississippi River between Rock Island, Illinois, and Davenport, Iowa, was opened for traffic. The steamboat interests saw this as a sure sign that a new and dangerous competitor had arisen, one that threatened their very existence. Two weeks after the opening of the bridge, on May 6, 1856, a steamboat, the *Effie Afton*, hit one of the piers of the bridge and mysteriously caught fire, destroying one of the wooden spans. The steamboat owners then sued the bridge company and demanded the removal of the bridge as a danger to shipping. The bridge company hired Abraham Lincoln to defend them, which he successfully did. The bridge was rebuilt, although it took some more years before the U.S. Supreme Court finally found in favor of the railroad interests. This "cause célèbre" was decisive in allowing railroad companies to construct bridges across navigable rivers. The case made such a noise that the Chicago *Daily Democratic Press* followed the proceedings from day to day. Of course, Chicago was much in favor of railroads, as opposed to

St. Louis, where the shipping business was concentrated. The text given here is not necessarily the exact words of Lincoln but the account of the reporter on duty.

Tuesday, September 22nd, 1857.

Mr. A. Lincoln addressed the jury: He said he did not purpose to assail anybody, that he expected to grow earnest as he proceeded, but not ill-natured. . . . He had no prejudice against steamboats or steamboatmen, nor any against St. Louis, for he supposed they went about as other people would do in their situation. St. Louis as a commercial place, may desire that this bridge should not stand, as it is adverse to her commerce, diverting a portion of it from the river; and it might be that she supposed that the additional cost of railroad transportation upon the productions of Iowa, would force them to go to St. Louis if this bridge was removed. . . .

The last thing that would be pleasing to him would be, to have one of these great channels, extending almost from where it never freezes to where it never thaws, blocked up. But there is a travel from East to West, whose demands are not less important than that of the river. It is growing larger and larger, building up new countries with a rapidity never before seen in the history of the world. He alluded to the astonishing growth of Illinois, having grown within his memory to a population of a million and a half, to Iowa and the other young and rising communities of the Northwest.

This current of travel has its rights, as well as that North and South. If the river had not the advantage in priority and legislation, we could enter into free competition with it and we would surpass it. This particular line has a great importance, and the statement of its business during little less than a year shows this importance. It is in evidence that from September 8, 1856, to August 8, 1857, 12,586 freight cars and 74,179 passengers passed over this bridge. Navigation was closed four days short of four months last year, and during this time, while the river was of no use, this road and bridge were equally valuable. There is, too, a considerable portion of time, when floating or thin ice makes the river useless, while the bridge is as useful as ever. This shows that this bridge must be treated with respect in this court and is not to be kicked about with contempt. . . .

What is reasonable skill and care? This is a thing of which the jury are to judge. I differ from them in saying that they [i.e., steamboat pilots] are found to exercise no more care than they took before the building of the bridge. If we are allowed by the Legislature to build a bridge, which will require them to do more than before, when a pilot comes along, it is unreasonable for him to dash on, heedless of this structure, which has been *legally put there*. The *Afton* came there on the 5th, and lay at Rock Island until next morning. When the boat lies up, the pilot has a holiday, and would not any of these jurors have then gone around there, and got acquainted with the place? Parker [pilot of the *Afton*] has shown here that he does not understand the draw. I heard him say that the fall from the head to the foot of that pier was four feet!! He needs information. He could have gone there that day and have seen there was no such fall. He should have discarded passion, and the chances are that he would have had no disaster at all. He was bound to make himself acquainted with it.

McCammon [a pilot on the *Afton*, but not in charge] says that "the current and the swell from the long pier, drove her against the long pier." Drove her towards the very pier from which the current came! It is an absurdity, an impossibility. The only reconciliation I can find for this contradiction, is in a current which White [one of the expert witnesses] says strikes out from the long pier, and then, like a ram's horn, turns back, and this might have acted somehow in this manner.

It is agreed by all that the plaintiffs' boat was destroyed; that it was destroyed upon the head of the short pier; that she moved from the channel, where she was, with her bow above the head of the long pier, till she struck the short one, swung around under the bridge, and there was crowded under the bridge and destroyed.

I shall try to prove that the average velocity of the current through the draw with the boat in it, should be five and a half miles an hour; that it is slowest at the head of the pier, swiftest at the foot of the pier. Their lowest estimate, in evidence, is six miles an hour, their highest twelve miles. This was the testimony of men who had made no experiment, only conjecture. We have adopted the most exact means. The water runs swiftest in high water, and we have taken the point of nine feet above low water. The water, when the *Afton* was lost, was seven feet above low water, or at least a foot lower than our time. Brayton [engineer of the bridge company] and his assistants timed the instruments—the best known instruments for measuring currents. They timed them under various circumstances, and they found the current five miles an hour, and no more. They found that the water, at the upper end, ran slower than five miles; that below it was swifter than five miles, but that the average was five miles. Shall men, who have taken no care, who conjecture, some of whom speak of twenty miles an hour, be believed, against those who have had such a favorable and well-improved opportunity? They should not even *qualify* the result. Several men have given their opinions as to the distance of the *Carson* [another steamboat in the vicinity], and I suppose if *one* should go and *measure* that distance, you would believe him in preference to all of them.

These measurements were made when the boat was not in the draw. It has been ascertained what is the area of the cross-section of the stream, and the area of the face of the piers, and the engineers say, that the piers being put there will increase the current proportionally as the space is decreased. So with the boat in the draw. The depth of the channel was 22 feet, the width 116 feet—multiply these and you have the square feet across the water of the draw, viz.: 2,552 feet. The *Afton* was 35 feet wide and drew five feet, making a fourteenth of the sum. Now one-fourteenth of five miles is five-fourteenths of one mile—about one third of a mile— the increase of the current. We will call the current 5½ miles per hour.

The next thing I will try to prove is that the plaintiffs' boat had power to run six miles an hour in that current. It has been testified that she was a strong, swift boat, able to run eight miles an hour up stream in a current of four miles an hour, and fifteen miles down stream. Strike the average and you will find what is her average—about 11½ miles. Take the 5½ miles, which is the speed of the current in the draw, and it leaves the power of the boat in that draw at six miles an hour, 528 feet per minute, and 8-4/5 feet to the second.

Next I propose to show that there are no cross currents. I know their witnesses say that there are cross currents—that, as one witness says, there are three cross currents and two eddies. So far as mere statement without experiment, and mingled with mistakes can go, they have proved. But can these men's testimony be compared with the nice, exact, thorough experiments of our witnesses? Can you believe that these floats go across the currents? It is inconceivable that they should not have discovered every possible current. How do boats find currents that floats cannot discover? We assume the position then that those cross currents are not there. My next proposition is that the *Afton* passed between the *S.B. Carson* and Iowa shore. That is undisputed. . . .

How was it that the *Afton*, with all her power, flanked over from the channel to the short pier without moving one inch ahead? Suppose she was in the middle of the draw, her wheel would have been 31 feet from the short pier. The reason she went over thus is, her starboard wheel was not working. I shall try to establish the fact that that wheel was not running, and, that after she struck, she went ahead strong on this same wheel. Upon the last point the witnesses agree—that the starboard wheel was running after she struck—and no witnesses say that it was running while she was out in the draw flanking over. Mr. Lincoln read from the testimony of various witnesses to prove that the starboard wheel was not working while she was out in the stream. . . .

The *Afton* came into the draw after she had just passed the *Carson*, and, as the *Carson* no doubt kept the true course, the *Afton* going around her, got out of the proper way, got across the current, into the eddy which is west of a straight line drawn down from the long pier, was compelled to resort to these changes of wheels, which she did not do with sufficient adroitness to save her. Was it not her own fault that she entered wrong? So far wrong, that she never got right. Is the defence to blame for that? . . .

The plaintiffs have to establish that the bridge is a material obstruction, and that they managed their boat with reasonable care and skill. As to the last point, high winds have nothing to do with it, for it was not a windy day. They must show "due skill and care." Difficulties going down stream, will not do, for they were going up stream. Difficulties with barges in tow, have nothing to do with it, for they had no barge. He said he had much more to say, many things he could suggest to the jury, but he would close to save time.

Source: Chicago *Daily Democratic Press*, September 24, 1857. Also printed in Roy P. Basler, ed., *The Collected Works of Abraham Lincoln* (New Brunswick, 1953) 2, 415–422.

Document 8
The American Sleeping Car, 1861

Foreign travelers in the United States always marveled at the convenience of the sleeping car, that typical American phenomenon, then still in its infancy. Anthony Trollope, already a famous English author, was suitably impressed by the sleeping car during his travels in America.

The lakes in America are cold, cumbrous, uncouth, and uninteresting; intended by nature for the conveyance of cereal produce, but not for the comfort of travelling men and women. So we gave up our plan of traversing the lake, and passing back into Canada by the suspension bridge at Niagara, we reached the Detroit River at Windsor by the Great Western line, and passed thence by the ferry into the city of Detroit.

In making this journey at night we introduced ourselves to the thoroughly American institution of sleeping-cars; that is, of cars in which beds are made up for travellers. The traveller may have a whole bed, or half a bed, or no bed at all as he pleases, paying a dollar or half a dollar extra should he choose the partial or full fruition of a couch. I confess I have always taken a delight in seeing these beds made up, and consider that the operations of the change are generally as well executed as the manoeuvres of any pantomime at Drury Lane. The work is usually done by negroes or coloured men; and the domestic negroes of America are always light-handed and adroit. The nature of an American car is no doubt known to all men. It looks as far removed from all bedroom accommodation, as the baker's barrow does from the steam engine into which it is to be converted by harlequin's wand. But the negro goes to work much more quietly than the harlequin, and for every four seats in the railway car he builds up four beds, almost as quickly as the hero of the pantomime goes through his performance.

The great glory of the Americans is in their wondrous contrivances, in their patent remedies for the usually troublous operations of life. In their huge hotels all the bell-ropes of each house ring one bell only, but a patent indicator discloses the number, and the whereabouts of the ringer is shown. One fire heats every room, passage, hall, and cupboard, and does it so effectually that the inhabitants are all but stifled. Soda-water bottles open themselves without any wire or strings. Men and women go up and down stairs without motive power of their own. Hot and cold water are laid on to all the chambers, though it sometimes happens that the water from both taps is boiling, and that when once turned on it cannot be turned off again by any human energy.

Everything is done by a new and wonderful patent contrivance, and of all their wonderful contrivances that of the railroad bed is by no means the least. For every four seats the negro builds up four beds, that is, four half-beds or accommodation for four persons. Two are supposed to be below on the level of the ordinary four seats, and two up above on shelves which are let down from the roof. Mattresses slip out from one nook and pillows from another. Blankets are added, and the bed is ready. Any over particular, an islander, for instance, who hugs his chains, will generally prefer to pay the dollar for the double accommodation. Looking at the bed in the light of a bed, taking as it were an abstract view of it, or comparing it with some other bed or beds with which the occupant may have acquaintance, I cannot say that it is in all respects perfect. But distances are long in America, and he who declines to travel by night will lose very much time. He who does so travel will find the railway bed a great relief. I must confess that the feeling of dirt on the following morning is rather oppressive.

Source: Anthony Trollope, *North America* (1862, repr. Gloucester: Allan Sutton, 1987), vol. 1, 173–74.

Document 9
The Pacific Railroad Act, 1862

After much partisan discussions in Congress about the route to be chosen for the transcontinertal railroad, the withdrawal of the southern delegates freed the way for President Lincoln to make his choice of the central route. This first Pacific Railroad Act was followed by several others when the help promised in the shape of land grants and U.S. bonds proved to be not enough to persuade private investors to risk their money in this giant undertaking. But the principles outlined in this first act remained valid throughout the construction of the first transcontinental railroad.

An Act to aid in the Construction of a Railroad and Telegraph Line from the Missouri River to the Pacific Ocean, and to secure to the Government the Use of the same for Postal, Military, and Other Purposes, July 1, 1862.

Be it enacted by the Senate and House of Representatives of the United States of America in Congress assembled, That [159 names of individuals] together with five commissioners to be appointed by the Secretary of the Interior, and all persons who shall or may be associated with them, and their successors, are hereby created and erected into a body corporate and politic in deed and in law, by the name, style, and title of "The Union Pacific Railroad Company" and by that name shall have perpetual succession, and shall be able to sue and to be sued, plead and be impleaded, in all courts of law and equity within the United States, and may make and have a common seal; and the said corporation is hereby authorized and empowered to lay out, locate, construct, furnish, maintain, and enjoy a continuous railroad and telegraph, with the appurtenances, from a point on the one hundredth meridian of longitude west from Greenwich, between the south margin of the valley of the Platte River, in the Territory of Nebraska, to the western boundary of Nevada Territory, upon the route and terms herinafter provided, and is hereby vested with all the powers, privileges, and immunities necessary to carry into effect the purposes of this act as herein set forth. The capital stock of said company shall consist of one hundred thousand shares of one thousand dollars each, which shall be subscribed for and held in not more than two hundred shares by any one person, and shall be transferable in such manner as the by-laws of said corporation shall provide. The persons hereinbefore named, together with those to be appointed by the Secretary of the Interior, are hereby constituted and appointed commissioners, and such body shall be called the Board of Commissioners of the Union Pacific Railroad and Telegraph Company, and twenty-five shall constitute a quorum for the transaction of business. . . .

SEC. 2. *And be it further enacted*, That the right of way through the public lands be, and the same is hereby, granted to the said company for the construction of said railroad and telegraph line; and the right, power, and authority is hereby given to said company to take from the public lands adjacent to the line of said road, earth, stone, timber, and other materials for the construction thereof; said right of way is granted to said railroad to the extent of two hundred feet in width on each side of said railroad where it may pass over the public lands, including all necessary grounds for stations, buildings, workshops, and depots, machines shops, switches, side tracks, turntables and water stations. The United States shall extinguish, as rapidly as may be the Indian titles to all lands falling under the operation of this act and required for the said right of way and grants hereinafter made.

SEC. 3. *And be it further enacted*, That there be, and is hereby, granted to the said company, for the purpose of aiding in the construction of said railroad and telegraph line, and to secure the safe and speedy transportation of the mails, troops, munitions of war, and public stores thereon, every alternate section of public land, designated by odd numbers, to the amount of five alternate sections per mile on each side of said railroad, on the line thereof, and within the limits of ten miles on each side of said road, not sold, reserved, or otherwise disposed of by the United States, and to which a preemption or homestead claim may not have attached, at the time the line of said road is definitely fixed: *Provided,* That all mineral lands shall be excepted from the operation of this act; but where the same shall contain timber, the timber thereon is hereby granted to said company. And all such lands, so granted by this section, which shall not be sold or disposed of by said company within three years after the entire road shall have been completed, shall be subject to settlement and preëmption, like other lands, a a price not exceeding one dollar and twenty-five cents per acre, to be paid to said company.

SEC. 4. [Commissioners will be appointed to issue patents to the lands after forty consecutive miles of railroad have been completed].

SEC. 5. *And be it further enacted,* That for the purposes herein mentioned the Secretary of the Treasury shall, upon the certificate in writing of said commissioners of the completion of forty consecutive miles of said railroad and telegraph, in accordance with the provisions of this act, issue to said company bonds of the United States of one thousand dollars each, payable in thirty years after date, bearing six per centum per annum interest, . . . to the amount of sixteen of said bonds per mile for such section of forty miles. . . .

SEC. 7. *And be it further enacted,* That said company shall file their assent to this act, under the seal of said company, in the Department of the Interior, within one year after the passage of this act, and shall complete said railroad and telegraph from the point of beginning as herein provided, to the western boundary of Nevada Territory before the first day of July, one thousand eight hundred and seventy-four: *Provided,* That within two years after the passage of this act said company shall designate the general route of said road, as near as may be, and shall file a map of the same in the Department of the Interior, whereupon the Secretary of the Interior shall cause the lands within fifteen miles of said designated route or routes to be withdrawn from preemption, private entry, and sale; and when any portion of said route shall be finally located, the Secretary of the Interior shall cause the said lands hereinbefore granted to be surveyed and set off as fast as may be necessary for the purpose herein named: *Provided,* That in fixing the point of connection of the main trunk with the eastern connections, it shall be fixed at the most practicable point for the construction of the Iowa and Missouri branches, as hereinafter provided. . . .

SEC. 9. [Covers the construction of the Kansas Pacific and Missouri Pacific railroads, to connect with the Union Pacific]. The Central Pacific Railroad Company of California, a corporation existing under the laws of the State of California, are hereby authorized to construct a railroad and telegraph line from the Pacific coast, at or near San Francisco, or the navigable waters of the Sacramento River, to the eastern boundary of California, upon the same terms and conditions, in all respects, as are contained in this act for the construction of said railroad and telegraph line first mentioned, and to meet and connect with the first mentioned railroad and telegraph line on the eastern boundary of California. . . .

Source: Congressional Papers, 37th Congress, Session II, chapter 120, 1862.

Document 10
Railroading in Wartime, 1863

During the Civil War railroads had become important elements in the warfare. The Federal government very soon set up a special organization, the U.S. Military Railroads, under Daniel C. McCallum, an experienced railroader. While McCallum organized the transportation expertly from headquarters, his commander in the field was Herman Haupt, an engineer of extensive experience and a knack for improvization. Toward the end of his career, in 1901, Haupt wrote down his reminiscences for posterity.

The long interval from January 26, 1863, when General Hooker took command, until May, 1863, was a period of comparative inactivity in military operations. The Army of the Potomac was encamped on the north side of the Rappahannock opposite Fredericksburg, and supplies were forwarded by river and rail via Acquia Creek. We were not troubled by guerilla raids or military interference. The trains were run with regularity by schedule, and the telegraph was left for the almost exclusive use of the military authorities.

The Construction Corps, during this period, was not idle, but performed services of great value in perfecting organization, procuring material, and preparing for rapid advance movements whenever they should be ordered.

A large number of bridge trusses were prepared in spans of 60 feet to be transported on flat cars, hauled by oxen to the sites of the bridges, and hoisted bodily into position by suitable portable machinery. These trusses were called "shadbellies" by the workmen from their peculiar shape.

A plan was also designed for a military truss bridge, the parts of which were interchangeable, and which could be put together without previous fitting, and with so much rapidity that, as my foreman, E.C. Smeed, expressed it, he could put the bridge together about as fast as a dog could trot.

Torpedoes were also prepared for blowing down bridges in operating on the communications of the enemy. These torpedoes consisted simply of an iron bolt with a head and washer of such diameter that they could be driven easily into a two-inch auger hole. Between the head and the washer was a tin case 8 inches long, open at both ends, filled with powder. Experiments were made in blowing up trunks of trees which proved their efficiency, and by means of them any ordinary wooden bridge could be thrown down in five minutes.

Other experiments were made on old sidings near Alexandria to determine the best mode of rapidly destroying tracks. The usual mode adopted by the enemy had been to tear up the rails, pile the cross ties, place the rails upon them, set the pile on fire, and bend the rails when heated. I found this mode entirely too slow, as several hours were required to heat the rails sufficiently and, when bent, we could generally straighten them for use in a few minutes, in fact, in less than one-tenth of the time required to heat and bend them

We had been experimenting for some time with no results that I considered satisfactory, when one day Smeed came into my office with a couple of U-shaped irons in his hands and exclaimed: "I've got it!" "Got what?" I asked. "Got the thing that will tear up track as quickly as you can say 'Jack Robinson,' and spoil the rails so that nothing but a rolling mill can ever repair them." "That is just what I want," was my reply; "but how are you to do it with that pair of horseshoes?"

He explained his plan. The irons were turned up and over at the ends so as firmly to embrace the base of the rail. Into the cavity of the U a stout lever of wood was to be inserted. A rope at the end of the lever would allow half a dozen men to pull upon it and twist the rail. When the lever was pulled down to the ground and held there, another iron was to be placed beside it, and another twist given, then the first iron removed and the process repeated four or five times until a corkscrew twist was given to the rail. After hearing the explanation, I said: "Think what it will do;

let us go at once and try it." Smeeds's plan was found to answer perfectly, and the problem of the simplest and quickest mode of destroying track was satisfactorily solved. . . .

> In a letter to Maj. Gen. H.W Halleck, then general in chief of the army of the United States, Haupt unfolded his plans for cavalry raids to destroy the enemy's communication with the use of his new-fangled portable instruments.

Washington, May 16, 1863.

. . . A thousand cavalry marching two abreast, and following each other closely, will occupy a space of one mile. At least one-half should be reserved for protection, leaving the other half for work. Suppose the working parties to be divided into squads of ten men, and that to each squad should be assigned the duty of removing and destroying twelve rails, supposed to be each 20 feet long. The number of squads in one mile will be 44, requiring 440 men, and leaving 560 for defense out of the thousand. Each squad should be supplied with the following implements: 2 U-shaped irons; 2 stout wooden levers, 12 feet long and 4½ inches diameter; 2 pieces of rope, each 6 yards long, to tie to the levers; 2 axes and 2 wooden wedges to place between levers and rails.

The levers can be cut from the woods, or stout fence rail can be used; the axes, ropes, and U-irons must be carried. The whole weight to be carried for a squad of ten men would be but twenty-five pounds; one pack-horse or mule would carry the implements for six or eight squads.

Five minutes is sufficient time to twist, bend, and remove a rail; in one hour the twelve rails, which form the task of a squad, could be destroyed. 440 men in the same time (one hour) will destroy a mile. 2,200 men in the same time can destroy five miles. 5,000 cavalry sent on an expedition to break communications, could detail 2,200 men for the work, leaving 2,800 for protection, and in one hour could effectually destroy five miles of track; they could then ride for two hours and destroy five miles more.

In destroying track it is best to pile and burn the cross ties. Each squad will have forty-eight ties to burn. To pile these ties, split two of them for kindling, pour over two canteens of coal oil, and set fire to the heap, will consume but fifteen minutes. A small detachment may be left to prevent residents in the vicinity from extinguishing the flames.

Heretofore it has been possible to operate effectually against the communications of an enemy only where there were important bridges that could be destroyed. The plans herein described for destroying track will permit communications to be broken wherever they can be reached, and in so effectual a manner that repairs will be impossible without new material, which, without tearing up some other road, it may be impossible for the enemy to procure.

A cavalry expedition, led by intelligent and dashing officers, provided with the appliances herein described, and with the bridge torpedoes for the destruction of bridges, could traverse the whole South and inflict irreparable damage upon the communications of the enemy. If a working force of 2,200 men can destroy five miles of track in one hour, and two or three men to a span, with the use of torpedoes, throw down the largest bridges in five minutes, the movement of the forces can be too rapid to admit of pursuit, except by cavalry, to prevent which the numerical strength should be great enough to oppose any possible force of cavalry that the enemy can bring against it. Fresh horses should be seized, wherever practicable, and abandoned ones shot.

The telegraph should be cut frequently; but instead of leaving the ends loose, the break should be at a pole, and the ends connected by small pieces of insulated wire, concealed by the insulators, so that the point of break would not be discernible.

On an expedition of this kind a few men, expert in repairs of track, bridges, and telegraph lines, would prove of great value. Still more important is it that the officers, and at least a portion of the force, say one or two men in each squad, should be actually drilled in laying track and in tearing it up, and in bending and twisting old and useless rails, if any can be found.

In the hope that the results of these experiments will prove beneficial for the service, they are respectfully submitted by

H. Haupt,
Brigadier-General,
In Charge of United States Military Railroads.

Source: Reminiscences of General Herman Haupt, written by himself (n.p., 1901), 185–87; 200–201.

Document 11
The Last Spike at Promontory, 1869

Maj. Gen. Grenville M. Dodge, chief engineer of the Union Pacific, was present at Promontory Point when the last spike of the first transcontinental railroad was driven on May 10, 1869. Forty years later he penned this eyewitness account of the event from memory; it may, therefore, not be quite true in every respect.

This ceremony was one of peace and harmony between the Union Pacific, coming from the east, and the Central Pacific, coming from the west. For a year or more there had been great contention and rivalry between the two companies, the Union Pacific endeavoring to reach Humboldt Wells, on the west boundary of Utah, and the Central Pacific rushing to reach Ogden, Utah, to give them an outlet to Salt Lake City. In the building of a Pacific steam road to connect the two oceans two lines were graded alongside of each other for 225 miles between Ogden and Humboldt Wells. Climbing Promontory Mountain, they were not a stone's throw apart.

When both companies saw that neither could reach its goal they came together and we made an agreement to join the tracks on the summit of Promontory Mountain, the Union Pacific selling to the Central Pacific fifty-six miles of its road back within five miles of Ogden and leasing trackage over that five miles to enable the Central Pacific to reach Ogden. These five miles were not only a part of the Union Pacific, but used by their line north to Idaho. This agreement was ratified by Congress. Each road built to the summit of Promontory, leaving a gap of about 100 feet of rail to be laid when the last spike was driven. The chief engineers of the Union and Central Pacific had charge of the ceremony and the work, and we set a day far enough ahead so that trains coming from New York and San Francisco would have ample time to reach Promontory in time to take part in the ceremonies.

On the morning of May 10, 1869, Hon. Leland Stanford, Governor of California and President of the Central Pacific, accompanied by Messrs. Huntington, Hopkins, Crocker and trainloads of California's distinguished citizens, arrived from the west. During the forenoon Vice-President T.C. Durant and Directors John R. Duff and Sidney Dillon and Consulting Engineer Silas A. Seymour of the Union Pacific, with other prominent men, including a delegation of Mormons from Salt Lake City, came in from the east. The National Government was represented by a detachment of "regulars" from Fort Douglass, Utah, accompanied by a band, and 600 others, including Chinese, Mexicans, Indians, half-breeds, negroes and laborers, suggesting an air of cosmopolitanism, all gathered around the open space where the tracks were to be joined. The Chinese laid the rails from the west, and the Irish laborers laid them from the east end, until they met and joined.

Telegraphic wires were so connected that each blow of the desending sledge [hammer] could be reported instantly to all parts of the United States. Corresponding blows were struck on the bell of the City Hall in San Francisco, and with the last blow of the sledge a cannon was fired at Fort Point. General Safford presented a spike of gold, silver and iron as the offering of the Territory of Arizona. Governor Tuttle of Nevada presented a spike of silver from his state. The connecting tie was of California laurel, and California presented the last spike of gold on behalf of that state. A silver sledge had also been presented for the occasion. A prayer was offered. Governor Stanford of California made a few appropriate remarks on behalf of the Central Pacific and the chief engineer [Dodge] responded for the Union Pacific. Then the telegraphic inquiry from the Omaha office, from which the circuit was to be started, was answered: "To everybody: Keep quiet. When the last spike is driven at Promontory Point we will say 'Done.' Don't break the circuit, but watch for the signals of the blows of the hammer. The spike will soon be driven. The signal will be three dots for the commencement of the blows." The magnet tapped one—two—three—then paused—"Done." The spike was given its first blow by President Stanford and Vice-President Durant followed. Neither hit the spike the first time, but hit the rail, and were greeted by the lusty cheers of the onlookers, accompanied by the screams of the locomotives and the music of the military band. Many other spikes were driven on the last rail by some of the distinguished persons present, but it was seldom that they first hit the spike. The original spike, after being tapped by the officials of the two roads, was driven home by the chief engineers of the two roads. Then the two trains were run together, the two locomotives touching at the point of junction, and the engineers of the two locomotives each broke a bottle of champagne on the other's engine. Then it was declared that the connection was made and the Atlantic and Pacific were joined together never to be parted.

The wires in every direction were hot with congratulatory telegrams. President Grant and Vice-President Colfax were the recipients of especially felicitous messages. On the evening of May 8th, in San Francisco, from the stages of the theatres and other public places, notice was given that the two roads had met and were to be wedded on the morrow. The celebrations there began at once and practically lasted through the 10th. The booming of cannons and the ringing of bells were united with other species of noise, making of which jubilant humanity finds expression for its feelings on such an occasion. The buildings in the city were gay with flags and bunting. Business was suspended and the longest procession that San Francisco had ever seen attested the enthusiasm of the people. At night the city was brilliant with illuminations. Free railway trains filled Sacramento with an unwonted crowd, and the din of cannon, steam whistles and bells followed the final message.

At the eastern terminus in Omaha the firing of a hundred guns on Capitol hill, more bells and steam whistles and a grand procession of fire companies, civic societies, citizens and visiting delegations echoed the sentiments of the Californians. In Chicago a procession of four miles in length, a lavish display of decoration in the city and on the vessels in the river, and an address by Vice President Colfax in the evening were the evidences of the city's feeling. In New York, by order of the mayor, a salute of a hundred guns announced the culmination of the great undertaking. In Trinity Church the Te Deum was chanted, prayers were offered, and when the services were over the chimes rung out "Old Hundred," the "Ascension Carol" and national airs. The ringing of bells on Independence Hall and the fire stations in Philadelphia produced an unusual concourse of citizens to celebrate the national event. In the other large cities of the country the expressions of public gratification were hardly less hearty and demonstrative.

Source: Grenville M. Dodge, *How We Built the Union Pacific and Other Railway Papers and Addresses* (Washington, D.C.: U.S. Printing Office, 1910), 67–70.

Document 12
The Race for Land Grants, 1870

Pioneer railroads were often highly dependent on government aid in the shape of land grants. Building out into unsettled country did not promise high traffic yields, and land was often the only item of real value in the company's books. Also, as land grants were often limited to a certain period of construction, all kinds of subterfuges were used to comply with the deadline. This story of the race into Indian Territory (modern Oklahoma) does not differ much from many others, and it gives some insight into the contemporary ideas about lands held by Native Americans.

We hastened back toward Parsons [Kansas], again crossing the great Kaw reservation, and meeting long trains of Indians, mounted on their shaggy ponies. This Neosho Valley line, which we had traversed, was the beginning of the present great trunk route from Sedalia to the Gulf. Work was begun on it, under a contract with the Land Grant Railway and Trust Company, in November, 1868, the line to extend from Junction City to Chetopa, on the frontier of the Indian Territory, a distance of 182 miles; and it was completed in October, 1870.

While this was in construction, the building of the line from Sedalia to Parsons was begun, and the whole route, 160 miles, was completed early in 1871. Meantime work was going forward, at lightning speed, in the Indian Territory. The manager of the line had made a bold stroke in order to be the first to reach the Cherokee country, and obtain permission to run a line through it, as well as to get conditional land-grants; and in May of 1870 occurred quite an episode in the history of railway building. On the 24th of that month the line had reached witin twenty-four miles of the southern boundary of Kansas. Much of the grading was unfinished; bridges were not up; masonry was not ready. But on the 6th day of June, at noon, the first locomotive which ever entered the Indian Territory uttered its premonitory shriek of progress. In eleven days twenty-six and a-half miles of completed rail were laid, four miles being put down in a single day. A grant of over 3,000,000 acres of land, subject, under treaty stipulations, to temporary Indian occupancy, has been accorded the Missouri, Kansas and Texas Railway Company, on the line of the road in the territory between Chetopa and the Red River. The question of the future disposition of the Indian Territory is interesting to the railroad builders, as they have extended their line through the great stretch of country, hoping that the fertile lands now waste may come into the market. Until it is opened to white settlement, or until the Indians adopt some new policy with regard to their lands, the Territory is, in many respects, a barrier to the best development of that portion of the South-west. The immense reservation, larger than all New England, extending over 60,000,000 acres, lying between Texas, with her 1,000,000 settlers, Arkansas, with her hardy 500,000, and Missouri and Kansas with their 2,000,000 of stout frontiers-men, is now completely given over to the Indian, and the white man who wishes to abide within its borders will find his appeal sternly rejected by an Indian Legislature, unless he marries into one of the dusky tribes and relinquishes his allegiance to Uncle Sam.

Source: Edward King, *The Southern States of North America* (London: Blackie & Son, 1875), 195–96.

Document 13
Railroading in the South after the Civil War, 1872

It was years after the end of the Civil War before some of the rail-roads in the South returned to some semblance of order. Mainte-nance was much behind schedule, rolling stock was in bad shape, and staff were badly paid and uninterested in the well-being of their companies. An added complication was that some of the rail-roads had fallen into the hands of northern "carpetbaggers," who were more interested in their own private gains than in serving the public. The Alabama and Chattanooga Railroad, where con-ductor Nimrod J. Bell served between 1872 and 1876, is a case in point. Two brothers from New England, John C. and Daniel N. Stanton, got hold of the A & C, helped by corrupt politicians in Montgomery, and started to milk it for their own purposes. Con-ductor Bell (born 1830, died circa 1899) is one of that rare breed of railroaders who penned memoirs later in life. His stories about the haphazard way of running trains on the Alabama & Chatta-nooga are sometimes hair-raising, but they give a clear picture of conditions on a southern railroad down on its luck.

I remember one time when the waters of the Tombigbee river were flowing over the lowlands, an engine with a train was rolling slowly over the bridge that crossed the river, the bridge gave way near the end just before the engine got off, and it went down in the water with the engi-neer and fireman on it, out of sight of those who were left to tell the story. A diving-bell was purchased and several efforts were made before the bodies were recovered. The engineer was a young man and had just been married. The baggage car went down on one end and also one coach, but I think they caught on some timbers. Some of those that were in them got out, and those that could not were helped out.

I was sent out of Chattanooga once after a heavy rainfall with an engine, a few box and flat cars, a baggage car and two coaches, and was instructed to go through to Meridian if I could possibly get over the road. I was early one Monday morning. I made pretty fair speed until I got west of Birmingham, when I found a place I thought not fit to run over before I would have it replaced. I had about twenty or twenty-five negroes on board, who were going to pick cotton in the Mississippi valley. I would hire them to help me and would also pick up section men when I could find any. I found the track torn up and embankments washed out in many places after I passed Tuscaloosa. Some places where I could get timber I would have trees cut down and build pens out of logs so as to put the track across the washout. I would pay my men off every night. I worked day and night until I got to Meridian. When I arrived there I went to an office, took a seat near a desk, crossed my arms on the desk, dropped my head on my arms and went to sleep and slept about four or five hours. When I awoke I started back to Chattanooga. I had not been in bed the whole week. . . .

I had a coach in my train one day when the front trucks were de-railed and the wheels on one side went in a ditch on the roadside. We were placing wood so as to put the wheels of the car back on the track, when a man who was a passenger came out to suggest how to put them back, as was invariably the case when an accident occurred, and is kept up to the present day by some passengers. When the man commenced to give instructions, I asked him if he wanted to help get the trucks of the coach back on the rails, and he said "Yes." I said to him then to help the boys bring wood, and so he went to carrying wood at once. . . .

A while after noon my passenger asked me where the dinner station was. I answered that there was none. He then asked where we got dinner. I answered that we did not get any. He then turned in and cursed out the man in New Orleans who sold him the ticket he had. He then cursed the road, and swore that he never would go over it again.

The hotels and boarding-houses along the road had quit letting the men have meals unless they would pay down for them, and this they could not do on account of not being paid off regularly. And on this account Mr. Stanton had several thousands dollars' worth scrip struck off as a kind of meal ticket. As well as I remember, they were issued in twenty-five and fifty cents slips, with the picture of a duck on one kind and a fine rooster on the other, and looked very nice when new. They went like Confederate money—were good for awhile, and anybody would take them, but soon played out. The men were paid with them as a part of their wages and they would get their meals with them, and sometimes grocerymen would take them. I knew one man who sold a house and lot and took Stanton scrip, as it was called, in payment for his property, and the scrip went dead on his hands. I think Mr. Stanton agreed to make it good in case it did fail, but a lawsuit was brought first and it was a long time before the man in question got anything, and when he did it was done by a compromise. After the scrip played out there was an arrangement made for the conductors to pay the men's board while on the road, out of their cash collections, a receipt being taken from the men who furnished the meals and the conductors turned the receipts in with their report as cash collections. . . .

I was running a mixed train one time when there was but one train each way a day. And the west-bound train had the right of track over the east-bound train, in case the regular place was missed. And the west-bound waited thirty minutes, and five minutes longer for variation of watches. One day when I was going west something got wrong with the engine, and the engineer stopped to fix it and we fell behind the schedule time. After the engineer finished the work on his engine, we went down to a well near by to get a drink of water. The engineer remarked that he had been feeling badly all the morning; he said he felt as if something was going to happen, adding: "I dreamed a dream last night that I dreamed just one year ago last night; and the next day my brother got killed."

We went on and could not make the meeting point for the east-bound train, so we side-tracked and waited our thirty minutes and five minutes for variation in watches, then backed out off the side track, as we had the right to the track, went ahead, but had only gone about half the distance to the station where both trains ought to have met, in case both had been on time, when we met the east-bound train on the main track. All that prevented a collison was both engines just having rounded a curve on to a straight piece of track, and both engines stopped just before they came together. My engineer was as mad as I ever saw. At that time the briers had taken possession of each side of the road up to the outside of the rails, at the place where the engines met. And all the injuries that any of the passengers received, were the ones inflicted by the briers, by which they were scratched when they jumped off the train into them. The conductor of the east-bound train said that the hands of his watch had been caught and he did not know it, and thought he had plenty of time to make the next station. The engineer said that his watch had stopped and he had left the station at a signal from the conductor, thinking the conductor had the right time. The engineer was allowed to run on, and the conductor was stopped off for thirty days, on account of the run which they had made.

Source: James A. Ward, ed. *Southern Railroadman: Conductor N.J. Bell's Recollections of the Civil War Era* (De Kalb: Northern Illinois University Press,1994), 92–103.

Document 14
An Example of a Prospectus to Sell Railroad Bonds to the Public, 1879

Every railroad company that wanted to sell its securities on the American or European market had to bring out a prospectus outlining its financial situation, the reason for issuing new shares or bonds, and the details of the loan in question. These prospectuses were issued in many languages apart from English, depending on the market a company or its financial agents was aiming at. Many were also untrustworthy, giving inflated figures and other untrue statements. The one given here is fairly straightforward and trustworthy.

THE ST. PAUL, MINNEAPOLIS AND MANITOBA RAILWAY COMPANY.
FIRST MORTGAGE 7 PER CENT, SINKING FUND LAND GRANT GOLD BONDS.
$12,000 PER MILE UPON COMPLETED ROAD AND 2,000,000 ACRES OF LAND.
INTEREST PAYABLE JANUARY AND JULY. PRINCIPAL DUE 1909.

The St. Paul, Minneapolis and Manitoba Railway Company has been organized out of the St. Paul and Pacific Railroad Company, the First Division of the St. Paul and Pacific Railroad Company, and the Red River and Manitoba Railroad Company, and now owns and is operating under the charter of the St. Paul and Pacific Railroad Company 565 miles of completed railway, running from St. Paul, Minnesota, and Minneapolis to the boundary line between the United States and the Province of Manitoba, where a connection is made with the Pembina Branch of the Canada Pacific Railroad with Winnipeg, including the railway from Minneapolis via St. Cloud to Alexandria.

The company also owns about 2,000,000 acres of fertile land in alternate sections, on each side of the lines. The country through which the railways pass is well settled, and furnishes a large and rapidly increasing local business, while the through traffic with Manitoba passes wholly over the company's lines. The company is building a line from Alexandria via Fergus Falls, to connect with its main line to Winnipeg, a distance of 90 miles, also 12 miles from Fisher's Landing to Grand Forks, which will be finished by the 1st of November next. This construction completes the system as originally projected. The company will then own 667 miles of completed and fully equipped road. The mortgage under which the above bonds are issued, covers the entire property of the company, (including the 2,000,000 acres of land), at the rate of $12,000 per mile of completed road. The proceeds of sales of land are specially devoted to a Sinking Fund, and are to be applied by the Trustees to the purchase of the bonds at or under 105 per cent, or to the retirement of the bonds by lot at a premium of 5 per cent. There is no prior indebtedness upon the property, except an old mortgage for $120,000 upon 10 miles of the railway, maturing in two years, and one of $366,000 on 80 miles due in 1893, both of which the company is prepared to pay off. The total amount of the bonds provided to be issued is $8,000,000, of which $6,700,000 is now to be issued. The entire issue has been sold by the company, and a limited amount is now offered to the public at 104 per cent, and interest from July 1st, the right being reserved to advance the price at any time.

The net earnings from the operations of these railways for the year ending December 31st, 1878, were $806,000, and for the first four months of 1879, $363,000. The total interest charge upon the entire loan is $560,000.

Purchasers can pay for the bonds on July 1st, from which date the bonds bear interest at 7 per cent, receiving the company's contract to deliver the bonds before September 1st, 1879, with the January 1st, 1880, coupons attached.

J.S. KENNEDY & CO., 63 William Street.
ROOSEVELT & SON, 32 Pine Street.New York, July 1st, 1879.

Source: Amsterdam Stock Exchange/author's collection.

Document 15
On an Emigrant Train across America, 1879

The Scot Robert Louis Stevenson (1850–94), then already becoming known as a novelist, traveled overland on an emigrant train in 1879, partly to see his future wife, whom he had met in France in 1876, in California, and partly for reasons of health, hoping that he could be cured of his chronic bronchial trouble. Some years later he became famous for his novels *Treasure Island* (1883), *The Strange Case of Dr. Jekyll and Mr. Hyde* (1886), and many others. His tale of adventure, pleasure, and suffering on the emigrant train was first published in Edinburgh in 1893 and later reprinted in many editions, at least one of them in America in 1895.

It was about two in the afternoon of Friday that I found myself in front of Emigrant House [opposite Omaha], with more than a hundred others, to be sorted and boxed for the journey. A white-haired official, with a stick under one arm and a list in the other hand, stood apart in front of us, and called name after name in the tone of a command. At each name you would see a family gather up its brats and bundles and run for the hindmost of three cars that stood awaiting us, and I soon concluded that this was to be set apart for the women and children. The second, or central car, it turned out, was devoted to men travelling alone, and the third to the Chinese. . . .

The families once housed, we men carried the second car without ceremony by simultaneous assault. I suppose the reader has some notion of an American railroad car, that long, narrow wooden box, like a flat-roofed Noah's ark, with a stove and a convenience, one at either end, a passage down the middle, and transverse benches upon either hand. Those destined for emigrants on the Union Pacific are only remarkable for their extreme plainness, nothing but wood entering in any part into their construction, and for the usual inefficacy of the lamps, which often went out and shed but a dying glimmer even while they burned. The benches are too short for anything but a young child. Where there is scarce elbow-room for two to sit, there will not be space enough for one to lie. Hence the company, or rather, as it appears from certain bills about the Transfer Station, the company's servants, have conceived a plan for the better accommodation of travellers. They prevail on every two to chum together. To each of the chums they sell a board and three square cushions stuffed with straw, and covered with thin cotton. The benches can be made to face each other in pairs, for the backs are reversible. On the approach of night the boards are laid from bench to bench, making a couch wide enough for two, and long enough for a man of the middle height; and the chums lie down side by side upon the cushions with the head to the conductor's van and the feet to the engine. When the train is full, of course this plan is impossible, for there must not be more than one to every bench, neither can it be carried out unless the chums agree. It was to bring about this last condition that our white-haired official now bestirred himself. He made a most active master of ceremonies, introducing likely couples, and even guaranteeing the amiability and honesty of each. The greater the number of happy couples the better for his pocket, for it was he who sold the raw material of the beds. His price for one board and three straw cushions began with two dollars and a half; but before the train left, and, I am sorry to say, long after I had purchased mine, it had fallen to one dollar and a half. . . .

The rest of the afternoon was spent in making up the train. I am afraid to say how many baggage-waggons followed the engine—certainly a score; then came the Chinese, then we, then the families, and the rear was brought up by the conductor in what, if I have it rightly, is called his caboose. The class to which I belonged was of course the largest, and we ran over, so to speak, to both sides; so that there were Caucasians among the Chinamen, and some bachelors among the families. But our own car was pure from admixture, save for one little boy of eight or nine, who had the whooping-cough. At last, about six, the long train crawled out of the Transfer Station and across the wide Missouri river to Omaha, westward bound. . . .

A great personage on an American train is the newsboy. He sells books (such books!), papers, fruit, lollipops, and cigars; and on emigrant journeys, soap, towels, tin washing-dishes, tin coffee-pitchers, coffee, tea, sugar, and tinned eatables, mostly hash or beans and bacon. . . . There were meals to be had, however, by the wayside; a breakfast in the morning, a dinner somewhere between eleven and two, and supper from five to eight or nine at night. We had rarely less than twenty minutes for each; and if we had not spent many another twenty minutes waiting for some express upon a side track among many miles of desert, we might have taken an hour to each repast and arrived in San Francisco up to time. For haste is not the foible of an emigrant train. It gets through on sufferance, running the gauntlet among its more considerable brethren; should there be a block, it is unhesitatingly sacrificed; and they cannot, in consequence, predict the length of the passage within a day or so. Civility is the main comfort that you miss. Equality, though conceived very largely in America, does not extend so low down as to an emigrant. Thus in all other trains, a warning cry of "All Aboard" recalls the passengers to take their seats; but as soon as I was alone with emigrants, and from the Transfer all the way to San Francisco, I found this ceremony was pretermitted; the train stole from the station without note of warning, and you had to keep an eye upon it even while you ate. The annoyance is considerable, and the disrespect both wanton and petty.

Many conductors, again, will hold no communication with an emigrant. I asked a conductor one day at what time the train would stop for dinner; as he made no answer I repeated the question, with a like result; a third time I returned to the charge, and then Jack-in-office looked me coolly in the face for several seconds and turned ostentatiously away. I believe he was half ashamed of his brutality; for when another person made the same inquiry, although he still refused the information, he condescended to answer, and even to justify his reticence in a voice loud enough for me to hear. It was, he said, his principle not to tell people where they were to dine; for one answer led to many other questions, as what o'clock it was? or, how soon should we be there? and he could not be eternally worried. . . .

It had thundered on the Friday night, but the sun rose on Saturday without a cloud. We were at sea—there is no other adequate expression— on the plains of Nebraska. I made my observatory on the top of a fruit-waggon, and sat by the hour upon that perch to spy about me, and to spy in vain for something new. It was a world almost without a feature; an empty sky, an empty earth; front and back, the line of railway stretched from horizon to horizon, like a cue across a billiard-board; on either hand, the green plain ran till it touched the skirts of heaven. Along the track innumerable wild sunflowers, no bigger than a crown-piece, bloomed in a continuous flower-bed; grazing beasts were seen upon the prairie at all degrees of distance and diminution; and now and again we might perceive a few dots beside the railroad which grew more distinct as we drew nearer till they turned into wooden cabins, and then dwindled and dwindled in our wake until they melted into their surroundings, and we were once more alone upon the billiard-board. The train toiled over this infinity like a snail; and being the one thing moving, it was wonderful what huge proportions it began to assume in our regard. It seemed miles in length, and either end of it within but a step of the horizon. Even my own body or my own head seemed a great thing in that emptiness. I note the feeling the more readily as it is the contrary of what I have read of in the experience of others. Day and night, above the roar of the train, our ears were kept busy with the incessant chirp of grasshoppers—a noise like the winding up of countless clocks and watches, which began after a while to seem proper to that land. . . .

To cross such a plain is to grow homesick for the mountains. I longed for the Black Hills of Wyoming, which I knew we were soon to enter, like an ice-bound whaler for the spring. Alas! and it was a worse country than the other. All Sunday and Monday we travelled through these sad mountains, or over the main ridge of the Rockies, which is a fair match to them for misery of aspect. Hour after hour it was the same unhomely and unkindly world about our onward path; tumbled boulders, cliffs that drearily imitate the shape of monuments and fortifications—how drearily, how tamely, none can tell who has not seen them; not a tree, not a patch of sward, not one shapely or commanding mountain form; sage-brush, eternal sage-brush; over all, the same weariful and gloomy colouring, grays warming into brown, grays darkening towards black; and for the sole sign of life, here and there a few fleeing antelopes; here and there, but at incredible intervals, a creek running in a cañon. The plains have a grandeur of their own; but here there is nothing but a contorted smallness. Except for the air, which was light and stimulating, there was not one good circumstance in that God-forsaken land.

At Ogden we changed cars from the Union Pacific to the Central Pacific line of railroad. The change was double welcome; for first, we had better cars on the new line; and, second, those in which we had been cooped for more than ninety hours had begun to stink abominably. Several yards away, as we returned, let us say from dinner, our nostrils were assailed by rancid air. I have stood on a platform while the whole train was shunting; and as the dwelling-cars drew near, there would come a whiff of pure menagerie, only a little sourer, as from men instead of monkeys. . . . The cars on the Central Pacific were nearly twice as high, and so proportionally airier; they were freshly varnished, which gave us all a sense of cleanliness as though we had bathed; the seats drew out and joined in the centre, so that there was no more need for bed-boards; and there was an upper tier of berths which could be closed by day and opened at night. . . .

From Toano [Nevada] we travelled all day through deserts of alkali and sand, horrible to man, and bare sage-brush country that seemed little kindlier, and came by suppertime to Elko. As we were standing, after our manner, outside the station, I saw two men whip suddenly from underneath the cars, and take to their heels across country. They were tramps, it appeared, who had been riding on the beams since eleven of the night before; and several of my fellow-passengers had already seen and conversed with them while we broke our fast at Toano. These land stowaways play a great part over here in America, and I should have liked dearly to become acquainted with them. . . .

When I awoke next morning, I was puzzled for a while to know if it were day or night, for the illumination was unusual. I sat up at last, and found we were grading slowly downward through a long snowshed; and suddenly we shot into an open; and before we were swallowed into the next length of wooden tunnel, I had one glimpse of a huge pine-forested ravine upon my left, a foaming river, and a sky already coloured with the fires of dawn. I am usually very calm over the displays of nature; but you will scarce believe how my heart leaped at this. It was like meeting one's wife. I had come home again—home from unsightly deserts to the green and habitable corners of the earth. . . .

Source: Robert Louis Stevenson, *The Amateur Emigrant from the Clyde to Sandy Hook* (Edinburgh, 1893, 107–33; republished as *Across the Plains, with other Memories and Essays* [London: Chatto & Windus, 1909]).

Document 16
Letter from the Brooks Locomotive Works Offering a Locomotive, 1879

After the general crisis that had begun in 1873, orders for steam locomotives fell rapidly; many railroads struggled to keep afloat. In the late 1870s, however, orders slowly picked up again, but manufacturers still had trouble selling their accumulated stock. This is a fairly typical letter from one of the leading locomotive works to a railroad company that might be interested. Apparently the builder sent out photographs of finished engines as advertisements for its products.

Dunkirk, N.Y., May 5, 1879.

J.P. Farley, Esq., General Manager St.Paul & Pacific RR,
St. Paul, Minn.

Dear Sir,

When you are in the market for additional locomotives we should
be pleased to submit specification and prices.

We have on our hands for immediate shipment one 14 × 22 shifting
engine, general design shown in photograph of *Elliot*, driving wheels 4 ft.
diam., weight 25 tons, an eight-wheel tender with a 1200 gallon "cut away"
tank, steel boiler, steel firebox, steel crossheads, built in our very best manner. Also nearly completed one 16 × 24 52-ton locomotive, general design
of the *J.E. Childs*, 5 ft. drivers, boiler of same material as the shifting engine.

If you are not in want of any engines at present, we solicite your
correspondence when you are.

Truly Yours,
M.L. Hinman, treasurer and secretary.

Source: James J. Hill Papers, James J. Hill Reference Library, St. Paul, Minn.

Document 17
Comparison of Several Reorganization Plans for a Bankrupt Railroad Company, 1890

The Missouri, Kansas & Texas Railway Company, or "Katy" for
short, was a firm with a good deal of foreign, chiefly Dutch and
English, funding in its capital structure. It had been incorporated
in 1865 as the Union Pacific, Southern Branch; changed its name
to the Missouri, Kansas & Texas Railway in 1869; was in receivership by 1874; was reorganized under ownership of Jay Gould
and went bankrupt again in 1888. Protective committees were
organized in Amsterdam and London, and each designed a plan
for reorganization, but with no results. Finally a combined Ameri-
can-English-Dutch group, known as the Olcott Committee, managed to reorganize the company successfully. New, lower-renting
securities were issued in exchange for old bonds; under all three
plans described below, bondholders lost some of their investment,
shareholders even more. The final Olcott plan differed from the
Olcott-Hoyt plan given here. The complicated figures given here
are a good example of the nature of such a reorganization,
wherein conflicting interests had to be reconciled. It should be
borne in mind that income bonds and common stock were of

doubtful value, as they paid interest or dividends only after all
other securities.

A: DISTRIBUTION.
Each 7% first consolidated mortgage $1000 of old company will be con-
verted into:
Amsterdam plan:
   $1163 in 4½% prior lien bonds + $300 in 5% preferred stock.
King-Adams (English) plan:
   $1000 in 5% first mortgage bonds + $400 in 5% second mortgage
   income bonds + $100 in cash.
Olcott-Hoyt plan:
   $1000 in 5% divisional first mortgage bonds (Northern Div.) + $35
   in cash + $35 in 4% divisional first mortgage bonds (Texas Div.) +
   $140 in 5% preferred stock.

Each old 6% Southern Branch bond of $1000 will be converted into:
Amsterdam plan:
   $1145 in 4½% prior lien bonds + $150 in 5% preferred stock.
King-Adams Plan:
   No details given.
Olcott-Hoyt plan:
   $1000 in 5% divisional first mortgage bonds (Northern Div.).

Each $1000 6% general consolidated mortgage bond will be converted into:
Amsterdam plan:
   $500 in 4½% first consolidated mortgage + $700 in 4½% second
   mortgage income bonds + $300 in 5% preferred stock.
King-Adams plan:
   $500 in 4% first mortgage bonds + $800 5% second mortgage income bonds + $50 cash.
Olcott-Hoyt plan:
   $1000 in 4% divisional first mortgage bonds (Texas Div.) + $170 in
   5% preferred stock.

Each $1000 5% general consolidated mortgage bond will be converted into:
Amsterdam plan:
   $500 in 4½% first consolidated mortgage + $625 in 4½% second
   mortgage income bonds + $150 common stock.

King-Adams plan:
> $500 in 4% first mortgage bonds + $600 in 5% second mortgage income bonds + $30 cash.

Olcott-Hoyt plan:
> $900 in 4% divisional first mortgage (Texas Div.) + $125 in 5% preferred stock.

Stockholders will receive new common stock after payment of respectively 10, 10 and 7½% assessment.

B. CAPITALIZATION.

Amsterdam plan:

4½% prior lien bonds,	$21,000,000
4½% first consolidated mortgage	$14,000,000
4½% second mortgage income bonds	$17,000,000
5% preferred stock	$17,000,000
common stock	$47,000,000

King-Adams plan:

5% first mortgage bonds	$18,000,000
4% first mortgage bonds	$14,000,000
5% second mortgage income bonds	$32,000,000
common stock	$47,000,000

Olcott-Hoyt plan:

5% first mortgage (Northern Div.)	$18,000,000
4% first mortgage (Texas Div.)	$28,000,000
5% preferred stock	$10,000,000
common stock	$47,000,000

C. FIXED CHARGES.

Amsterdam plan:

prior lien	$945,000
first consolidated	$630,000

King-Adams plan:

5% first mortgage	$900,000
4% first mortgage	$560,000

Olcott-Hoyt plan:

5% first mortgage (Northern Div.)	$900,000
4% first mortgage (Texas Div.)	$1,120,000

NB The fixed charges, the interest to be paid by the company on the first mortgage and consolidated mortgage loans would be $1,575,000 for the Amsterdam plan; $1,400,000 for the King-Adams plan; and $2,020,000 for the Olcott-Hoyt plan. Interest on second mortgage bonds to be paid only after all other liabilities have been paid, dividend on preferred stock only if earned, dividend on common stock only to be paid when anything is left after payment of all other liabilities.

D. CONTROL.

Amsterdam plan:

By voting trustees in interest of income bonds, until interest earned.

King-Adams plan:

By Union Trust Company, details not given.

Olcott-Hoyt plan:

By Colgate-Hoyt Committee for three years.

Source: Amsterdam Stock Exchange, author's collection.

Document 18
Rules for Employees of a Railroad Company, 1893

Labor for railroad companies was always strongly regulated. Lower-level employees especially had to comply with strict regulations and in case of disobedience faced severe disciplinary measures or immediate dismissal without recourse to mediation. The extracts from the Rules and Regulations of the Chicago & North-Western Railway of 1893 as given here are fairly typical of the period. It will be noted that these instructions are rather one-sided, outlining only the duties of the employees, not their rights or the responsibilities of the railroad company toward its workers.

General Instructions.

1. The Rules herein set forth supersede all prior rules and instructions, in whatsoever form issued, which are consistent therewith. . . .

4. Every employe[!] of this Company whose duties are in any way prescribed by these rules must always have a copy of them at hand when on duty, and must be conversant with every rule. He must render all the assistance in his power in carrying them out, and immediately report any infringement of them to the head of his department.

5. Disobedience of orders, or violation of rules, will be sufficient cause for immediate dismissal from the service of the Company;

but suspension from duty may be substituted, at the discretion of the proper officer.

6. If any one is in doubt as to the meaning of any rule, or special order, application must be made at once to proper authority, for an explanation. Ignorance cannot be accepted as an excuse for neglect or omission of duty.

7. Each person in the employ of the Company is to devote himself exclusively to its service, and is not to engage in any other business, except on permission from the General Superintendent. Employes who are liable to be called upon for duty at any time must keep the proper officer fully advised of any change in residence.

8. Employes must be civil and obliging to all with whom they are brought in contact, especially in their relations with passengers and the public. Answer questions politely and endeavor to give satisfactory information. No violent disputes or altercations will be permitted under any circumstances.

9. All employes will be on the constant lookout to protect the interests of the Company, and to this end will report at once anything coming under their notice detrimental to its best interests; give full particulars in writing of all cases of damage to persons or property, or any negligence or misconduct on the part of other employes.

10. No person, whatever his rank, will be allowed to absent himself from duty without permission from the head of the department in which he is engaged. . . .

12. Intoxication, or even the occasional use of of intoxicating liquors, on the part of the employes, will be sufficient reason for dismissal.

13. An employe discharged from any department shall not be employed in any other, without the consent of the head of the department from which he was discharged.

14. Minors must not be employed in the train service.

15. Employes must wear the prescribed badges or uniforms while on duty.

16. Every precaution must be taken to prevent loss or damage by fire. No rubbish, oily waste, rags, or waste paper must be allowed

to accumulate in the offices, depots or buildings of the Company. Matches, oil and lamps shall be kept separate and in secure and safe places. Chimneys, pipes and stoves must be known to be safe and secure, and for that purpose examined frequently.

17. Yardmen, trainmen, and other employes, are directed to communicate with the Superintendent of the Division at once, if they are aware of any defects in the track, bridges, culverts, platforms, etc., whereby an accident might happen.

18. Employes are strictly forbidden to make charge for, or receive any fee or reward for service performed in the line of duty.

19. All communications of importance, especially those concerning the safety of trains, track or bridges, shall always be made in writing, except where it is absolutely impossible to do so.

20. The use of the telegraph must be restricted to actual necessity and only resorted to in matters of importance, and where an immediate answer is necessary.

21. Employes will be held responsible for the prudent and economical use of all supplies and material furnished them. Order, cleanliness and economy are enjoined upon all in the care and use of the property, tools, material, etc., entrusted to them.

22. Mail agents, express messengers, parlor and sleeping car conductors and porters, news agents, and persons in charge of individual cars, are subject while on duty to the rules governing employes of the Company.

Source: Chicago & North Western Railway, Rules and Regulations for the Government of Employes of the Operating Department, 1893. Collection of H. Roger Grant.

Document 19
A Secret Agreement between Railroad Leaders and Bankers about the Reorganization of the Northern Pacific Railroad, 1896

During the later years of the nineteenth century, American bankers, led by J. Pierpont Morgan, and railroad tycoons came together in an attempt to avoid wasteful competition, by establishing spheres of influence of competing railroads. Many of these agreements were unknown to the general public, the common stockholders, or the government agencies. When they became known, the press raised an outcry that in time led to more regulation and control. This document is typical of many such secret deals.

MEMORANDUM OF A CONFERENCE held in London on the 2nd of April, 1896, between

Mr. J. PIERPONT MORGAN, representing his own interests and those of his firm, MESSRS. J.P. MORGAN & CO., New York.

LORD MOUNT STEPHEN and MR. JAMES J. HILL on their own behalf and representing the interest of the Great Northern Railway and its stockholders.

MR. ARTHUR GWINNER representing the interests of the Deutsche Bank, Berlin, whereof he is one of the directors.

I.

The so-called London Agreement having been found impracticable has been abrogated, and it has been decided that the Northern Pacific Railroad Company shall be re-organized independently of the Great Northern Railway or any other company or interest. Mr. Hill and Lord Mount Stephen will do all in their power to further this object; Mr. Hill will discourage Northern Pacific Branch Line Bondholders who might approach him with a desire to create a competition, thereby forcing the Northern Pacific to allow higher prices or better conditions to these branch roads.

II.

The Great Northern Railway Company and the re-organized Northern Pacific Railroad Company shall form a permanent alliance, defensive, and in case of need offensive, with a view of avoiding competition and aggressive policy and of generally protecting the common interests of both companies.

The four parties hereto subscribing promise to use their best endeavors towards the loyal fulfilment of this purpose of friendly and harmonious working of the two systems, with insistence of good faith on the part of the operating officials in maintaining rules and rates fixed by the respective superior officials and Boards of Directors.

III.

All competitive business, such as for instance the transports for account of the Anaconda Copper Company, shall be divided upon equitable terms between both companies. Tariff wars and rate cutting shall be absolutely avoided. Neither party shall in future ingress into the other's territory by new construction or purchase or acquiring of control of existing lines.

IV.

The parties hereto subscribing agree to procure, as far as may be in their power, to maintain the Oregon Railway and Navigation Company and its reorganized successor company as an independent corporation keeping good and equitable relations with the Great Northern, Northern Pacific and other neighbouring companies. The object of the Great Northern and Northern Pacific Companies shall be simply to prevent others securing control of the O.R.& N. Co., and to maintain rates on and by the same, permitting the Union Pacific, Quincy, or any other company to use the O.R.& N. Company lines upon fair and equal terms.

V.

Mr. J.P. Morgan and Mr. Gwinner will arrange to offer Lord Mount Stephen and Mr. Hill jointly to purchase such common stock and preferred stock of the re-organized Northern Pacific Company as may become the property of the Northern Pacific Syndicate and may be available for sale, pursuant to the provision of article 13 of the Syndicate agreement. Such stock shall be offered before distribution to Syndicate members or being otherwise disposed of to Lord Mount Stephen and Mr. Hill jointly, but only upon terms which shall be at least as beneficial to the Syndicate as any terms at the time offered by any other party.

VI.

Lord Mount Stephen and Mr. Hill hereby jointly instruct Messrs. J.P. Morgan and Company and the Deutsche Bank to purchase for their account N.P. securities to a total maximum cost of three million dollars.

$ . . . Northern Pacific Consolidated Mortgage Bonds at not exceeding $55. per cent.

$ . . . Northern Pacific Railroad Preferred Stock at not exceeding $15. per cent.

$ . . . Northern Pacific Railroad Common Stock at not exceeding $3. per cent.

This order shall be in force until cancelled in writing. Messrs. J.P. Morgan and the Deutsche Bank promise to use their best endeavors towards the most favorable execution of these purchases which are entrusted as far as the Consols are concerned to the Deutsche Bank, Berlin, and as far as the stock is concerned to Messrs. Morgan.

Messrs. Morgan shall give due advice to Mr. Hill and the Deutsche Bank shall give due advice for account of Lord Mount Stephen and Mr. Hill to Messrs. J.P. Morgan & Co. of New York, of all purchases made and the bankers shall debit the respective accounts with the cost of such purchases together with all brokerage and outlay for expenses, plus a commission of half per cent. on the nominal amount of the securities purchased. Mr. Hill and Lord Mount Stephen unless otherwise to be agreed upon, will for the securities thus bought, pay one week after the same shall be placed at their disposal respectively.

The Deutsche Bank will return to Messrs. Morgan two-thirds of the commission it receives and Messrs. Morgan will return to the Deutsche Bank one-third of their commission.

VII.

Messrs. J.P. Morgan & Company and the Deutsche Bank will purchase for their own respective accounts, and at their discretion Northern Pacific Consols, old Preferred or old Common Stock to the aggregate outlay of dollars five hundred thousand each party. Until the time when Messrs. Morgan or the Deutsche Bank shall desire to sell or otherwise dispose of the securities thus acquired, Mr. Hill and Lord Mount Stephen shall have the option jointly to purchase from Messrs. Morgan and the Deutsche Bank, respectively, these bonds and stocks, and this at an advance of ten dollars per cent on the nominal amounts of the bonds and stocks respectively. Until this option is made use of or shall have lapsed Lord Mount Stephen and Mr. Hill shall have the right of vote on the securities purchased by Messrs. Morgan and the Deutsche Bank for their own accounts.

VIII.

During the five years following the termination of the voting trust provided for in the plan of re-organization of the Northern Pacific Railway Co. of 16th March, 1896, Messrs. J.P. Morgan & Co. and the Deutsche Bank agree to exercise their rerspective vote or any proxies they may control, in favour of so many candidates to the Board of Directors of the re-organized N.P.Co. as shall be proposed to them by Lord Mount Stephen and Mr. Hill jointly and be proportionate to the holding of Northern Pacific Stock by the Great Northern parties as shown from time to time, provided always that in the judgment of both Messrs. Morgan and of the Deutsche Bank the Great Northern Company and parties shall continue to use their best endeavors towards the permanent prosperity of the re-organized Northern Pacific Company.

During the same time and in the same manner Lord Mount Stephen and Mr. Hill will exercise their respective vote or any proxies they may control of stock of the re-organized Northern Pacific Company in favour of such candidates to its Board of Directors as may be proposed to them by Messrs. J.P. Morgan & Co. and the Deutsche Bank jointly and of a number of candidates proportionate to the holding of Northern Pacific Stock represented by Messrs. Morgan and the Deutsche Bank from time to time.

THIS MEMORANDUM OF AGREEMENT has been executed and signed in four copies and delivered to the parties here respectively, who mutually bind themselves to its loyal execution in good faith and agree not to make known any part of it without the express consent of all the four parties.

[Signed] J. Pierpont Morgan
Mount Stephen
Jas. J. Hill
Arthur Gwinner.

Source: James J. Hill Papers, Northern Pacific Reorganization, James Jerome Hill Reference Library, St. Paul, Minnesota.

Document 20
American Hoboes, 1898

The hobo was a typical American phenomenon. Tramps roamed the country in the nineteenth and twentieth centuries and used the railroad for free rides. Some were in search of work, especially in the harvesting season; others were just tramping around without clear destinations. They rode freight trains, in empty boxcars, or "rode the rods," assuming a most uncomfortable and dangerous position clinging to the underframe of a car. A distinct camaraderie between hoboes developed over the years, warning colleagues against railroad "bulls," railroad policemen, who regularly tried to chase them off. Irregular hobo camps near railroad yards were established; there a certain code of honor was observed by the real hoboes, information was exchanged, and food was

shared. Few of the hoboes left written testimonies to their way of
life, but here is a memoir produced late in life by one who did—
Charles P. Brown, better educated than average.

Now the little town of Fargo is located in the Redriver Valley on the
west bank of the Redriver, and the Redriver Valley in North Dakota and
Minnesota is known to be one of the greatest wheat growing districts in
the world, and there were hundreds of men flocking into Fargo, for this
was the distributing point for the great wheat fields, and boy, I never saw
so much growing wheat before nor since.

Well as near as I can remember, it was around about the third or
fourth of August, 1898, when Pat and I reached Fargo, and the wheat was
a little too green to cut as yet, so the farmers were not taking on any help
just then, and the outcome of it was, there was a small army of hobo wheat
harvest hands waiting for the big work to start, and the most of them were
living just outside of the town in hobo camps along the river banks. Now
in the slang of the hobo, these camps are known as the jungles, and you
will always find them located where the men can get fire-wood and water.

Now as Pat and I had taken up with two other boys, we all four went
out into the jungles and made us a camp, and we each one would throw
in some money and make up a jackpot, then a couple of us would go into
town and buy some groceries, and bring them back to the jungles and cook
a big can of mulligan-stew, for we done all of our cooking and eating in
the jungles. We only eat two meals a day, but oh boy, they sure did taste
good. No doubt you wonder what we used for cooking utensils in the
jungles. Well in all hobo jungle camps, there is all sorts of tin cans, ranging from the well known tomato can, up to the big five gallon square oil
cans, and the hoboes cut the tops out of these different cans, and use them
to cook with, and they also use the big oil cans to boil up with (boil and
wash their clothes). We used to take one of the big square cans and cut it
off about two inches from the bottom and use it (that is the bottom part)
to fry bacon and eggs and potatoes in, just like a skillet or frying pan, and
we would use the one gallon fruit cans to boil food in, and the small
tomato cans to drink our coffee out of.

Now after a guy has bummed around over the country long enough
to get wise to himself, after he cooks a meal in a jungle camp, he will always wash up the cans and frying pans that he has used and leave them
in good order for the next fellow, for that is the code of the hoboes in the
jungles, specially among the old time hoboes.

And you can always tell when a gay cat has been in camp, for he leaves the cans all dirty and scattered every which way. (A gay cat is a green horn who has not hoboed long enough yet, to get wise to the ways of the road.) And if one of these guys comes around where some old seasoned hoboes are cooking up a feed, the old timers will all begin to hiss, and holler scat, for they can tell by his looks and actions that he is a gay cat, and they don't want him around, but some times on the other hand if they are a gang of professional yeggs [thieves], they might invite the gay cat to have some feed with them, for in many cases they can use a green horn in their business as a lookout, or a stool-pigeon to bring them information as to the lay of the store, post office, or any other place in a small town that they have planned on robbing.

There is a big difference between the working stiff that lives in the jungles, and hoboes around over the country, beating his way from place to place while looking for work, and the regular professional hobo yegg, that won't work at all, but lives by plying his trade as a thief and a robber.

He and his brother yeggs will lay around in the jungles outside of a small town or city, while they scheme and plan to rob some postoffice, or crack the safe in some store or small bank, and railroad men in the train service soon became able to tell the difference between the two classes, for the hobo working man in most cases is very frank, and will talk and answer questions, for he has nothing to conceal, while on the other hand, the hobo yegg is a hard-boiled, surly cuss that keeps his trap shut, and you will most always find him keeping off to himself when riding in a boxcar where there are other hoboes, for he does not care to mix with anybody except his own kind.

Well, to get back to my story, as I said before, we four boys done our cooking and eating in the jungles, for the days were hot, but the nights were pretty cool, so instead of sleeping by camp fires in the jungles, like many other hoboes did, we would go out into the Northern Pacific train yards where they had many boxcars stored, waiting to be used in the wheat rush, and sleep in a boxcar on a bed of straw that we would fix up for ourselves.

We would take off our shoes and coats, and spread the coats over the upper part of our bodies, covering up our chests, shoulders and head, so that our warm breath would keep us warm, for that is the best way to keep warm when you have only got your coat to cover yourself with.

Well, after we had laid around Fargo for about a week, we four boys made up our minds to beat it up to Grand Forks, N.D., which was the next division point north of Fargo on a branch line of the Great Northern.

Now I will explain at this time that the railroads up in that part of the country at this season of the year are in the same fix as the farmers, for they have to hire the floating element of railroad men (known as boomers) to help handle and move their trains during the big wheat rush, just the same as the farmers have to hire the floating hobo working men known as stiffs, to help them harvest the wheat.

Now these boomer railroad men (sometimes called boomer rails) go up into that part of the country to make a stake while the wheat rush is on, for they go jumping around over the country working first for one railroad and then another whenever business is good, and many of them are kept on the go for they have violated rule "G" so often that they in many cases have got such bum records that they have to work under a flag and phoney references. (Rule "G" in the book of rules, says that a man cannot, and must not use intoxicating liquors. And working under a flag, with phoney references, means that a boomer is working under another name, and has sprung false service letters on the railroad officials.) But when business is good and the railroads have a rush of some kind and their yards are blocked and they need experienced men to move their trains, they will forget all about the boomers bad faults and will almost give him a French kiss on both cheeks until the rush is over for they know that these men are all around railroad men, and can hit the ball and play the game wherever they put them, but just as soon as the rush is over and they do not need them any longer, they start cutting the board and laying them off, and just because they have to go chasing around over the country looking for another job, the companies blame them for being boomers. I will never be able to understand why railroad companies always hate a boomer like a rattlesnake when business is slack and they don't need them, but this is well known fact in the railroad world.

Well, to get back to my story, there were many boomers come up to this part of the country, to make a stake through the wheat rush, and by picking up bo money from the harvest hands that rode their trains, and as they was out after all the jack that they could get, they sure was hostile, and it was dig up or hit the grit.

Now us boys had made it up among ourselves, that if the train crews were hostile, and chased us off, that instead of us all trying to stick together we would each and every one look out for himself, and if we did get separated we would go on and wait for each other in Grand Forks.

So one night we grabbed a train of empty boxcars headed north on the G.N. but the shacks were trying to keep everybody off that did not come across with a piece of change, and I got separated from the rest of the boys, but as I figured that they were on the train some place, I stayed on thinking that I would meet them somewhere further up the line, so I rode out about thirty miles from Fargo to a storage yard at a little place called Alton Junction, where the crew set their train out, and then returned to Fargo light (with just the engine and caboose).

And as it was just breaking day, I went over to the jungles and waited there for the rest of the boys, but after laying there all day and they did not show up, I figured it out to myself that they had not made it out of Fargo, as I had done. So that evening I grabbed a southbound train and beat it back to Fargo, and the next day while I was looking for them, I met some fellows that we had talked with a few days before, and one of them told me that he was pretty sure that he saw them in one of the Employment offices the day before where they were shipping men out to Montana, on a railroad grading job for the N.P. railroad...

Source: H. Roger Grant, ed., *Brownie the Boomer: The Life of Charles P. Brown, an American Railroader* (De Kalb: Northern Illinois University Press, 1991), pp. 20–24. Used with permission.

Document 21
Railroad Excursions Offered by the Phillips-Judson Company, 1898

By the end of the nineteenth century, several companies had organized conducted excursions to Colorado and the West Coast for travelers who wanted to avoid the bother of procuring tickets, hotel accommodations, meals, and such themselves. The A. Phillips & Co. (founded 1880) and the Judson & Co. Personally Conducted Overland Excursions (1889) joined forces in 1898 under the name of Phillips-Judson Consolidated Overland Excursions and offered a choice of excursions by train to the natural wonders of the West.

Our Route.

We leave Chicago every Thursday at 6.00 P.M. from the Union Passenger Station, via Chicago & Alton R.R., passing through Joliet, Bloomington, and cross the Mississippi River at Louisiana, arriving at Kansas City Friday morning. After breakfast, we resume our journey, leaving Kansas City at 10.00 A.M. via Missouri Pacific R.R., and the day is spent in traveling through the finest fruit and farming lands in the State of Kansas. Saturday morning we reach Pueblo; having had breakfast, there is time for a stroll through the active little city before again resuming our journey. At 12.45 noon, we leave Pueblo on the World-Renowned Scenic Line of the Denver & Rio Grande. Passing Canon City we see to the right the State Penitentiary of Colorado, and the convicts at work in the quarries, and then in a few minutes we are in the Royal Gorge, one of the most wonderful works of nature: Imagine a narrow chasm only 60 feet wide, the Arkansas River rushing madly alongside the railway embankment, and the crags towering aloft 2,500 feet above you.

After several hours spent in passing through the most delightful scenery, we arrive at Leadville, famous for its mines, and for being the highest city in the world; being 10,218 feet above sea level. Leaving Leadville we go over the Tennessee Pass, through the Grand Canon, and reach Glenwood Springs, noted for its fine hotel, and Hot Springs, of great curative powers; darkness overtakes us, and we can very safely make the promise that the day just passed will be ever looked back to by the passengers with the very greatest pleasure. Arriving at Grand Junction at midnight, we leave there on the scenic line of the Rio Grande Western R.R., and shortly pass the Colorado State line and are in Utah. Sunday forenoon is spent in passing through scenery equal to the day before, the town of Provo, and through the valley of the Jordan, till we finally approach the famous and beautiful city of Salt Lake, where we see the great Mormon temple. Arriving at Ogden, the terminus of the Rio Grande Western R.R., at 1.30 P.M., Mountain Time, we leave at 1.10 P.M., Pacific Time, by Southern Pacific line, and the last stage of the journey is commenced. We shortly have a magnificent view of the Great Salt Lake. Fifty two miles west of Ogden we come to Promontory, noted for being the junction point of the Southern Pacific and Union Pacific railroads in 1869, thus enabling the passenger to make the overland journey by rail instead of by wagon, as in the days of the "forty-niners." Monday morning finds us at Reno, a mining town, and during the day most interesting views may be had of the Humboldt River and the Nevada Canon.

Arriving at Sacramento, passengers whose destination is on the Mt. Shasta Route of the Southern Pacific, such as Red Bluff, Marysville, or

Portland, Ore., and Oregon and Washington points, have to change cars—from there having a through Pullman Tourist Sleeping Car to destination. Monday night our San Francisco passengers arrive at their destination.

Those of our passengers destined to Southern California points leave Sacramento at 5.15 P.M., and pass through the great San Joaquin Valley, the vineyard of California, whose length from North to South is 250 miles and is sixty wide. We arrive at Los Angeles on Tuesday afternoon at 1.20 P.M., having made one of the most interesting and enjoyable trips it is possible to make to the Pacific Coast. Those in our parties going farther than Los Angeles receive every possible assistance from our manager in starting for their respective destinations. . . .

Tourist Cars.
The Tourist Cars used with our personally conducted parties are built by Pullman Co., specially for our use, and are in all respects superior to the Tourist Cars usually run on other lines. They have upholstered spring seats and backs, and the toilet arrangements are much improved. They are furnished with regular Pullman equipment of hair mattresses, curtains, tables, carpets, blankets, sheets, pillows, pillow-slips, and all necessary toilet articles. A colored porter will be in attendance with each car. Through cars are run without change from Chicago to San Francisco and Los Angeles, thus saving our passengers from having the annoyance of changing cars and hand-baggage en route.

Baggage.
Can be checked through from starting point to any Pacific Coast point to which tickets can be purchased. One hundred and fifty pounds of baggage checked free on each full ticket, and seventy-five pounds will be checked on each half ticket. Excess baggage will be charged for at regular rates, which will be collected by the road issuing through baggage cheks. We assist our patrons in checking baggage, etc., and handle and transfer all hand-baggage when changing cars.

Sleeping Car Rates.
A completely furnished double berth in a tourist sleeping car from Chicago, Bloomington, or St. Louis to California costs only $6.00, and from Kansas City only $5.00, or $9.50 less than the same accommodations in a Palace Sleeper. Each double berth will accommodate two persons without extra sleeper charge; but passengers desiring the exclusive use of a

berth can obtain it for the price named. Charges for berths are uniform via all lines. There is no free sleeping car service to California over any route. . . .

Management.

Our managers go through from the Atlantic to the Pacific Coast with each party, attending to the wants of the passengers, and will be assisted by experienced and accommodating colored porters, whose duties are to wait upon and assist members of the party. We have the exclusive use of all cars occupied by our passengers, and ample room is provided for all who accompany our parties. We leave Chicago with our west-bound parties, from Chicago & Alton R.R. Depot, corner of Canal and Adams streets, and Bloomington, St. Louis and Kansas City from the Union depots of those cities. . . .

Passengers with our parties will not be put to the inconvenience of being disturbed at night, by conductors requiring to be shown tickets. Our managers will take charge of all tickets, and conductors look to them for the tickets for the party.

Meals.

We stop en route at first-class eating houses. Our passengers are afforded the same privileges as the occupants of Pullman Palace Sleeping Cars or other first-class cars, in the matter of meals at Dining Halls or in Dining Cars en route. Lunch counters are at every eating-station, where tea, coffee, etc., can be obtained, and other small wants supplied. We recommend passengers to provide themselves with lunch baskets with drop handles, so as to go under the seats.

Source: Brochure of Phillips-Judson Consolidated Excursions, 1898. Collection of H. Roger Grant.

Document 22
A Railroad Wreck in Popular Music, 1903

Railroad wrecks always held a kind of morbid attention for the press and the public. Ghoulish descriptions were printed and the horrors of a wreck exaggerated to almost unbelievable proportions. When Southern Railway's mail train No. 97 derailed at high speed on Stillhouse Trestle, just of north of Danville, Virginia, on September 27, 1903, it was nothing out of the ordinary. The engineer, fireman, conductor, and several postal clerks were killed, but the train had not been carrying passengers. Yet for some reason this wreck caught the public fancy and was immortalized in a song.

"Wreck of the Old 97"

September 27, 1903, Danville, Virginia

On a cold frosty morning in the month of September
When the clouds were hanging low,
Ninety-seven pulled out of Washington station
Like an arrow shot from a bow.

Old Ninety-seven was the fastest mail train
That was ever on the Southern line,
But when she got to Monroe, Virginia
She was forty-seven minutes behind.

They handed him his orders at Monroe, Virginia,
Saying "Steve, you're way behind time.
This is not thirty eight, but it's Old 97
You must put her in Spencer on time."

Steve Broady said to his black greasy fireman,
"Just shovel in a little more coal,
And when we cross the White Oak Mountain
You can watch Old 97 roll."

It's a mighty rough road from Lynchburg to Danville
And the line's on a three mile grade.
It was on that grade that he lost his airbrakes
And you see what a jump he made.

He was going downhill at ninety miles an hour
When the whistle broke into a scream.
He was found in the wreck with his hand on the throttle
And scalded to death by the steam.

Now ladies you must all take fair warning
From this time ever more.
Never speak harsh words to your true loving husbands
They may leave you and never return.

Source: Public domain, repr. Katie L. Lyle, *Scalded to Death by the Steam*, 27.

Document 23
Letters from Banker Jacob H. Schiff to
President Theodore Roosevelt, 1907

During the early years of the twentieth century the railroad industry came under ever closer scrutiny by the government. All abuses and shady practices had been exposed; the law originally establishing the Interstate Commerce Commission had been largely an empty gesture, but the public, led by the press, clamored for legislation that would effectually end the railroad monopoly. Bankers and railroad leaders opposed this trend but to little avail; the Hepburn Act of 1907 did indeed greatly enlarge the powers of the ICC. President Theodore Roosevelt was no friend of monopoly or big business, and his attorney general, Philander Knox, was even less so. Banker Jacob H. Schiff, known as a moderate man in the business world, tried in vain to convince Roosevelt that more restrictions of the railroad industry would lead to disaster. But his emphasis on the word "confidence" in the following letters reveals the center of the problem: there was no confidence left between the railroads and the public. By 1907 the railroad industry had gone too far in abusing its position of monopoly.

March 24, 1907.

Dear Mr. President,

When about a month ago I had the honor of an interview with you, you said to me, "Mr. Schiff, I have nothing to avenge, but I wish to make certain that we are protected in the future against the abuses of the past." In this every good citizen should agree with you and uphold you, and it appears to me the time has come to act upon what you have said to me. We are dealing no longer with a theory but with a condition. Events have traveled fast. We are confronted by a situation not only serious, but which, unless promptly taken in hand and prudently treated, is certain to bring great suffering upon the country. Confidence in values has become thoroughly shaken; there is absolutely no sale for securities, even of the most approved character, either at home or abroad; and unless the distrust, which has grown so intense of late, can speedily be removed, all work of railway improvement and new construction—of which there is so much required—will before long have to cease. The effect of this will be far-reaching and will be felt in the activities of the entire country. I am neither an alarmist nor a pessimist, but I can readily see whither we are rapidly drifting.

There can be little doubt that whatever railway legislation the Administration may ask from the next Congress will be granted. In fact, with the passions which have been aroused, it is not at all unlikely that Congress will go farther than you would probably wish it to go, and laws may be placed on the statute book, the enactment of which will later on be regretted. It is not the money situation, which is likely to right itself before long, but the uncertainty as to what may be the final outcome of the present agitation which is at the bottom of the growing distrust. To permit this situation to continue until after the meeting of Congress next winter, and to further grow in intensity, as it no doubt will, will be certain to bring about intolerable conditions. A public statement on your part, such as is said to have been suggested, may, to some extent, quiet the troubled waters, but—if I may be permitted to say so—its effect will not be far-reaching.

There is, as far as my judgment goes, only one remedy which will cure the situation in which we find ourselves: the prompt coming together of the railroads and the people, in a mutual endeavor to right what has been wrong, to remedy what needs to be cured. This can only be done through the initiative of the Administration. As matters have shaped themselves, there can be little doubt that the railroads will be found eager in the desire to support any reasonable legislation tending to remedy the shortcomings and abuses which have been laid bare, and providing such further safeguards as may suggest themselves.

I am convinced that if it be practicable, on your part, to bring together a committee representative of the railroad interests and the Interstate Commerce Commission, with a view to work out the details of legislative measures, such as shall commend themselves to your Administration, with the purpose that these be presented to the next Congress, with the committee's endorsement, a relationship can be established between the people on the one hand and the railroads on the other, such as has never before existed; and that the very effort to accomplish this will speedily restore confidence and dispel the clouds which are now gathering in so threatening a manner. If what I have suggested can be carried into effect through your initiative, it will prove constructive statesmanship of the highest order, which, I repeat, will save the country much suffering.

Trusting that this may have your consideration, I am, with expressions of high respect,

Yours most faithfully,
Jacob H. Schiff.

March 28, 1907.

Dear Mr. President,

You have been good enough to write me fully in reply to my letter to you of the 24th inst., and this I deeply appreciate. I also thank you for sending me copy of your last annual message to Congress, calling my attention to certain utterances this contains, and while I have again read it, I also wish to assure you again, as I have had the opportunity to do before this, that personally I not only know, but thoroughly understand, the sincerity and propriety of your position. Perhaps you will remember that I have only recently taken the opportunity to say personally to you—and I do not wish to recall of this a single iota—that I feel that the next generation will be better and happier because of your having been President, but that I also feared that the present generation would have yet to go through much suffering because of your stern and uncompromising attitude in important questions, and because of the manner in which changes in economic conditions, which in your opinion had become necessary, are forced upon the country and upon the interests involved.

Five years ago—after you had ordered suit to be brought for the dissolution of the Northern Securities Company—you did me the honor to discuss with me the attitude you had taken, and permitted me to present to you and Attorney General Knox my own views upon the situation which had been created. Perhaps you will recall that, among other things, I then said that it appeared to me we were entering upon a thorny path, which would finally lead to radicalism becoming rampant. I cannot now but feel that we are rapidly drifting towards such a condition. A more careful and prudent treatment of the difficult economic problems, which, five years ago or longer, you had rightly discerned needed solution, would have made possible for a long time the preservation of the material prosperity of the country, the proper maintenance of which is after all the real basis of the happiness of the people.

It is unfortunately human nature that the majority of the people will rather get things for nothing than pay adequate and proper value, and while I thoroughly understand that to support this is entirely foreign to you, the multitude today believes that it is right on their part to demand corporation service at such remuneration as the people alone shall dictate. At this time we are before two paths both terminating at the point it is desired to reach. The one is a short cut, but it leads across rocks and abysses, and if taken, we shall have to suffer and be exhausted before or when we reach our destination. The other path may be somewhat longer, but it avoids the rough places; it gives opportunities for rest on the way, and while it will bring us to the destination we seek somewhat later, we shall arrive there without much suffering and shall be ready to march on without having ultimately to rest or recover from the exhaustion which we would have experienced had we chosen the short cut.

Need I explain, Mr. President, the simile? Certainly the theories and practices which are wrong in the railroad business should be corrected as speedily as is practicable—certainly the abuses which have crept in should be made to cease. But must and can the far-reaching changes which need be made in what it has taken half a century to build up and develop be brought about in half a decade? And more than that, should not those who necessarily will be affected to so great an extent, the owners and their experienced representatives, be called into consultation as to the best and safest manner in which the momentous changes to which it is properly intended to give the form of law should be determined and their carrying into effect be proceeded with? Mr. Morgan—the big man he is—has perhaps acted somewhat impulsively, but I can understand what was in his mind when he recently suggested that a few representative railroad men hold a conference with you.

If instead of Mr. Morgan, who after all represents a class against which, unfortunately, great prejudice now exists, you as the head of the American people, in whom the people properly and fortunately have every confidence, will propose that the Interstate Commerce Commission, as the representative body of the Government, and the representatives of the railroads, chosen in such a manner as the railroad interests may themselves determine, come together with the view of arriving at a solution of the difficult problems involved, I cannot but believe that the good which will result will be immeasurable. You have taken action in a somewhat similar situation, when in the autumn of 1902 you brought about peace between the anthracite coal operators and the miners, a peace which has now remained undisturbed almost five years. I can only repeat, that unless something is done—through such a measure as I have indicated, or any other which may be practicable—so that confidence be restored in railroad affairs and properties, unless the conviction can be brought to investors not only in the United States, but also abroad, that the people and the railroads are going to come together and solve the existing differences in mutual confidence, actuated by the desire that justice shall be done to all, we shall enter upon the most serious and probably most disheartening period in our economic history.

I repeat, the present is a money situation to a small extent only. The intelligent attitude of Secretary Cortelyou [George Bruce Cortelyou, 1903–1905 Secretary of Commerce and Labor, 1905–1909 Postmaster-General] and the prudent measures he is taking will soon restore equilibrium in the money market, and indeed, if the present conditions of distrust continue and spread we shall, before long, be faced by too great an abundance of loanable funds. What is needed are measures through the application of which this insane fear that the railroads and the people are getting more and more apart and that destructive legislation is, in consequence, likely to be enacted, can be removed, so that confidence may be restored, and the work of upbuilding and development of the great highways of trade and commerce can be continued, instead of, as is threatened, being seriously interrupted to the lasting injury of the prosperity of the country and the happiness of its people.

I have again to ask, Mr. President, that you pardon the frankness with which I am writing, and feel assured that even if I move in what is commonly designated as "Wall Street atmosphere," I have the sincere conviction that you have no other intention but to do what is eventually to the interest of the people, to whatever class they may belong, or in whatever position the may find themselves.

Most sincerely yours,
Jacob H. Schiff.

Source: Cyrus Adler, *Jacob H. Schiff: His Life and Letters* (Garden City, NY: Doubleday, Doran and Cy., 1928; repr. Grosse Pointe, Mich.: Scholarly Press, 1968), 1, 44–50.

ANNOTATED BIBLIOGRAPHY

Abdill, George B. *Civil War Railroads*. Burbank, Calif.: Superior, 1961. Well illustrated popular history of the railroads during the Civil War.

Adler, Dorothy R. *British Investment in American Railways 1834–1898*. Charlottesville: University Press of Virginia, 1970. Useful survey of British financial influence in the American railroad industry.

Ambrose, Stephen E. *Nothing Like It in the World: The Men Who Built the Transcontinental Railroad 1863–1869*. New York: Simon and Schuster, 2000. A well written popular history of the building of the Union and Central Pacific roads as from the point of view of the men involved.

Anderson, George L. *Kansas West*. San Marino, Calif.: Golden West Books, 1963. Study of the construction of the Kansas Pacific Railroad.

Athearn, Robert G. *Rebel of the Rockies: A History of the Denver and Rio Grande Western Railroad*. New Haven, Conn.: Yale University Press, 1962. Study of the leading railroad in Colorado and its builder, William S. Jackson.

———. *Union Pacific Country*. First edition 1971, reprinted Lincoln and London: University of Nebraska Press, 1976. Scholarly account of the impact of the Union Pacific Railroad on the country it traversed.

Bain, David H., *Empire Express: Building the First Transcontinental Railroad*. New York: Viking, 1999. A highly readable, well documented, and well researched account of the epic story of the first transcontinental.

Baker, George P. *The Formation of the New England Railroad Systems*. Cambridge, Mass.: Harvard University Press, 1937. Business history of the railroads in New England.

Bartky, Ian R. *Selling the True Time: Nineteenth Century Timekeeping in America*. Stanford, Calif.: Stanford University Press, 2000. Useful study of the problems before the establishment of a national time in America.

Beebe, Lucius. *The Central Pacific & the Southern Pacific Railroads*. Berkeley, Calif.: Howell North, 1963. Popular and well illustrated history of both companies from the early days to the present.

———. *The Overland Limited*. San Diego, Calif.: Howell North, 1963. Highly readable and well illustrated history of one of the best-known luxury trains.

Black, Robert C., III. *The Railroads of the Confederacy*. Chapel Hill: University of North Carolina Press, 1998. Exhaustive and well documented study of the southern railroads during the Civil War.

Bogen, Julius I. *The Anthracite Railroads:. A Study in American Railroad Enterprise*. New York: Ronald Press, 1927. Study of eastern coal railroads.

Botkin, B.A., and Alvin F. Harlow, eds. *A Treasury of Railroad Folklore: The Stories, Tall Tales, Traditions, Ballads and Songs of the American Railroad Man*. New York: Bonanza Books, 1953. Popular stories and songs about railroads.

Brown, John K. *The Baldwin Locomotive Works 1831–1915: A Study in American Industrial Practice*. Baltimore, Md.: Johns Hopkins University Press, 1995. Exhaustive study of one of the leaders of American locomotive construction.

Bryant, Keith L., Jr. *Arthur E.Stilwell: Promoter with a Hunch*. Nashville, Tenn.: Vanderbilt University Press, 1971. Solid biography of a colorful railroad promoter.

———. *History of the Atchison, Topeka and Santa Fe Railway*. First edition 1974; reprinted Lincoln: University of Nebraska Press, 1982. Scholarly history of the Santa Fe.

Burgess, George H., and Miles C. Kennedy. *Centennial History of the Pennsylvania Railroad Company, 1846–1946*. Philadelphia: Pennsylvania Railroad Company, 1949. Official history of one of the great railroads in America.

Buss, Dietrich G. *Henry Villard: A Study of Transatlantic Investments and Interests*. New York: Arno Press, 1978. The role of Villard in the railroads of the Pacific Northwest.

Carosso, Vincent P. *The Morgans: Private International Bankers 1854–1913*. Cambridge, Mass.: Harvard University Press, 1987. Study of the role of the House of Morgan in American finance.

Casey, Robert J., and W.A.S. Douglas. *Pioneer Railroad: The Story of the Chicago and North Western System*. New York: McGraw-Hill, 1948. Popular history of one of the country's leading railroads.

Chandler, Alfred D. *The Railroads: The Nation's First Big Business*. New York: Harcourt, Brace and World, 1965. Study of the railroads as the first large-scale business organizations.

———. *The Visible Hand: The Managerial Revolution in American Business*. Cambridge, Mass.: Harvard University Press, 1977. Sweeping study of the role of railroads in the development of modern business organization.

Chernow, Ron. *The House of Morgan: An American Banking Dynasty and the Rise of Modern Finance*. New York: Simon and Schuster, 1990. Study of one of America's greatest banking houses, very much involved in railroad reorganization.

Clark, John E., Jr. *Railroads in the Civil War: The Impact of Management on Victory and Defeat*. Baton Rouge: Louisiana State University Press, 2001. Recent scholarly study of the organization of rail transportation on both sides during the Civil War.

Cochran, Thomas C. *Railroad Leaders 1845–1890: The Business Mind in Action*. Cambridge, Mass.: Harvard University Press, 1953. Study of railroad managers, with extensive excerpts from correspondence.

Cohen, Norm. *Long Steel Rail: The Railroad in American Folk Song*. Urbana: University of Illinois Press, 1981. The role of railroads in popular music.

Condit, Carl W. *The Port of New York: A History of the Rail and Terminal System from the Beginnings to Pennsylvania Station*. Chicago: University of Chicago Press, 1980. Very detailed study of all railroads in and around New York City until about the first decade of the twentieth century. A second volume takes the story forward to the present day.

Cronon, William. *Nature's Metropolis: Chicago and the Great West*. New York: Norton, 1991. Study of the development of Chicago and the role played by the railroads.

Cunningham, John T. *Railroads of New Jersey: The Formative Years*. Andover, N.J.: Afton, 1997. Regional sudy of nineteenth century railroads.

Daggett, Stuart. *Railroad Reorganization*. First edition 1908; reprinted New York: Augustus M. Kelley, 1967. Old but still useful study of the reorganization of bankrupt railroads.

———. *Chapters on the History of the Southern Pacific*. First edition 1922; reprinted New York: Augustus M. Kelley, 1966. Business history of the Central and Southern Pacific, still useful, as there is no modern study of these companies during the nineteenth century.

Davis, Burke, *The Southern Railway*. *Road of the Innovators*. Chapel Hill: University of North Carolina Press, 1985. Scholarly study of the role played by the Southern Railway in the development of the American railroad industry.

Denevi, Don. *The Western Pacific*. Seattle, Wash.: Superior, 1978. History of one of the last mainlines built in America.

Derleth, August. *The Milwaukee Road: Its First Hundred Years*. New York: Creative Age Press, 1948. Popular history of one of the Granger railroads.

Dilts, James D. *The Great Road: The Building of the Baltimore and Ohio, the Nation's First Railroad, 1828–1853*. Stanford, Calif.: Stanford University Press, 1993. Study of the early years of the pioneer of American railroads.

Dodge, Grenville, *How We Built the Union Pacific Railway*. Washington, D.C.: U.S. Printing Office, 1910. Written from memory—colorful but not always dependable.

Dozier, Howard D. *A History of the Atlantic Coast Line Railroad*. First edition 1920;

reprinted New York: Augustus M. Kelley, 1971. Classic work on this leading southern railroad.

Droege, John A. *Passenger Terminals and Trains.* First published 1916; reprinted Milwaukee, Wis.: Kalmbach, 1969. Technical description of recent passenger stations and operations, by an author from the railroad industry.

Ducker, James H. *Men of the Steel Rails: Workers on the Atchison, Topeka & Santa Fe Railroad, 1869–1900.* Lincoln: University of Nebraska Press, 1983. Social history of workers of one large railroad company.

Edson, William D. *Railroad Names: A Directory of Common Carrier Railroads Operating in the United States 1826–1997.* Fourth edition. Privately published, 1999. Most useful survey of all railroads that ever operated in America.

Engelbourg, Saul, and Leonard Bushkoff. *The Man Who Found the Money: John Stewart Kennedy and the Financing of the Western Railroads.* East Lansing: Michigan State University Press, 1996. Biography of railroad financier.

Fogel, Robert W. *Railroads and American Economic Growth.* Baltimore, Md.: Johns Hopkins University Press, 1964. Controversial study of the part played by railroads in the economic development of America.

————. *The Union Pacific: A Case of Premature Enterprise.* Baltimore, Md.: Johns Hopkins University Press, 1960. Study of the reasons for the lack of economic importance of the UP in its early years.

Frey, Robert L., ed. *Railroads in the Nineteenth Century: Encyclopedia of American Business History and Biography.* New York: Facts On File, 1988. Very useful volume for students of general railroad history.

Gamst, Frederick C., ed. *Early American Railroads: Franz Anton Ritter von Gerstner's 'Die innern Communicationen' (1842–1843).* Stanford, Calif.: Stanford University Press, 1997. Translation of the extensive description of early American railroads by an outstanding Austrian engineer.

Gates, Paul W. *The Illinois Central Railroad and Its Colonization Work.* First edition 1934; reprinted New York: Johnson Reprint, 1968. Pioneering study of the land policy of the Illinois Central.

Goodrich, Carter. *Government Promotion of American Canals and Railroads, 1800–1890.* New York: Columbia University Press, 1960.

Gordon, John S. *The Scarlet Woman of Wall Street: Jay Gould, Jim Fisk, Cornelius Vanderbilt, the Erie Railway Wars, and the Birth of Wall Street.* New York: Weidenfeld and Nicholson, 1988. Popular history of the scandals surrounding the Erie in the 1860s.

Gordon, Sarah H. *Passage to Union: How the Railraods Transformed American Life, 1829–1929.* Chicago: Ivan R. Dee, 1996. Social history of the role played by railroads in America.

Grant, H. Roger. *The North Western: A History of the Chicago & North Western*

Railway System. De Kalb: Northern Illinois University Press, 1996. The modern standard history of an important railroad.

———. *We Took the Train*. De Kalb: Northern Illinois University Press, 1990. Collection of personal accounts of railroad travel.

———, ed. *Brownie the Boomer: The Life of Charles P. Brown, an American Railroader*. De Kalb: Northern Illinois University Press, 1991. A rare inside view of life on the railroad in the first decade of the twentieth century.

Grant, H. Roger, and Charles W. Bohi. *The Country Railroad Station in America*. Sioux Falls, S.Dak.: Center for Western Studies, 1988. Study of the role played by the railroad depot in American towns.

Greenberg, Dolores. *Financiers and Railroads 1869–1889: A Study of Morton, Bliss & Company*. Newark: University of Delaware Press, 1980. Study of one of the American banking houses involved in railroad finance.

Griswold, Wesley S. *A Work of Giants: Building the First Transcontinental Railroad*. London: Frederick Muller, 1962. Readable and well documented story of the building of the Union and Central Pacific.

Gross, Joseph. *Railroads of North America*. Third edition. Privately published, 2000. Useful survey of all railroads that ever operated in America.

Haney, Lewis H. *A Congressional History of Railways in the United States*. First edition 1908; reprinted New York: August M.Kelley, 1968. Old but still useful survey of the involvement of Congress with railroads.

Harlow, Alvin F. *The Road of the Century: The Story of the New York Central*. New York: Creative Age Press, 1947. Popular history of one of the great railroad companies.

———. *Steelways of New England*. New York: Creative Age Press, 1946. Popular history of all railroads in the area.

Hayes, William E. *Iron Road to Empire: The History of 100 Years of the Progress and Achievements of the Rock Island Lines*. New York: Simmons Boardman, 1953. Popular history of one of the pioneering railroad companies.

Herr, Kincaid. *The Louisville & Nashville Railroad 1850–1963*. First edition 1943; reprinted Lexington: University Press of Kentucky, 2000. Updated version of a classic work on one of the great railroads of the South.

Hidy, Ralph, Muriel E. Hidy, Roy V. Scott, and Don L. Hofsommer. *The Great Northern Railway: A History*. Boston: Harvard Business School Press, 1988. Exhaustive study of one of the great American railroads.

Hilton, George W. *American Narrow Gauge Railroads*. Stanford, Calif.: Stanford University Press, 1990. Definitive study of narrow-gauge railroads in America.

Hilton, George W., and John F. Due. *The Electric Interurban Railways in America*. Stanford, Calif.: Stanford University Press, 1960. Well researched survey of all interurban companies in America.

Hofsommer, Don L. *The Southern Pacific, 1901–1985*. College Station: Texas A & M University Press, 1986. Although primarily covering the twentieth century, this study gives a useful overview of the earlier history.

Holton, James L. *The Reading Railroad: History of a Coal Age Empire*. Vol. 1, *The Nineteenth Century*. Laury's Station, Pa.: Garrigues House, 1989. Detailed and well illustrated history of one of the leading anthracite carriers of the eastern seaboard.

Hungerford, Edward. *Men of Erie: A Story of Human Development*. New York: Random House, 1946. Popular history of the Erie Railroad.

Husband, Joseph. *The Story of the Pullman Car*. First published 1917; reprinted Grand Rapids, Mich.: Black Letter Press, 1974. Popular history of Pullman's sleeping cars.

Jackson, Robert W. *Rails across the Mississippi: A History of the St. Louis Bridge*. Urbana and Chicago: University of Illinois Press, 2001. Well researched and in-depth study, covering all aspects of the construction of the first large steel railroad bridge in America.

Jensen, Oliver. *The American Heritage History of Railroads in America*. New York: Bonanza Books, 1981. Popular and lavishly illustrated history of railroads.

Jessen, Kenneth. *Railroads of Northern Colorado*. Boulder, Colo.: Pruett, 1982. Solid regional study.

Johnson, Arthur M., and Barry E. Supple. *Boston Capitalists and Western Railroads: A Study in the Nineteenth-Century Railroad Investment Process*. Cambridge, Mass.: Harvard University Press, 1967. Study of the role of the Boston capital market in the development of western railroads.

Josephson, Matthew. *The Robber Barons: The Great American Capitalists 1861–1901*. First edition 1932; reprinted San Diego and New York: Harcourt Brace Jovanovich, 1962. Lively and colorful story about the great American business tycoons, including many railroad leaders.

Klein, Maury. *The Great Richmond Terminal: A Study in Businessmen and Business Strategy*. Charlottesville: University Press of Virginia, 1970. Scholarly study of the predecessor of the Southern Railway.

———. *History of the Louisville & Nashville Railroad*. New York: Macmillan, 1972. History of one of the great railroads of the South.

———. *The Life and Legend of Jay Gould*. Baltimore, Md.: Johns Hopkins University Press, 1986. Most recent biography of this controversial railroad financier.

———. *The Life and Legend of E.H. Harriman*. Chapel Hill: University of North Carolina Press, 2000. Most recent scholarly biography of a great railroad tycoon.

———. *Union Pacific: Birth of a Railroad 1862–1893*. New York: Doubleday, 1987. Exhaustive study of the first transcontinental railroad. A second volume,

Union Pacific: The Rebirth 1894–1969 (New York: Doubleday, 1989) takes the story from the Harriman era into the twentieth century.

Lambie, Joseph T. *From Mine to Market: The History of Coal Transportation on the Norfolk and Western Railway.* New York: New York University Press, 1954. Study of one of the biggest coal haulers of the East.

Larson, John Lauritz. *Bonds of Enterprise: John Murray Forbes and Western Development in America's Railway Age.* Cambridge, Mass.: Harvard University Press, 1984. Study of one of the leading developers of western railways.

Lavender, David. *The Great Persuader.* Garden City, N.J.: Doubleday, 1970. Biography of Collis P. Huntington, the California railroad tycoon.

Lewis, Oscar. *The Big Four.* New York: Knopf, 1938; reprinted Sausalito, Calif.: Comstock, 1971. History of the four men behind the Central Pacific— Stanford, Hopkins, Huntington, and Crocker.

Licht, Walter. *Working for the Railroad: The Organization of Work in the Nineteenth Century.* Princeton, N.J.: Princeton University Press, 1983. Study of the first two generations of railroad workers.

Lindsey, Almont. *The Pullman Strike: The Story of a Unique Experiment and of a Great Labor Upheaval.* Chicago: University of Chicago Press, 1942; reprinted 1964. Good study of one of the nastiest strikes of the nineteenth century.

Lyle, Katie L. *Scalded to Death by the Steam: Authentic Stories of Railroad Disasters and the Ballads That Were Written about Them.* Chapel Hill, N.C.: Algonquin Books, 1988. Collection of stories of accidents and disasters on the railroad.

Malone, Michael P. *James J. Hill: Empire Builder of the Northwest.* Norman: University of Oklahoma Press, 1996. Most recent biography of this master railroader.

Marshall, James. *Santa Fe, the Railroad That Built an Empire.* New York: Random House, 1945. Popular study of one the great American railroad companies.

Martin, Albro. *Enterprise Denied: Origins of the Decline of American Railroads, 1897–1917.* New York: Columbia University Press, 1971. Solid study of the role of government in limiting the freedom of railroad management.

———. *James J. Hill and the Opening of the Northwest.* New York: Oxford University Press, 1976. Study of the role played by Hill and his Great Northern Railway in the development of the Northwest of America.

Masterson, V.V. *The Katy Railroad and the Last Frontier.* Columbia: University of Missouri Press, 1988. Study of the Missouri, Kansas & Texas Railroad.

Mencken, August. *The Railroad Passenger Car: An Illustrated History of the First Hundred Years with Accounts by Contemporary Passengers.* First edition 1957; reprinted Baltimore, Md.: Johns Hopkins University Press, 2000. Short survey with very interesting accounts of early rail travel.

Mercer, Lloyd J. *Railroads and Land Grant Policy: A Study in Government Intervention.* New York: Academic Press, 1982. Role of government in helping pioneer railroads on their feet.

Meyer, Balthasar H. *History of Transportation in the United States before 1860.* Reprinted New York: Peter Smith, 1948. Study of all means of early transportation.

Mickelson, Sig. *The Northern Pacific Railroad and the Selling of the West.* Sioux Falls, S.Dak.: Center for Western Studies, 1993. Influence of the NP Railroad on the opening of the Northwest.

Middleton, William D. *Landmarks on the Iron Road: Two Centuries of North American Railroad Engineering.* Bloomington: Indiana University Press, 1999. Study of railroad bridges, tunnels, docks, etc. of the nineteenth and twentieth centuries.

———. *The Time of the Trolley.* Milwaukee, Wis.: Kalmbach, 1967. Popular and well illustrated history of the streetcar in America.

Miller, John A. *Fares Please! A Popular History of Trolleys, Horse-Cars, Street-Cars, Buses, Elevateds, and Subways.* New York: Dover, 1960. History of urban transportation.

Miner, H. Craig. *The St. Louis–San Francisco Railroad: The Thirty-fifth Parallel Project, 1853–1890.* Lawrence: University Press of Kansas, 1972. Study of one of the less successful transcontinental projects.

Morris, Juddi. *The Harvey Girls: The Women Who Civilized the West.* New York: Walker, 1997. Study of the Harvey Houses on the Santa Fe system and their waitresses.

Myrick, David F. *New Mexico's Railroads: A Historical Survey.* Second edition. Albuquerque: University of New Mexico Press, 1990. Solid survey of all railroads in the state.

———. *Railroads of Nevada and Eastern California.* 2 vols. First edition 1962; reprinted Reno: University of Nevada Press, 1992. Exhaustive study of all railroads in the region.

Nelson, Scott Reynolds. *Iron Confederacies: Southern Railways, Klan Violence, and Reconstruction.* Chapel Hill: University of North Carolina Press, 1999. Railroads and politics in the South after 1865.

Norris, Frank. *The Octopus: A Story of California.* First edition 1901; reprinted New York: Airmont, 1969. A novel set around 1900 in a California under the thumb of the Southern Pacific Railroad.

Oss, S.F. van. *American Railroads as Investments: A Handbook for Investors in American Railroad Securities.* London: Effingham Wilson, 1893. Handy survey of all American railroads operating in the last decade of the nineteenth century, with financial performances.

Overton, Richard C. *Burlington Route: A History of the Burlington Lines.* Lincoln: University of Nebraska Press, 1965. Scholarly history of the Chicago, Burlington & Quincy Railroad.

————. *Burlington West: A Colonization History of the Burlington Railroad.* New York: Russell and Russell, 1967. Study of the efforts of the CB & Q Railroad to people the regions it traversed.

Prince, Richard E. *Atlantic Coast Line Railroad: Steam Locomotives, Ships and History.* First edition 1966; reprinted Bloomington: Indiana University Press, 2000. History of the ACL and its constituents.

————. *Seaboard Air Line Railway: Steamboats, Locomotives and History.* First edition 1969; reprinted Bloomington: Indiana University Press, 2000. History of the SAL and its constituents.

Reed, S.G. *A History of the Texas Railroads and of the Transportation Conditions under Spain and Mexico, and the Republic and the State.* Houston: St. Clair, 1941. Exhaustive study of the development of roads and railroads in Texas.

Renz, Louis T. *The History of the Northern Pacific.* Fairfield, Wash.: Ye Galleon Press, 1980. History of the second transcontinental railroad.

Richter, William L. *The ABC-CLIO Companion to Transportation in America.* Santa Barbara, Calif.: ABC-CLIO, 1995. Useful encyclopedia of topics on transportation by rail, road, water and air.

Riegel, Robert Edgar. *The Story of the Western Railroads from 1852 through the Reign of the Giants.* First edition 1926; reprinted Lincoln: University of Nebraska Press, 1964. Older but still useful survey of western railroading.

Sarnoff, Paul. *Russell Sage: The Money King.* New York: Ivan Obolensky, 1965. Biography of a shady railroad financier who preferred to operate in the background.

Saunders, Richard, Jr., *Merging Lines: American Railroads 1900–1970.* De Kalb: Northern Illinois University Press, 2001. Although concentrating on the post-World War I period, a good and highly readable survey of earlier mergers.

Schwantes, Carlos A. *Railroad Signatures across the Pacific Northwest.* Seattle: University of Washington Press, 1993. Solid economic and cultural history of the area and its railroads.

Shaw, Robert B. *A History of Railroad Accidents, Safety Precautions and Operating Practices.* Privately published, 1978. Solid study of railroad accidents and the measures taken to prevent them.

Signor, John R. *The Los Angeles and Salt Lake Railroad Company: Union Pacific's Historic Salt Lake Route.* San Marino, Calif.: Golden West Books, 1988. Popular and well illustrated history of this cross-country railroad.

Simons, Richard S., and Francis H. Parker. *Railroads of Indiana.* Bloomington: Indiana University Press, 1997. Excellent study of all railroads in the state.

Smalley, Eugene V. *History of the Northern Pacific Railroad.* New York: Putnam, 1883. History of the second transcontinental railroad.

Starr, John William. *Lincoln and the Railroads.* First edition 1927; reprinted New York: Arno Press, 1981. Study of President Lincoln's involvement with the railroads in America.

Stilgoe, John R. *Metropolitan Corridors: Railroads and the American Scene.* New Haven, Conn.: Yale University Press, 1983. Highly original study of the impact of railroads on cultural life in America.

Stover, John F. *American Railroads.* Second edition. Chicago: University of Chicago Press, 1997. Solid survey of American railroad history up to the present day.

————. *History of the Baltimore and Ohio Railroad.* West Lafayette, Ind.: Purdue University Press, 1987. Solid history of a pioneer railroad.

————. *History of the Illinois Central Railroad.* New York: Macmillan, 1975. Well-researched history of one of the American trunk lines.

————. *The Railroads of the South: A Study in Finance and Control.* Chapel Hill: University of North Carolina Press, 1955. Survey of southern railroads after Reconstruction.

————. *The Routledge Historical Atlas of the American Railroads.* New York and London: Routledge, 1999. Useful survey of American railroading and railroad leaders from early beginnings to the present.

Stromquist, Shelton. *A Generation of Boomers: The Pattern of Railroad Labor Conflict in Nineteenth Century America.* Urbana: University of Illinois Press, 1987. Study of working conditions and strikes on the railroads.

Swank, Walbrook D., ed. *Train Running for the Confederacy 1861–1865: An Eyewitness Memoir.* Charlottesville, Va.: 1990. Rare insight in the life of a train conductor during the Civil War.

Taylor, George Rogers. *The Economic History of the United States.* Vol. 4, *The Transportation Revolution 1815–1860.* First edtion 1951; reprinted Armonk, N.Y.: M.E. Sharpe, 1977. Solid study of transportation in America during the first half of the nineteenth century.

Taylor, George Rogers, and Irene Neu. *The American Railroad Network 1861–1900.* Cambridge, Mass.: Harvard University Press, 1956. Succinct survey of the gradual development of the network, with the different gauges shown.

Trautmann, Frederick, ed. *A Prussian Observes the American Civil War: The Military Studies of Julius Scheibert.* Columbia: University of Missouri Press, 2001. One of the best studies of the Civil War by a contemporary foreign observer.

Trelease, Allen W. *The North Carolina Railroad, 1849–1871, and the Modernization of North Carolina.* Chapel Hill: University of North Carolina Press, 1991. Exhaustive study of the role played by the railroad in the development of the state.

Turner, George Edgar. *Victory Rode the Rails: The Strategic Place of the Railroads in the Civil War.* Indianapolis, Ind.: Bobbs-Merrill, 1953. First study of the role of railroads on both sides during the war.

Vance, James E. *The North American Railroad: Its Origin, Evolution and Geography.* Baltimore, Md.: Johns Hopkins University Press. Study of the influence of geography on the development of railroads.

Veenendaal, Augustus J., Jr. *The Saint Paul & Pacific Railroad: An Empire in the Making, 1862–1879.* De Kalb: Northern Illinois University Press, 1999. Complete history of the predecessor of the Great Northern Railway.

———. *Slow Train to Paradise: How Dutch Investment Helped Build American Railroads.* Stanford, Calif.: Stanford University Press, 1996. Exhaustive study of the role played by Dutch investors in the financing of the American railroad network.

Ward, James A., ed. *Southern Railroad Man: Conductor N.J. Bell's Recollections of the Civil War Era.* De Kalb: Northern Illinois University Press, 1994. Edition of a rare personal account of railroading during the war years.

Watson, Don, and Steve Brown. *From Oxteams to Eagles: Texas & Pacific Railway.* Cheltenham, Ont.: Boston Mills Press, 1973. Popular history of one of the lesser-known transcontinentals.

Webb, William. *The Southern Railway System: An Illustrated History.* Erin, Ont.: Boston Mills Press, 1986. Well written and well illustrated history of one of the great railroads of the South.

Weber, Thomas. *The Northern Railroads in the Civil War 1861–1865.* First edition 1952; reprinted Bloomington: Indiana University Press, 1999. Study of the role of the railroads in the war effort of the Union.

White, John H., Jr. *American Locomotives: An Engineering History, 1830–1880.* Second revised edition. Baltimore, Md.: Johns Hopkins University Press, 1997. Definitive history of the first fifty years of American steam locomotives.

———. *The American Railroad Freight Car.* Baltimore, Md.: Johns Hopkins University Press, 1993. Definitive study of the construction of freight cars.

———. *The American Railroad Passenger Car.* Baltimore, Md.: Johns Hopkins University Press, 1978. Definitive Study of the construction of passenger cars.

———. *A Short History of American Locomotive Builders in the Steam Era.* Washington, D.C.: Bass, 1982. Succinct and very useful survey of the locomotive industry in America.

Williams, John Hoyt, *A Great and Shining Road: The Epic Story of the Transcontinental Railroad.* New York: Times Books. A popular story of the building of the Union and Central Pacific.

Wilson, Neill C., and Frank J. Taylor. *Southern Pacific: The Roaring Story of a Fighting Railroad.* New York: McGraw-Hill, 1952. Popular history of one of the transcontinental railroads.

INDEX

About the Author

Augustus J. Veenendaal is senior research historian at the Institute of Netherlands History in The Hague, the Netherlands. He is the author of numerous articles and books on American and Dutch railroad history.